D0927349

effective learning & teaching in

MATHEMATICS & its applications

Edited by peter kahn & joseph kyle

the institute for learning and teaching
in higher education

THE TIMES
HIGHER
EDUCATION SUPPLEMENT

KOGAN
PAGE

First published in 2002

Kogan Page Limited
120 Pentonville Road
London N1 9JN
UK

Stylus Publishing Inc
22883 Quicksilver Drive
Sterling VA 20166-2012
USA

British Library Cataloguing in Publication Data

A CIP record for this book is available from the British Library.

ISBN 0 7494 3569 0

Typeset by Saxon Graphics Ltd, Derby
Printed and bound in Great Britain by Biddles Ltd, Guildford and King's Lynn
www. biddles.co.uk

Contents

About the editors

Peter Kahn is the Teaching Development Officer at the University of Manchester and is also Honorary Teaching Fellow in the Department of Mathematics there. He was previously a Lecturer in Mathematics at Liverpool Hope University College. He has recently written a study guide for students, *Studying Mathematics and its Applications* (Palgrave, 2001).

Joseph Kyle is Senior Lecturer and Director of Undergraduate Studies in the School of Mathematics and Statistics at the University of Birmingham. He coordinates the activity that relates to mathematics of the Learning and Teaching Support Network (LTSN) Mathematics, Statistics and Operational Research (OR) Network and is an associate editor of the Institute of Mathematics and its Applications (IMA) journal, *Teaching Mathematics and its Applications*.

About the specialist contributors

Afzal Ahmed is a Professor of Mathematics Education and Director of the Mathematics Centre at University College Chichester. He was a member of the Cockcroft Committee and has worked internationally in mathematics education. He is currently a member of the International Commission for the Study and Improvement of Mathematics Teaching (CIEAEM) and co-editor of the IMA journal, *Teaching Mathematics and its Applications*.

John Appleby is Director of the Engineering Foundation Year at Newcastle University, and Senior Lecturer in Engineering Mathematics. He is the principal author of DIAGNOSYS, an expert-system diagnostic test for mathematics and other subjects, and co-edited *Teaching Undergraduate Mathematics* (Imperial College Press, 1998).

Clifford Beevers attended Manchester University as an undergraduate and a postgraduate in the 1960s and currently teaches at Heriot-Watt University in Edinburgh. He is Director of the CALM Project for Computer Aided Learning in Mathematics and co-director of the Scottish Centre for Research into Online Learning and Assessment.

Robert Burn has taught mathematics in a variety of institutions since 1963, including Homerton College and Exeter University. His last post before retiring was as Professor of Mathematics Education at Agder University College, Norway. He served as editor of the Teaching and Learning Undergraduate Mathematics newsletter from 1993 to 2000 and he is a member of the editorial board of *Educational Studies in Mathematics*. He has published several mathematical text-books, including *A Pathway to Number Theory* (Cambridge University Press, 1997) and *Numbers and Functions* (Cambridge University Press, 2000).

Neil Challis is Head of Mathematics at Sheffield Hallam University. Following a spell as a mathematician in industry, he has for many years been teaching mathematics to students on various mathematics, engineering and science degrees. He is an associate editor of *Teaching Mathematics and its Applications*.

William Cox lectures in mathematics at the University of Aston. He has taught mathematics to students from a wide range of disciplines and abilities. He has published extensively on mathematical education and is a founder member of the Midlands Mathematics Consortium, a research network formed to study the transition to university mathematics.

Tony Croft is Manager of the Mathematics Learning Support Centre at Loughborough University and is a consultant in Applicable Mathematics for the LTSN Mathematics, Statistics and Operational Research (OR) Network.

Neville Davies is Director of the Royal Statistical Society Centre for Statistical Education and a Professor at Nottingham Trent University.

Janet Duffin works in the Department of Mathematics at the University of Hull as a support tutor under the Mathematics Advisory and Counselling Service. She is primarily involved in helping undergraduates who are experiencing difficulty with the mathematics required of them in their degree work.

Terence Etchells is currently a Senior Lecturer in Mathematics at Liverpool John Moores University and uses computer algebra significantly in the teaching and assessment of mathematics on undergraduate degree programmes there. His interest in computer algebra systems started during his early career in a comprehensive school teaching mathematics in the early 1980s. He has developed many ideas and strategies for the introduction of computer algebra into teaching and published and lectured widely throughout the world on this subject over the last decade.

Harry Gretton is a Principal Lecturer in Mathematics at Sheffield Hallam University, and has taught in higher education for too many years! He is well known for his work on the use of technology in mathematics education, and is also a qualified NVQ assessor.

Stephen Hibberd is a Senior Lecturer in Mathematical Sciences at Nottingham University. He is an applied mathematician with multidisciplinary research interests in modelling. Teaching interests include the mathematical education of engineers, diagnostic testing and learning support for students at the school/university interface, and the development of modelling skills through project activities for final year undergraduates.

Derek Holton is Professor of Pure Mathematics at the Univerity of Otago, Dunedin, New Zealand. His mathematical research is in the area of graph theory where he has worked on matchings and cycles. He has been interested in all aspects of mathematics education for quite some time. He recently completed the chairing of an International Commission on Mathematical Instruction (ICMI) study on the teaching and learning of mathematics at university level. The resulting study volume of the same name was published by Kluwer Academic Press in 2001. Derek is also involved in a Web site for primary teachers (www.nzmaths.co.nz).

Ken Houston is Professor of Mathematical Studies at the University of Ulster and has taught in higher education for many years. He has written extensively on the teaching and learning of mathematics, particularly mathematical modelling. He is an associate editor of *Teaching Mathematics and its Applications*, and is the Chair or past Chair of several national and international conferences and committees.

Carl Leinbach is a Professor of Mathematics and Computer Science at Gettysburg College, Gettysburg, Pennsylvania in the United States. He wrote his first book, *Calculus as a Laboratory Course* (Prentice-Hall, 1974), on technology for students who had access to a mainframe computer programmable in FORTRAN 70 or BASIC. Since then he became interested in computer algebra systems and was a beta tester for DERIVE. He has published several articles on the use of computer algebra in the teaching of university mathematics courses.

John Mason has taught mathematics for over 40 years and has worked at the Open University for over 30 years. He remains focused on supporting those who wish to think mathematically, and those who wish to support others who wish to think mathematically. *Thinking Mathematically* (Addison Wesley, 1982) and *Learning and Doing Mathematics* (Macmillan, 1988) are just two of the many books, pamphlets and papers which he has written for students and teachers. His concerns and interests have led him to examine the role of mental imagery in mathematical thinking, the role of metaphor and metonymy in how choices are made when thinking mathematically, and the design of tasks intended to promote mathematical thinking.

Neville Neill is a Senior Lecturer in mathematics at the University of Ulster. He has been a Course Director, Placement Tutor and Faculty Advisor on Enterprise in Higher Education. He is currently University Assessor for South China Agricultural University and overseas editor for a series of books on mathematics education in German-speaking countries.

Jane Paterson studied at Glasgow, The Open and Napier universities. She is an author for the Scholar project at Heriot-Watt University (see http://scholar.hw.ac.uk/) and a tutor for The Open University.

Peter Petocz is a Senior Lecturer in Statistics in the Department of Mathematics at the University of Technology, Sydney, Australia. As well as his work as an applied statistician, he has been involved in statistics and mathematics education for two decades, both as a practitioner and researcher. He has produced several videos and has investigated the effect of video-based materials on learning in mathematics and statistics, the design of introductory statistics courses and (together with Anna Reid) students' conceptions of learning and teaching in statistics.

David Pountney is a Principal Lecturer and Subject Leader for Mathematics and Statistics at Liverpool John Moores University. He teaches mathematics, including the use of computer algebra systems, to specialist mathematics undergraduates and non-specialists such as engineering and science students, and he has published textbooks and numerous articles related to the teaching of mathematics and mathematics applications. In particular, he and his co-authors were co-chairs of the 4th International *DERIVE*-TI89/92 (Computer Algebra in Mathematics Education) at Liverpool John Moores University in July 2000.

Anna Reid is a Senior Lecturer in Academic Development (Learning and Teaching) at Macquarie University, Sydney, Australia. Her research has focused on the areas of conceptions of learning and teaching in higher education and the relations between learning and perception of work. She has developed university policy in relation to group work, work-based and flexible learning, assessment and evaluation, academic leadership and postgraduate supervision. She works with academics on quality development and review of teaching, and courses with a focus on the integration of generic attributes, inclusivity and diversity.

Honor Williams is a Reader in Mathematics Education and Dean of the Faculty of Sciences at University College Chichester. The main focus of her research, development and publications concern the role of assessment in enhancing learning and teaching of mathematics at school and tertiary level. She has contributed to the IAEA (International Association of Educational Assessment) as well as the International Commission on Mathematical Instruction (ICMI) studies, and has directed projects on Teaching, Learning and Assessing Mathematics at sixth form and university level.

Acknowledgements

The editors are grateful to Sally Brown and Jonathan Simpson for their roles in bringing this book to publication. We would also like to thank all of the contributors for sharing their experience of, and insight into, learning and teaching mathematics and its applications. Finally, we are grateful to John Blake for his foreword.

Forewords

Mathematics dates from antiquity, built upon the minds of the world's intellectual giants: Euclid, Pythagoras, Archimedes, Newton, Euler, Gauss, Einstein and many, many others. It is perhaps the most developed science, deploying a huge corpus of theory and technique. Music, art and mathematics transcend all cultures but perhaps mathematics most of all is universal, for it is a truly common language, regrettably appreciated by and accessible to far too few of us.

Among the sciences, mathematical sciences have undergone extraordinary growth over the last decade, primarily stimulated by advances in computing facilities, both software and hardware. The advancement of science, indeed society more generally, has always depended upon mathematics and will do so even more in the future.

Communicating this corpus of knowledge, understanding the theoretical and logical base and deploying this knowledge to the benefit of mankind is one of the biggest challenges facing education at the beginning of this new century (or millennium!). It is therefore pleasing to see a text on *Effective Teaching and Learning in Mathematics and its Applications*, edited by Peter Kahn and Joseph Kyle, with chapters by leading practitioners in the discipline of mathematics, statistics and operational research. Chapters in the book cover the key areas of assessment (diagnostic, formative, summative), learning developments, course design and reflection, application of mathematics in modelling phenomena, the analysis of data and preparation for future employment. There is also recognition of the need to support the non-specialists who need mathematics or statistics for the full understanding and appreciation of their own discipline.

I strongly encourage you to read the chapters of this book, implement and further develop the ideas and concepts relevant to your interests, but to also draw your colleagues' attention to the book as well, for there is much to understand about the learning, teaching and assessment of mathematics, statistics and operational research.

Professor John R Blake
Director, LTSN Mathematics, Statistics and Operational Research Network
School of Mathematics and Statistics, The University of Birmingham
http://www.mathstore.ac.uk

I am delighted to see in print this latest volume in the Effective Learning and Teaching series. The editors are to be congratulated on the immense amount of hard work they have invested in putting together this important contribution to the literature on learning and teaching in mathematics. Teaching maths is never easy and I am sure that readers will find much useful information and advice in this book as well as useful contact information and references to further reading. I am particularly happy to see the contributions that have been made by our colleagues in the LTSN subject centre, since it is imperative that the ILT and subject centres work together to provide a 'joined up' approach to supporting staff working in teaching and the support of learning in higher education.

The ILT is now at an important stage in its development with more than 10,000 members as we go to press, 112 programmes in higher education teaching and learning accredited by the ILT and a full programme of publications, activities and events on offer. Now with members in the majority on our governing council, active on all our committees and working parties and getting involved in the running our members' forums and other events, members are increasingly taking charge of shaping and directing the policy and direction of the organisation.

This book has a part to play in the ILT's mission to enhance the status of teaching, improve the experience of learning and support innovation in higher education. I commend it to you, whether you are an ILT member or not and welcome the contribution it makes to the higher education context.

Sally Brown
Director of Membership Services
Institute for Learning and Teaching

Preface

Setting the scene

Recent years have seen a greater focus on learning and teaching in mathematics and its applications in higher education. What should the typical undergraduate programme contain and how should it be taught? How best do we serve the needs of those who require mathematics as part of their study of another discipline? There will, no doubt, be many valid answers to these questions. And it is one of the strengths of this text that it attempts to cover a fair slice of the spectrum of these views.

As we write, there is in the UK what we might refer to as the 'official' answer, embodied in the December 2001 draft of the Quality Assurance Agency for Higher Education (QAA, 2000) Benchmarking statement, which covers mathematics, statistics and operational research (QAA, 2001). In this we see that a graduate who has reached the modal level should be able to:

- Demonstrate a reasonable understanding of the main body of knowledge for the programme of study.
- Demonstrate a good level of skill in calculation and manipulation of the material within this body of knowledge.
- Apply a range of concepts and principles in loosely defined contexts, showing effective judgement in the selection and application of tools and techniques.
- Develop and evaluate logical arguments.
- Demonstrate skill in abstracting the essentials of problems, formulating them mathematically and obtaining solutions by appropriate methods.
- Present arguments and conclusions effectively and accurately.
- Demonstrate appropriate transferable skills and the ability to work with relatively little guidance or support.

The authors of this statement go to some lengths to qualify and set the context for this list. In particular it is stressed that 'students should meet this standard in an overall sense, not necessarily in respect of each and every of the statements listed'

(QAA, 2001). There is no attempt to set a 'national curriculum' but a clear generic description of the type of skills and qualities we should look to be fostering in our programmes.

Not surprisingly, many of the themes in the bullet points above surface again and again in the chapters that follow. At the same time we have been keenly aware that the learning experiences of students who have to engage with mathematics and its applications cover a wide spectrum. This will range from foundation level material, preparing students for entry to other numerate disciplines, to advanced level specialist mathematical study at or near the contemporary frontiers of the subject. It is our intention therefore that the tone of this text is both contemporary and inclusive.

Identifying the audience

The main purpose of this book is to serve as a guide for everyone who contributes to the learning experiences of students who have to engage with mathematics and its applications. Although it is anticipated that college and university-based lecturers, whether newly appointed or experienced, will constitute the core readership, many others including engineers and scientists, educational developers, teaching assistants and those in staff development units should also find something of interest and value in what follows. Departmental heads and those involved in mentoring other members of staff will also find the book helpful.

Moreover, although the editors are based in the UK, the themes developed are not unique to any one country but, rather like mathematics itself, are applicable across international boundaries.

Explaining the aim

Throughout the book, the underlying aim of the authors is to assist those engaged in facilitating learning and teaching in mathematics and its applications at higher education level. The contributors are firmly grounded in the discipline and have followed quite specific briefs relevant to mathematics and its applications. In the use of the term mathematics, we have allowed our authors a reasonable amount of latitude, believing that the context renders the necessary clarity. Typically, the term 'mathematics' is used by the contributors to refer both to mathematics itself and to applications of mathematics. Thus, this text does not focus on generic aspects of learning and teaching in higher education for which there is now a substantial and rapidly expanding literature.

Nor is the book intended as a direct classroom resource with immediately 'consumable' exercises and activities. There are abundant materials of this nature available, as can be seen by visiting www.mathstore.ac.uk, the Web site of the Learning and Teaching Support Network (LTSN) Mathematics, Statistics and

Operational Research (OR) Network. (It is worth noting in passing that the Mathematics, Statistics and OR Network supports learning and teaching within these disciplines in the UK, as part of the wider network of subject centres called the LTSN.) Instead, the book seeks to explain the challenges of mathematics and its applications in education and give examples of good practice from experienced facilitators in the field. Hence, it provides a guide for reflective practice and offers routes to explore wherein readers may develop their own pedagogic principles.

In planning any text of this nature, a number of sub-headings arise almost naturally. These are:

- Teaching and the support of learning.
- Design and planning of learning activities.
- Assessment and giving feedback to students.
- Effective environments and student learning support systems.
- Reflective practice and personal development.

In this book we have endeavoured to see that this fifth point is not seen as isolated or independent from the other points above, but rather features as a crucial component in them all. It is no accident that these are descriptions of the five key areas of professional activity as identified by the UK's Institute for Learning and Teaching in Higher Education (ILT) and we are happy to see the aims of this text aligned closely with the work of the ILT.

Clearly, professional commitment to teaching and the support of learning needs to be espoused by all engaged in higher education. However, it may well be argued that such commitment is particularly apposite for contemporary mathematics and its applications. There are clear signs that the wider world is becoming aware of the issues, many of them international, that currently surround the discipline. Whether it is as a result of changing policy affecting school mathematics or whether it is the impact of rapidly developing technology, we face many new challenges in our discipline. Furthermore, the range and diversity of those engaged in learning our subject is considerable and is destined to become wider still in the near future.

An important consideration for the editors and the contributors has been to maintain a clear focus on those issues that are almost unique to mathematics and its applications. On one hand it is the science of strict logical deduction and reasoning, which are very severe taskmasters both for the learner and the teacher. On the other hand the breadth of the applicability of mathematics is immense. Mathematics is fundamental not only to much of science and technology but also to almost all situations that require an analytical model-building approach, whatever the discipline. In recent decades there has been an explosive growth of the use of mathematics in areas outside the traditional base of science, technology and engineering. Even in considering the development of Web-based resources, mathematics with its specialist symbols and fonts presents challenges that do not disturb many other disciplines or, it would seem, those developing commercial software.

A further factor in the design of the content has been to offer an insight into a range of approaches for teachers and learners. We know that, in the UK at least, 'most teaching comprises formal lectures' and that more innovative methods are only used 'occasionally' (QAA, 2000). Similarly we learn that most assessment strategies rely on formal examinations and, more damagingly, that in some cases too narrow a range of assessment methods had led to deficiencies in the measurement of learning. There is clearly some value therefore in exploring, as many of the subsequent chapters do, tried and tested alternatives to the traditional approaches.

Outlining the structure

The book is divided into two main parts. Part A focuses on issues that are common to learning and teaching across mathematics and its applications as a whole and at any level. It takes in such topics as the use of technology, assessment and course design. Part B, beginning at Chapter 10, focuses on specific areas of mathematics and its applications. It also covers specific contexts, such as learning and teaching that involves non-specialist students of mathematics.

Chapter 1 is designed to provide a context for later contributions. The focus is on the transition from largely school mathematics to further study of the subject at a higher education level. There is a close analysis of what skills might be expected from various backgrounds and advice on how to use and interpret the results of initial assessment or diagnosis of students' mathematical abilities. Thus Chapter 1 sets the scene and tells us exactly where we are when we start to work with our students.

In Chapter 2, we explore the contrast between the ways in which mathematics is discovered and the ways in which it is presented, especially to students. It looks therefore at the nature of the process that leads students to develop an understanding of formal mathematical structures. The initial focus is on the role of pattern recognition and conjecture, taking particular account of proof, and leads on to a wider consideration of the role that special cases play in the genetic process.

This chapter is appropriately followed by the topic of Chapter 3, which takes as one of its starting points the idea that for the student the genesis of a new mathematical concept or result is very often an active process. This, the authors claim, is a powerful argument in favour of active learning, by which they mean learning where the students' minds are actively engaged in creating knowledge through interacting with their teachers, peers and the subject matter.

Chapter 4 begins with a concise resume of the standard technical terms that have now become part of the assessment landscape. There then follows a survey of various attempts to use the computer to assist in assessing mathematics. There is a discussion on matching assessment to learning outcomes and a substantial section outlining good practice in the design of assessment elements. The chapter closes with a look at what developments are likely to emerge in the near future.

As an acknowledgement of the ever-increasing power and ease of access of computer technology one of the themes in Chapter 4, that of computer-assisted assessment, is examined in greater detail in Chapter 5. Technology continues to have a significant impact on the learning, teaching and assessment of mathematics throughout higher education establishments worldwide. In this chapter the authors look particularly at the impact of computer algebra systems, that is to say software systems that can perform symbolic as well as numerical manipulations and which include graphical display capabilities. Examples include *Mathematica*, *Maple*, *Macsyma* and DERIVE. Some of these systems are available not only on PCs but also on hand-held 'super-calculators' such as the TI-92 plus and the TI-89. The chapter concentrates on the use of DERIVE to illustrate the issues raised, but these issues are generic in nature and the translation to other systems is straightforward.

The increasingly important area of transferable skills is the topic for Chapter 6. The authors here take the point of view that transferable skills are best taught and practised in the context of a student's main study: mathematical sciences. In other words, the development of these skills should be embedded in the mathematics curriculum. After describing the range of skills that come under this heading, the authors describe how one might go about embedding transferable skills in the curriculum.

Such an approach is also advocated within Chapter 7, which addresses a common challenge, that of designing courses that open up mathematics to students in ways that both attract them and serve their needs. The author argues that while it is essential that courses are built around mathematical considerations, course designers also need to take account of wider issues. Taking learning outcomes as the fundamental element of design, the author shows how the remaining elements of course structure fall more naturally into place. In order to illustrate these principles the author includes a number of case studies, two of which seek to draw on the approach of problem-based learning.

Chapter 8 explores the notion of the Total Learning Environment, a concept in which all participants, curriculum, assessments, evaluations and perceptions are considered to be part of the one learning entity. In many ways this draws together themes from earlier chapters. In this chapter, the authors describe the various components of the Total Learning Environment through the use of a model, which although it might vary from institution to institution, highlights the important issue of improving student learning at all levels. The approach is illustrated through a case study of how one mathematics department used this model to improve the first-year mathematics learning environment.

As indicated above, there is an increasing emphasis being given to the concept of the reflective practitioner and Chapter 9 concentrates on the role of reflection in learning from experience as a lecturer or tutor. After considering some reasons for engaging in active reflection in the first section, some suggestions are made concerning effective ways to use memories of incidents as the basis for methodical reflection with a view to improving the learning and teaching experience. It is argued that an important corollary of such reflection is that it is possible to help students develop more efficient and effective learning processes, and one of the ways of doing this is by engaging them in a similar process of reflection.

For many students of other disciplines in higher education 'mathematics' means 'numeracy'. Chapter 10 examines the related issues that have always posed something of a problem for the university sector, especially for students studying subjects other than mathematics. The chapter begins with a case study examining how numeracy support has developed at one university. From this detailed consideration of one approach to developing students' numeracy one can distil more general issues inherent in offering numeracy support. The chapter concludes by giving a wider picture of the current situation in the UK, using case studies from a selection of other universities.

An allied but quite distinct issue is that of providing support for the mathematical requirements of the non-specialist student. Chapter 11 explores both the needs of non-specialist students of mathematics and the ways in which these needs might be met more effectively than is presently the case. In the context of this chapter, 'non-specialists' are students who come to university to read subjects other than mathematics, either as single- or joint-honours students, but for whom mathematics is nevertheless a compulsory part of their university experience. These students may be contrasted with the wider body of students considered in the previous chapter, where the focus was on all students in higher education and their subsequent employment-related needs. After an initial consideration of who should teach non-specialists, the chapter goes on to review a number of recent reports and the concerns they raise about the state of mathematics education of non-specialists in universities. The author then looks at some practical steps that might be taken and concludes by suggesting future measures that will go some way to ensure that the problems that have been highlighted are tackled in a serious way.

In October 1970, the *Mathematical Gazette* carried an article describing 'What makes a mathematician?' in which we were told that 'in the application of mathematics, one needs an appreciation of model-making'. Now more commonly referred to as mathematical modelling, this area has become increasingly important over the intervening years and is examined in Chapter 12. The term 'mathematical modelling' is closely connected to the concept of a mathematical model but reflects more the higher-level interactive skills of formulating, analysing, evaluating and reporting of physical situations through the use of mathematical models. This chapter discusses the main features of this complex, interactive, multifaceted activity that is based on applying mathematics. Some structural features of the process are delineated after which there are concrete suggestions on implementing these ideas at various levels in the curriculum.

Statistics is often regarded as being difficult to understand, especially by non-specialist students of the subject. If for no other reason it merits a full and separate chapter. In Chapter 13, the author outlines the issues pertinent to this relatively youthful branch of knowledge. The case is persuasively argued that for many students, especially non-specialists, a data-driven approach to learning statistics has best chance of success. The approach is illustrated with a description of the innovative Web-based random data selector. The chapter then describes a new approach to teaching statistics that has been developed in the motor industry and could be deployed with good effect in engineering departments.

Mathematics graduates are rightly seen as possessing considerable skill in abstract reasoning, logical deduction and problem solving, and for this reason they find employment in a great variety of careers and professions. However, these skills are rarely well developed when they enter higher education. In particular there is very little appreciation of the central role of proof in mathematics and hardly any real facility in the various styles of proof and logical reasoning. In Chapter 14 we examine these issues and look at some suggestions for developing these much valued skills.

The conclusion to the book in Chapter 15 seeks to draw out a number of characteristics of effective learning and teaching in mathematics and its applications. The chapter takes each of the identified characteristics in turn, drawing out their role in effective learning and teaching and looking to see how future practice might take greater account of them. While it is relatively straightforward to draw out various characteristics of effective learning and teaching, it is more challenging to ensure that one's own practice is in fact effective. The chapter thus ends by considering the professional development of lecturers and tutors with regard to their teaching, both on an individual basis and more widely.

Finally, the book also gives pointers to a variety of resources that are available to support learning and teaching in mathematics and its applications. In particular, the Internet allows access to a vast range of resources, and one person's selection is provided in the Appendix. Otherwise, references to a number of texts on learning and teaching in mathematics are given in the section on further reading. Several of these place an emphasis on specific aspects, such as giving lectures.

And now ... ?

Read the book! Engage with it and reflect upon it. We would encourage you frequently to consider how you might apply or adapt the ideas proposed in this text to your own practice. Even where you disagree with the text, we would hope that you would take steps to enhance your understanding of the contentious issue and possibly to adapt your own teaching as a result. Our aim in presenting this text is to help all who are looking to improve the learning experiences of students as they study one of the most inspiring and most challenging subjects in higher education.

References

Quality Assurance Agency for Higher Education (QAA) (2001) *QAA Subject Overview Report for Mathematics, Statistics and Operational Research*, QAA, Bristol, http://www.qaa.ac.uk/revreps/subjrev/All/QO7_2000.pdf

QAA (2001) *Draft Benchmarking Document for Mathematics, Statistics and Operational Research*, QAA, Bristol, http://www.qaa.ac.uk/crntwork/benchmark/phase2/mathematics.pdf

Part A

Issues in learning and teaching

1

The transition to higher education

John Appleby and William Cox

Introduction

The transition from one educational stage to another is usually a difficult and uncertain process. Examples include the first day at school, the primary/secondary interface, GCSE to A level (in the UK), school to university and even embarking upon postgraduate research. This article considers the transition to university and how we might better influence students' prior expectations and preparation for this new phase of their life. In addition, we look at the implications for the current curriculum of the common problems of the transition as well as discussing initial assessment of students as they enter higher education (HE).

In mathematics there has been a great deal of recent publicity about the issues around the transition to HE, especially in the UK. Notable among these are the report from the London Mathematical Society (1992) and the more recent publication by the Engineering Council (2000). Other commentators include Cox (1994), Lawson (1997) and Gardiner (1997). Mustoe (1992), Sutherland and Pozzi (1995) and others look at the problem as it affects engineering programmes. Developments that impact on these issues include: changes in school/pre-university curricula, widening access and participation, the wide range of degrees on offer in mathematical subjects, IT in schools and social factors. In the UK, problems arising in the transition are mentioned in many Quality Assurance Agency (QAA) Subject Review reports in Mathematics, Statistics and Operational Research (MSOR), and also in some engineering Subject Review reports.

Various reports, including those listed above, point to the changes in schools as the source of problems in the transition, and make recommendations as to how things could be put right there. Indeed, in response to wider concerns about literacy and numeracy, recent government initiatives within the UK have, perhaps, partially restored some of the skills that providers of numerate degrees need; and these might feed into HE in the next decade. As well as changes at primary level, there is much talk of extending these to the 11–13 age group. But notwithstanding such changes, it is doubtful that we will ever return to a situation where school qualifications are designed solely as a foundation for HE, ensuring that any chosen university entrant will be capable in all the skills required by any university programme with a mathematics component.

However, difficulties in transition are caused not just by changes in school curricula, but also by changes in the ability range, in student attitudes and expectations, student financial burdens, in the resourcing available in HE, and in the curricula we expect them to undertake. Some of these are not at all under our control, and the best we can do is to be aware of them and how they affect our students. Others, including curriculum design and, to an extent, pastoral support, may need attention if those who choose our courses are to have the best chance of success. We might also usefully consider what our students know about our courses when they choose them, and how they might prepare themselves a little before they come: in attitude as well as in knowledge. For example, Loughborough University sends new students a revision booklet before they come (see Croft, 2001; and also the discussion in Chapter 11). Since 50 per cent of MSOR providers within England have been criticized for poor progression rates in Subject Reviews, it is clear that there is much to be done.

We can make an analogy with the position of English as a Second Language provision in adult education, where students apparently equally well qualified have widely variable skills and needs. An important component of such provision is rigorous initial assessment to determine students' current skills profiles before designing a realistic programme that will meet their needs. We are not used to this in HE because there are usually a large number of students and they are traditionally expected to be capable of catching up for themselves if need be, and we are used to the idea that they have already covered everything that we need. It is therefore likely that a system of initial assessment will form an important part of our degree programmes, especially in the transition phase (see the section on initial assessment below).

Understanding the transition to higher education

A recent Teaching and Learning Undergraduate Mathematics (TaLUM) symposium categorized the issues impacting on the HE transition in mathematics as follows:

- The nature of mathematics: does 'mathematics' mean the same thing to schoolteachers, mathematics lecturers, engineering lecturers, etc? Mathematics taught in the context of mathematics honours courses and in 'service' courses for students whose study focuses on other relevant disciplines may be seen as having quite different purposes, by lecturers as well as students.

- Social component. HE is more student centred, students are less biddable, there are financial, emotional and other conflicting pressures.
- Diversity. There is wider participation, wider access, more variable backgrounds and more variable requirements.
- University requirements. Expansion in HE has led to a wide range of not always clearly articulated aims and objectives, so that entry qualifications no longer specify adequately what students should know and be able to do; some attempts have been made to address this through the work of the QAA.
- School provision. This is no longer geared to feed a coherent spectrum of HE institutions, and university staff are sometimes ignorant of it. There have been changes in school curricula in other subjects such as physics, which used to provide useful support and motivation for students learning mathematics.
- University provision. There are changes in content and style of university teaching compared with school. This is partly due to the fact that many university teachers are not trained (based on an assumption of self-motivated, able students).

The TaLUM symposium further noted that the following were also needed:

- Representation. There is a need to expand fora for school and university teachers to air views and concerns, debate issues, etc; the Learning and Teaching Support Network (LTSN) subject centres may now contribute to this within the UK.
- Liaison. There is a need for closer liaison between schools and universities.

The preceding list focuses on changes in the transition to HE, attempting to list some of the main categories of reasons for the increased difficulties. It is also useful to consider the students and their perspective, the university including its staff and its courses, and the change that is required for the one to adapt to the other. In this section we explore the contrast between attitudes and characteristics typical of lecturers and those of students, together with our intentions and expectations, usually implicit, of the course and of the students. We examine the curriculum in more detail in the following section.

University lecturers were not typical students even at the time they were students, and, in many cases, that was 10, 20, or even 40 years ago. We liked our subject, worked adequately if not hard, and also perhaps had a style of learning that was atypical. Understanding what we were doing, finding out for ourselves, checking our results, as well as having a natural bent for mathematics, were likely to be our characteristics. This attitude continues (except that there is far more emphasis on research compared to teaching these days), and we probably most like teaching those who are interested and make an effort. Most of us probably had family members who had been to university: not true for many students for some years after any major expansion.

In addition, we may well have enjoyed reading as a pastime, perhaps did not have a telephone or television in our lodgings, and certainly did not have a mobile phone or access to the Internet. We probably did not have term-time work, and also spent less on clothes, entertainment and drink, etc. School teaching also followed a different style as well as different syllabuses, with more routine practice though perhaps with fewer topics and possibly no calculator. On the other hand, we were less used to visiting the library, interviewing people, project work and group work and more used to textbook problems little connected with everyday problems. Furthermore, we also did not have to address the issues associated with IT and transferable skills, both of which are discussed in other chapters.

Our current student group, as well as having a great variety of qualifications and ability, also have variety in social background, age, work experience and ambitions or intentions. Lastly, some students, especially mature ones, may have had some gap since they last formally studied mathematics.

Other factors not often mentioned are the changes in other areas of the school curriculum. In the UK the most obvious are that double mathematics A level, formerly common for applicants to mathematics, physics or engineering courses, is now rare, and the changes in physics. Far fewer sixth-formers now study physics, so much so that many engineering courses now accept students without this qualification, but also the nature of Physics A level has changed. Partly because GCSE Mathematics contains no calculus, A level Physics has become less quantitative, and topics like simple harmonic motion and dimensional analysis are missing. Apart from the actual topics, this may also contribute to a relatively 'Pure' view of mathematics (at A level) as a subject with its own laws, rather than as a tool for describing the real world. It may also be relevant that in English, as well as in mathematics, there has been a reduced emphasis on standard techniques and the need for accuracy, and increased emphasis on creative use.

In the past we have not always been explicit about what we expect from students, and indeed, what we are trying to achieve in our undergraduate courses. Clearly, knowledge of the subject has been pre-eminent as an aim, with the implicit aim of understanding. After all, if *we* generally seek to understand what we do, and want to learn more, then it is easy to assume that the same is, or should be, true for our students. Thus our assessment methods have focused on skill at solving standard types of problems, with the real aims pursued incidentally (Ball *et al*, 1998). A student like ourselves will, in achieving mastery, attempt a wide range of problems and try to understand why the methods work when they do. However, a typical student (and, to an extent, this was always true) will see the assessment task as the mastery of a restricted skill and, in focusing on this problem type alone, may fail to make the connections we expect and achieve even that mastery. Therefore, to address the needs of a typical student, we must address the curriculum, be prepared to change it if necessary, as well as to prepare students for it (see following section).

A further area worth consideration is that of the change of pattern of learning as the student comes to HE. Instead of a school pattern, in which the majority of work is supervised in class or closely directed, students find that the majority of their work is undirected and unsupervised. In addition, they are expected to make use of a wide range of resources – books (and finding their way round the library and the Web), notes, handouts, computer-based materials – and new patterns of work: choosing their own tasks, managing their own time, and group work of a different kind. In the section on initial assessment below we consider further how we might address some of these issues for the new student.

The curriculum

We have two aims in considering the curriculum: Is the curriculum appropriate? How can we help students to cope with it? Moreover, we might consider various aspects of the curriculum including: syllabuses, assessment, resources, time-tabling and scheduling, style versus content, knowledge versus understanding, mathematics honours versus service teaching, and progression in several of the above over the three or four years of the course.

In this chapter, we can only reflect on the broader issues of what constitutes an appropriate curriculum, and offer some suggestions about the second question: how can we best support students, especially in the early days of their course? However, our reflections on transition should feed into discussions about the course as a whole. To some extent, we have to accept that an appropriate curriculum is one that our students can cope with (see Chapters 7 and 8 for a fuller discussion of curriculum design and related issues).

It is now a major challenge to match the first and subsequent years' curriculum to the skills profile of what might be a wide range of incoming students. So many assumptions made about their background are now out of date. For example, consider the case of the integral:

$$\int \frac{1}{4x^2 - 1} \, dx$$

which might occur as part of solving a differential equation in the first year of a typical mathematics degree programme, taking mostly students with around A level B grade standard. Twenty years ago the typical lecturer might have written the bald steps on the board as:

$$\int \frac{dx}{(2x-1)(2x+1)} \, dx = \frac{1}{2} \int \left(\frac{1}{2x-1} - \frac{1}{2x+1} \right) dx$$

$$= \frac{1}{2} \int \frac{dx}{2x-1} - \frac{1}{2} \int \frac{dx}{2x+1}$$

$$= \frac{1}{4}\ln|2x + 1| - \frac{1}{4}\ln|2x + 1| + C$$

$$= \frac{1}{4}\ln\left|\frac{2x - 1}{2x + 1}\right| + C$$

with little explanation, and very little or no time actually studying the method of integration.

In fact, five distinct techniques are used, namely:

- difference of two squares;
- partial fractions;
- substitutions for $2x - 1, 2x + 1$;
- integral of reciprocal;
- properties of logs.

For a class today of grade B students even the individual steps of the above argument could be beyond a significant proportion (greater than 50 per cent). Putting them together therefore represents a significant learning task. This is no longer a case of revision with a few reminders, and such students can no longer be sent off to sort the details out for themselves without help. Time and resources must be allowed in the curriculum for the students to consolidate their skills in areas such as this. For engineering students, more revision of these skills has been routine for longer, but there have been changes in the examination. As well as a simpler integrand, the method of integration will probably be given. Other examples of changes over time include specifying all steps in examples, rather than most, specifying methods of solution for differential equations, and giving intermediate results in problems, which reduces the requirement for analysis and for accuracy.

So a continual rethink of the curriculum is required if even good A level students are not to be continually bombarded by the need to call instantly on basic skills that they simply do not have. It is easy to view this as 'dumbing down', falling standards, etc, and to begrudge the extra time needed for catching up. But this is nothing new, and there is little point in wasting time on recriminations: we simply have to work with the students we have. Against this, we must avoid a boring curriculum; methods are more interesting, relevant and memorable if seen as part of a whole and in context rather than in isolation.

Defining the curriculum in terms of learning outcomes

Encouraged by the programme of subject reviews within the UK we have become more explicit about our aims and objectives, or aims and learning outcomes, as they are now formulated. Specifically, a learning outcome is a statement of a performance under certain conditions to a certain standard (see Gronlund, 1978; Mager, 1990). We do not claim that what has been written always reflects properly what we do, nor that we act on what we say is our intention. Nonetheless, it seems a good thing at least to try to be more explicit. This will help us to decide what we expect/desire in incoming students. This of course will depend on our programme, and such things as the student body: honours or service.

Under the broader heading of aims, the issue of who we are teaching will often predominate. For non-specialists, the needs of the discipline must be considered. They often need fairly advanced ideas early on, such as partial differentiation, and even partial differential equations, also some Fourier analysis ideas, etc, where we would prefer to build up more slowly. On the other hand, the early introduction of applications is good for motivation and in providing a framework for the strategic side of mathematics. For mathematics honours, the needs of the subject are important, and the desired outcomes are expressed more in terms of mathematical thinking. Contrast the 'mathematics toolkit' view, with rapid progress initially and competence in tackling science, engineering or economics problems with deeper understanding and a sound basis for further study in mathematics.

Departments fall into categories – not all are completely different – so we may benefit from others' efforts here, and there will always be some overlap in basic requirements (though the level of fluency required may vary). The curriculum to which these students are to be inducted will be based on the entry level, background qualifications, and so on, as well as somewhat varying aims. Realistically, we also have to accept students with gaps in their knowledge, and with partial (and variable) familiarity with some of this material.

We need to express what we want the students to know in terms of learning outcomes that are specific but not unwieldy. This should help us to design a valid and reliable assessment strategy. Some learning outcomes will inevitably be joint or multi-skill, such as integration by partial fractions. Such a learning outcome could strictly be broken down into separate skills, but this is unrealistic, and also neglects our wish that they can do the whole of such a problem. That is, the skills of analysis and synthesis are neglected by decomposition into, and assessment as, separate skills. This example is, however, scarcely a multi-step problem, as the student has probably learned the whole as one routine procedure (see Smith *et al*, 1996; Ball *et al*, 1998; Galbraith and Haines, 2000). The hierarchical network of skills underlying the expert-system diagnostic test DIAGNOSYS attempts a practical compromise by a limited breaking down of problems into component skills (see the example in the next section).

There are different types or levels of learning outcomes, from factual knowledge to advanced cognitive skills. The standard classification of learning outcomes is Bloom's taxonomy. As it stands this is impracticable for useful teaching purposes, and many authors (see, for example, Smith *et al*, 1996; Ball *et al*, 1998; Galbraith and Haines, 2000) have adapted and simplified it. Recently, Smith *et al* (1996) have defined the 'Mathematical Assessment Task Hierarchy': MATH. The categories in this taxonomy are shown in Table 1.1.

Table 1.1 Mathematical Assessment Task Hierarchy

Group A	Group B	Group C
factual knowledge	information transfer	justifying and interpreting
comprehension	application in new situations	implications, conjectures and comparisons
routine use of procedures		evaluation

As Smith *et al* (1996) observe, most exam papers are biased towards Group A skills, as indeed are most textbooks. Ball *et al* (1998) describe how assessments can be designed to create a diversity of assessments and learning activities and assess across the full range of learning outcomes. For incoming students, we tend to focus on Group A tasks: essential skills we need to rely on before advancing to the higher cognitive skills B and C. Although we often bemoan the absence of a 'deep approach' in our students, as well as work, study, analytical, problem solving, self-correction and self-critical skills, these must really be developed over time. The diagnostic tests we know of focus on the basics typified by Group A though some offer partial steps for reduced marks, and, ironically, a traditional type test, using fewer, longer, questions, does depend more on higher skills.

Ideally, all contributors to the provision should be involved in specifying the requirements of students, with wide consultation, because:

- It clarifies and publicizes staff expectations and opens them to scrutiny.
- It informs everyone about the real background of students.
- It informs all staff about what their students will know for future years.
- It informs curriculum design in subsequent years.

There will be areas of disagreement in attempting to specify such starting knowledge, as well as an educational process for staff (perhaps one of the underlying problems in university mathematics teaching is that, in a highly hierarchical and interdependent subject, we have often failed, in the past, even to discuss our several aims and assumptions). However, without some agreement, it is unlikely that the process will be at all effective.

If we are looking at our initial curriculum, trying to match it to the students we have, we must also look at the consequences for later years (and the MMath degree is one such outcome). However, we must also not forget the need to challenge students and to reach topics that relate to current applications and problems. There are also areas where a greater willingness to investigate and research, together with modern computational and algebra tools, permits extended explorations in mathematics, providing always that there is a secure basis on which to build.

We have said little about other aspects of the curriculum, but the best constructed syllabus may fail if the coursework load and deadlines set by other staff distract the student from steady progress in mathematics. We can only urge awareness of the issue here.

Initial assessment and what to do with it

Having discussed how we might describe the curriculum and the requirements this implies for incoming students, we now consider what initial assessment is capable of doing and should attempt to do.

Part of the problem is that students often have partial knowledge of a topic: familiarity not fluency. For example, the higher-level syllabuses at GCSE include fractional indices, but students who have not done mathematics beyond that level will often be found deficient even in manipulation of positive indices. Clearly they need practice in using indices, but lengthy re-teaching of the topic may turn students off, and they may assume they know things better than they do. It may be that they can do a question on just that skill, but fail to recognize it in context. One might say, 'a little algebra is a dangerous thing'!

Some departments/providers already make an initial assessment in the form of 'diagnostic tests' and 'remedial' provision (Edwards, 1996). While well meaning, such provision has a stigma attached to it whereas it should be seen as an essential part of good educational practice designed to 'audit' what students know before moving on, so here we use the term 'initial assessment'. A further danger to be aware of is that poor performance at this stage may lower students' expectations of themselves. The need for such initial assessment exists at all levels, from the Higher National Diploma to Cambridge honours mathematics programmes (Engineering Council, 2000); the variability in our entrants implies careful provision to support them and enable them to reach their full potential. We must try to determine what students know, not what either we or they think they know.

Having identified what we would like them to know, we must decide how we will determine what they do know, that is, to what extent they have attained each learning outcome. This depends on a range of things: entry qualifications, ability, attitude and motivation, learning style, etc. There are a number of possible sources of information:

- entry qualifications;
- pre-university syllabuses;
- diagnostic tests/initial assessment.

In themselves, entry qualifications are of limited use, and information is not always easy to obtain at present. Grades B to D at A level seem like a lottery, in that no knowledge of any particular topic can be relied upon (Chandler, 1997; Cox, 2000). Even a student with an A grade can have substantial gaps on topics we expect. However, some rough idea of the 'average' knowledge of students with a given grade can be usefully discerned following appropriate analysis of the results of objective tests. Note that other factors affecting the transition to HE, such as learning styles, intelligence and motivation, are not usually measured by school qualifications.

Pre-university syllabi are not all that useful, as there is no guarantee about what has been covered. For example, the terms 'polynomial' and 'rational function' are used frequently in defining syllabuses but many students do not seem to know these terms.

Initial assessment can be useful in pinning down detailed knowledge, though we must accept performance 'on the day' can be variable, and also dependent on such factors as wording, context and choice of symbols. To be valid and reliable, initial assessment must be based on clearly specified learning outcomes. Such assessments are used:

- To provide occasional updates for designing curricula, combating false expectations of staff, and researching into students' backgrounds.
- Annually, to help individual students, allocate them to support groups or fully streamed classes.

The opinion of the staff is often the least useful guide to what students are likely to know. They are often unaware of recent developments in pre-university education and the implications for students' knowledge and skills. This is vividly illustrated in the work of Adamson, Byrom and Clifford (1998). These authors tested mechanical engineering entry students on their performance in basic ideas of physics, mathematics, and even spelling and grammar. They also surveyed staff on their prior expectations of the students' results. In many areas the staff expectations were twice what the students could actually achieve.

In mathematics a recent survey by Sutherland and Dewhurst (1999) has investigated the mathematical knowledge expected of entrants to HE across a wide range of disciplines. In a large number of areas it is possible to compare these expectations with the likely prior performance values for incoming students at different levels (Cox, 2001b). Preliminary findings are that there is again a significant gap between expectations and actuality, and one can estimate the mismatch for each outcome and so better inform staff expectations. Because of extensive retirements and the rate of change in schools and colleges, we can no longer rely just on 'common sense' or teaching 'folklore' among experienced teachers. However, we can now get information from new sources (eg LTSN and QAA Subject Review Web sites) and process it more easily.

So we need to survey incoming students on an agreed list of key learning outcomes to audit their strengths and weaknesses. This may amount to 100 or so learning outcomes, if we avoid breaking down every question into components so it can be realistic to test in all, and also at different levels. The structure of mathematics can be used to avoid re-testing, as in DIAGNOSYS. For example, a weaker student who cannot simplify both of $(\frac{1}{2})^{-1}$ and $x^2 x^3$ need not be tested on $x^{-2} x^{-3}$, while a better student who can do the third can be presumed to be able to do the first two.

Currently, some 40 per cent of institutions use some sort of initial assessment. This may be a one-off test, paper or computer based, or several tests, interviews, seminars, etc. Ideally the mode should be chosen for effectiveness rather than convenience. Some criterion-based tests (see Engineering Council, 2000) require students to achieve mastery (eg an 80 per cent score) in selected topics through repeated attempts at tests.

Tests are often parochial, aimed at the institution's own students. However, wider communication through the Web and through LTSN, especially where tests can be customized to local aims (not a problem for paper-based tests, and some computer-based tests also permit this) should enable surveys of a wider range of students (Cox, 2001a) and the use of initial assessment tools more widely.

When we do know what students' specific problems are, we must find the most effective way of dealing with them. Here we concentrate on helping them to adapt to the curriculum on offer. We do not have time to re-teach all the topics in A level and earlier that might be missing, ie teaching uniformly across all topics; we must focus on limited areas and/or students in terms of what is needed and how it is delivered. For example, it is found (Cox, 2000) that 'A level equivalent' students entering HE through non-standard entry routes have problems with expanding brackets (70 per cent can expand two sets of brackets satisfactorily, but only 40 per cent can do three with facility and speed), whereas most A level students have no problems here. Also note context and variety of forms $1 - x(2 - x)$ may be misread as $(1 - x)(2 - x)$, and $(2 - x)(1 - x)$ is significantly more difficult than $(x - 2)(x + 1)$ for weaker students, though to us they probably seem equivalent. So in this case students probably need lots of exercises (with answers), rather than teaching as such, and maybe a short test.

Students may or may not be familiar with inequalities, but few are fluent in their usage, so this topic is best done from scratch as part of the main curriculum, not regarded as 'remedial' at all. Students with high grades are usually confident with rules of differentiation, whereas others usually less so. In this case ab initio teaching (especially of the topic 'function of a function') is needed. The whole of calculus must be taught for non-A level groups, carefully paced, with graded exercises and tutorial support, matching the teaching, learning and assessment strategy to the problem.

Institutions have tried many ways to provide initial and continuing support (Edwards, 1997). Whether these are successful or not often depends on the abilities, attitudes and motivation of students and staff, and an approach that may be effective in one environment may be useless in another. Here we describe some things that have been tried, as identified from MSOR Subject Review reports and the literature.

Additional modules or courses

Some providers mount specific modules/courses designed to bridge the gap, ranging from single modules focusing on key areas of A level Mathematics to one year Foundation courses designed to bring under-qualified students up to a level where they can commence the first year proper. Specific modules devoted to consolidate and ease the transition to university should be integrated as far as possible with the rest of the programme so that lecturers on parallel modules are not assuming too much of some students. Foundation years should provide a measured treatment of key material; a full A-level course is usually inappropriate in one year.

There are a number of computer-based learning and assessment packages (see, for example, Chapter 5) that can be used to supplement the curriculum. They are best used integrated fully with the rest of the curriculum, linked strategically with the other forms of teaching and with the profiles and learning styles of the individual students. It is well accepted that simply referring students with specific weaknesses to 'go and use' a computer package is rarely effective. Some students have problems that are deep-rooted, requiring intensive 'guide by your side' teaching, and struggling alone in front of a computer is the last thing they need. On the other hand many middle-ability students may be happy to work through routine material on the computer, thus freeing up teachers to concentrate on the more pressing difficulties. Computer-based learning materials have met with mixed success and they certainly do not constitute an easy or cheap option.

Streaming is another way in which the curriculum can be adapted to the needs of incoming students as a means of easing the transition. 'Fast' and 'slow' streams, 'practical' and 'more theoretical' streams and others are being used by a number of providers (for example, Savage, 2001, at the University of Leeds). With streaming or support modules, there can be real problems ensuring that all students in the group are kept interested but are enabled to tackle the next stage of the course together.

Another important aspect of matching the curriculum to incoming students is that of the varying attitudes of students and how we influence them or take them into account. Shaw and Shaw (1997, 1999) studied the attitudes and motivation of students, classifying them in various groups that could be used in designing teaching, learning and assessment strategies. Such a classification may help in designing initial assessment targeted at specific types of students for example.

Environment providing support and resources to aid in catching up

Providing a genuinely supportive environment is hard work, with no short cuts possible. The most effective providers in this respect simply spend a lot of time and patience and resources on students. Regular formative (if you can get students to do it) and summative coursework is often a strong feature of good support provision, with fast turnaround in marking and feedback that promotes learning. Subject Reviews often cite tardy return of coursework and unhelpful or non-existent feedback as prime weaknesses in this area, while another regular criticism is the similarity of coursework and examination questions. This is not the way to support students, even if it does raise pass rates, since it fails to develop independent learning skills in the students. Another common criticism is coursework weighting, as students may be able to pass, almost whatever their performance in the examinations. Again, easing the transition in this way is simply deferring the problem. A balance has to be struck between being too helpful, a short-term fix, and encouraging students to overcome their own deficiencies and problems.

Some providers have introduced learning centres, mathematics workshops and surgeries, as a means of supporting students in an individual and confidential way (Lawson, Halpin and Croft, 2001). There are some excellent examples of good practice here, and the concept is commendable and usually a very cost-effective use of resources. One can spread the cost by extending the facility to cover all students requiring mathematical help across the institution. If we include students whose study involves the use of statistics, art students enquiring about Mandelbrot sets, and management students asking about the butterfly effect, then every single student in the institution might be covered. One institution took 'surgeries' literally and used a GP's announcement system to call students to the next available lecturer!

Keeping close track of students and their performance as a means of giving individual support is used in many cases (see, for example, the Feedback and Monitoring System (FAMOS) at the University of Southampton; Quality Assurance Agency for Higher Education, 2000). While this is obviously a prerequisite to supporting students at an individual level, it is again necessary to draw a fine balance between providing a helping hand and a permanent crutch. Partly as a response to high failure and non-completion rates some providers have introduced such measures as attendance registers and compulsory meetings with personal tutors. One might ask if this is really the way to breed independent lifelong learners endowed with mature self-discipline.

Some institutions take the opportunities offered by an induction/freshers' week to start the process of transition with such things as initial assessments. Some send out materials during the summer, helping the students to prepare themselves and find out what they are in for. At the very least this shows students that their individual difficulties are of concern to the institution and can be a useful icebreaker in initial meetings with personal tutors.

In providing assistance to first-year students there is a growing trend in the use of second- and third-year students in a mentoring role, supporting, but not replacing, experienced staff. Such student mentors go under a number of names – peer tutors, 'aunties', 'gurus', etc – but the main idea is for them to pass on their experiences and help others with their problems. Having gone through these problems themselves recently, they are in a position to understand and empathize with struggling first-year students. Some mentors are paid or receive other benefits. In at least one institution such students receive credit towards their own qualifications in terms of the development of transferable skills that the work evidences. Reviewers report that both parties usually benefit, the mentors from the transferable skills they develop and the achievements they can add to their curricula vitae, and the students from the help they receive. It is of course essential that the mentors are trained for their role, and that this provision is monitored carefully. Finally, the scheme must be properly resourced and administered, not run on an ad hoc basis.

Regular, small group tutorials are often used to support students, sometimes run by postgraduates (with comments as for student mentors above). They should be carefully focused, requiring experience and a great deal of hard work. It is an area in which staff development could – but often does not – play an important role. By their nature, such tutorials are very difficult to observe, but nevertheless reviewers have reported some very good practice and find that it is possible to recognize good-quality tutoring in action.

Some providers now bring in schoolteachers, or liaise in other ways with schools. This can be very effective and rewarding for all parties, with obvious benefits in the greater appreciation by schoolteachers of the students' difficulties. In work on expectations of incoming students' mathematical background (Cox, 2001b) it was found that the expectations of an experienced schoolteacher were much closer to the reality than those of many academic staff; not surprising you might think, but what is salutary is the degree of the difference.

While emphasizing that supporting students is hard work for staff, we must not forget that it also requires hard work from the students. A large amount of the routine basic skills of mathematics is learnt only by repetitive practice; why should mathematics be different from any other worthwhile activity? The motivation for such drudgery is that it will be useful in the end. Teachers can play an important role in reassuring students of that and in making the process as efficient as possible, by for example graduating the difficulties of exercises and providing lots of easy problems as well as tougher ones.

Providing a safety net and time to catch up

Some institutions do not have a resit policy, that is, students carry failures forward, retaking and restudying topics while learning new material in parallel. This may be used as a strategic device for getting students through by extra study over the summer. However, this may be demoralizing for the students, who should be accommodated within the normal curriculum if possible. In one institution entry standards were lowered one year to increase intake numbers to target. This led to about a dozen students coming in with lower grades than usual. Every one of these students, and only these students, failed exams in the summer and had to take resits. Properly planned support would be much better than this.

Conclusions

Transition to another situation and phase of education or employment will always cause some problems for students or any of us. We must aim to reduce the likelihood of these problems, diagnose those that remain, and offer support to those affected.

To do this, we must first be aware of what these actual or potential problems are; the early section on Understanding the Transition focused on this area. To reduce the incidence of these problems requires changes to our curriculum, in delivery and assessment as well as content, but also better pre-course information and, where we can, pastoral and other support.

Within our subject area, it is helpful to identify specific weaknesses in students' knowledge or skill, especially with topics we have taken for granted in the past. Such initial assessment, if carefully related to the actual needs of the curriculum to follow, can enable us to help the students fill vital gaps, or become aware of persistent needs for which support may be made available.

Despite what many of us see as problems with students' level of preparation for HE, and with resourcing, we must strive in all this to continue to make mathematics challenging, interesting, worthwhile, and avoid what really is 'dumbing down', that is, treating mathematics as simply a collection of facts or procedures to be memorized.

References

Adamson J, Byrom, T and Clifford, H (1998) Further comparative studies in the prior knowledge assessment of BEng (Hons) course entrants, *International Journal of Mechanical Engineering Education*, **26**, pp 177–96

Ball, G *et al* (1998) Creating a diversity of mathematical experiences for tertiary students entrants, *International Journal of Mechanical Engineering Education*, **29**, pp 827–41

Chandler, S (1997) A-level mathematics examinations as a fair assessment of the needs of students post-GCSE Intermediate and Higher Tiers, *Teaching Mathematics and its Applications*, **16**, pp 157–59

Cox, W (1994) Strategic learning in A-level mathematics?, *Teaching Mathematics and its Applications*, **13**, pp 11–21

Cox, W (2000) Predicting the mathematical preparedness of first year undergraduates for teaching and learning purposes, *International Journal of Mathematical Education in Science and Technology*, **31**, pp 227–48

Cox, W (2001a) Inter-institutional collaboration on easing the transition to university, *MSOR Connections*, **1**(1), pp 5–8

Cox, W (2001b) On the expectations of the mathematical knowledge of first year undergraduates, *International Journal of Mathematical Education in Science and Technology*, to appear

Croft, A (2001) *Algebra Revision booklet*, Loughborough University, Loughborough

Edwards, P (1996) *Implementing Diagnostic Testing for Non-specialist Mathematics Courses*, Open Learning Foundation, London

Edwards, P (1997) Just how effective is the mathematics diagnostic test and follow-up support combination?, *Teaching Mathematics and its Applications*, **16** (3), pp 118–21

Engineering Council (2000) *Measuring the Mathematics Problem*, The Engineering Council, London

Galbraith, P and Haines, C (2000) Conceptual mis(understanding) of beginning undergraduates, *International Journal of Mathematical Education in Science and Technology*, **31**, pp
651–78

Gronlund, N E (1978) *Stating Objectives for Classroom Instruction*, 2nd edn, Macmillan, New
York

Lawson, D, Halpin, M, and Croft, A (2001) After the diagnostic test – what next?, *MSOR
Connections*, **1**(3), pp 19–23

London Mathematical Society (1992) *The Future for Honours Degree Courses in Mathematics
and Statistics*, The London Mathematical Society, London

Mager, J F (1990) *Preparing Instructional Objectives*, 2nd edn, Kogan Page, London

Quality Assurance Agency for Higher Education (QAA) (2000) *Subject Review Report
Q70/2000 for University of Southampton*, QAA, Bristol

Savage, M D (2001) Streaming in mathematics for Physics students at Leeds, private
communication

Shaw, C T and Shaw, V F (1997) Attitudes of first-year engineering students to mathematics
– a case study, *International Journal of Mathematical Education in Science and Technology*,
28(2), pp 289–301

Shaw, C T and Shaw, V F (1999) Attitudes of first-year engineering students to mathematics
– a comparison across universities, *International Journal of Mathematical Education in Science
and Technology*, **30**, pp 47–63

Smith, G *et al* (1996) Constructing mathematical examinations to assess a range of
knowledge and skills, *International Journal of Mathematical Education in Science and
Technology*, **27**, pp 65–77

Further reading

Anderson, J *et al* (1998) Do third-year mathematics undergraduates know what they are
supposed to know? *International Journal of Mathematical Education in Science and Technology*,
29, pp 401–420

Appleby, J C and Anderson, A (1997) Diagnostic testing of mathematics and mechanics on
entry, in *The Mathematical Education of Engineers II*, eds S Hibberd and L R Mustoe,
Institute of Mathematics and its Applications, Southend-on-Sea

Barry, M D J and Steele, N C (eds) (1991) *A Core Curriculum in Mathematics for the European
Engineer*, Swiss Federal Institute of Technology, Switzerland

Burn, R, Appleby, J and Maher, P (1998) *Teaching Undergraduate Mathematics*, Imperial
College Press, London

Clifford, H (1994) A comparison of expectations and achievements in a prior knowledge
assessment of BEng (Hons) course entrants, *International Journal of Mechanical Engineering
Education*, **22**, pp 55–68

Gardiner, A (1997) Rediscovering mathematics?, *Teaching Mathematics and its Applications*,
16, pp 145–47

Hirst, K E (1996) *Changes in A-level Mathematics from 1996*, University of Southampton,
Southampton

Houston, K (ed) (1994) *Innovations in Mathematics Teaching*, Staff and Educational
Development Association, Birmingham

Hunt, D N and Lawson, D A (1996) Trends in mathematical competency of A-level
students on entry to university, *Teaching Mathematics and its Applications*, **15**(4), pp 167–73

Hunt, D N and Lawson, D A (1997) Common core – common sense?, in *The Mathematical Education of Engineers, II*, ed S Hibberd and L R Mustoe, pp 21–26, Institute of Mathematics and its Applications, Southend-on-Sea

Kitchen, A (1996) A-level mathematics isn't what it used to be; or is it?, *Mathematics Today*, May/June

Lawson, D (1997) What can we expect from A-level mathematics students?, *Teaching Mathematics and its Applications*, **16**(4), pp 151–56

Micallef, M J (1997) Mathematics A-level as preparation for university mathematics-based programmes?, *Teaching Mathematics and its Applications*, **16**, pp 160–64

Mustoe, L R (1992) Clinging to the wreckage – mathematics for engineers in the 1990s, *Institute of Mathematics and its Applications Bulletin*, **28**, pp 99–102

Rycraft, M (1997) The mathematical knowledge of some entrants to HE in the UK, *International Journal of Mathematical Education in Science and Technology*, **28**(3), pp 411–17

Sutherland, R and Pozzi, S (1995) *The Changing Mathematical Background of Undergraduate Engineers: A review of the issues*, The Engineering Council, London

Sutherland, R and Dewhurst, H (1999) *Mathematics Education Framework for Progression from 16–19 to HE*, Graduate School of Education, University of Bristol, Bristol

2

The genesis of mathematical structures

Robert Burn

Introduction

The lecturer's strength

When a lecturer in mathematics is appointed, this is normally on the strength of his or her research; not just on the fertility of his or her ideas, but also on the proven capacity to present them for publication according to the accepted norms. In mathematics itself the accepted norms generally have a deductive structure: definition, theorem, proof, corollary. This sequence has some degree of necessity about it. One needs terms from a definition in order to articulate a theorem, a proof to justify it and then corollaries to show its significance. Expounding mathematics according to this deductive sequence makes it as easy as can be for the logic to be checked. And where applications of mathematics are concerned the focus typically will be on a systematic presentation of the finished mathematical theory. Because these are the kinds of format in which the lecturer has established his or her expertise, it is not surprising that when lecturing or when writing a textbook, these are the formats a lecturer commonly uses. These formats are needed for convincing one's peers; they are rarely the most helpful for a student beginning to learn the subject.

The phenomena of learning mathematics and didactical inversion

In his *Didactical Phenomenology of Mathematical Structures* Hans Freudenthal (1983) distinguished between different phenomena in mathematics education:

- The articulation of formal structures, their logical connections and their applications are the substance of the phenomenon of *mathematics*.
- The interactions between teacher and student, and the activities engineered by the teacher for the student are a *didactical* phenomenon.
- The experiences that the student goes through in learning some mathematics are a *genetic* phenomenon of a psychological nature.

That these three kinds of phenomena are distinct from one another goes without saying. Someone appointed as a lecturer in mathematics has demonstrated his or her expertise in understanding and generating the first of these, and we will presume the lecturer's familiarity with the relevant phenomena of mathematics in all that follows. What we will attempt to describe in the rest of this chapter is the mathematical thinking that generates a mathematical product – the *genetic* phenomenon – so that this may inform didactic choice. As Freudenthal says in his preamble, 'No mathematical idea has ever been published in the way it was discovered' (Freudenthal, 1983: ix).

This points to a divergence between formal mathematical structures and their genesis. We highlight the distinction between genetic process and formal product in Table 2.1. Freudenthal claimed that mathematical practice often led to a didactical inversion in which the genetic sequence was reversed in exposition. While the psychological processes are those that create the product, the ordinary conventions of lecturing offer the product first and then expect the genetic processes to take place as the succeeding exercises are attempted. And yet, however unhelpfully deductive or formal the teacher's exposition may be, each student coming to the subject afresh will go from not knowing to knowing, a path of personal discovery, and although that process will rarely copy all of the steps of the original discovery, it is a genetic process leading to a formal product. The best pedagogy is informed by knowledge of both genetic and formal structure and the difference between them.

This chapter will thus explore the nature of the genetic process that leads students to develop an understanding of formal mathematical structures. We will initially focus on the role of pattern recognition and conjecture, taking particular account of proof. This leads into a wider consideration of the role that special cases play in the genetic process. The remainder of the chapter then focuses on considering the genetic process in the context of the specific mathematical structures of concepts, axioms and definitions and sets. The detailed consideration of specific mathematical structures and types of structure plays an important role throughout the chapter in illustrating the genetic process. The more theoretical approach taken in this chapter complements the approach taken in Chapter 3 where a variety of perspectives, including an understanding of the divergence between mathematical structures and their genesis, provide the basis for developing active learners of mathematics. Furthermore, while this chapter pays particular attention to pure mathematics, the principles exposed are also relevant to applications of mathematics.

Table 2.1   Genetic processes and formal products

Genetic	Formal
process	product
heuristic	deduction
meaning	definition
guess, conjecture	theorem
examples	logic
plausible reasoning	convincing
test	proof
counter-example	contradiction
specialize	generalize
modelling process	physical theory

The genetic phenomenon
Pattern recognition and conjecture

A fine example of a genetic study, using historical rather than psychological data, was the investigation of Euler's theorem about the vertices, edges and faces of a polyhedron, $V - E + F = 2$, by Imre Lakatos (1976). The details of how mathematicians responded to counter-examples to the theorem as originally proposed is in sharp contrast to a standard modern presentation of the theorem in which all the snags that emerged are captured and ruled out in the way the theorem is now formulated.

Those who attended the 2nd International Congress for Mathematics Education (ICME-2) in Exeter in 1972 were given copies of a little pamphlet put together by George Pólya under the title *As I Read Them*. It contained 10 quotations (or paraphrased quotations) about learning and discovery, and was reproduced by Howson (1973). The author found three of Pólya's quotations especially apt in describing the experience he had had while doing research in the foundations of geometry for his PhD. These were:

> We should give no small share of the credit to Democritus who was the first to state the result though he did not prove it [*just guessed it*]. ... the method I used did not furnish an actual demonstration [*just a suggestion, a guess. ...Yet*] I foresee that this method, once understood, will be used to discover other theorems which have not yet occurred to me, by other mathematicians, now living or yet unborn.
>
> (Archimedes)

> [*First guess, then prove: that's the way to do it.*]

> Thus all human cognition begins with intuitions, proceeds from thence to conceptions, and ends with ideas.
>
> (Kant)

[*Learning begins with action and perception, proceeds from there to words and concepts, and should end in desirable mental habits.*]

The object of mathematical rigour is to sanction and legitimate the conquests of intuition, and there never was any other object for it.

(J Hadamard)

The illumination here was that without an idea that one believed in, or had a hunch about, there was nothing to try to prove. The genesis of mathematics lies in experiment, trial, hunch, guesswork and intuition. In mathematical terms, the formulation of conjectures or hypotheses, making guesses and suppositions, play an important and necessary role in the development of research, even when further work clarifies the status of guesswork, and conjectures either get no mention (when they are false) or are called theorems (if they can be justified) when the work is finally published. For the research worker, the generation of conjectures is a necessary step in the growth of his or her knowledge. The ideas that students pick up may be false or may be open to refinement. Either way, they share some aspects of a conjecture. A pedagogy that deals regularly in conjectures and their refinement will be touching the genetic processes more often than one that only provides systematic deduction.

One of the common features to emerge from research on undergraduates learning mathematics is their attitude to proof. Students commonly say that they learn proofs because lecturers require them in examinations, and they do not associate the word *proof* with *convincing* or *justifying*. This makes the learning of proofs a kind of circus trick rather than something that satisfies a rational mind. When a theorem and proof are presented as a *fait accompli* all one can do is to memorize them. *After* memorization, understanding may indeed grow from the experience of applying the theorem. This is the didactical inversion to which Freudenthal referred. The natural step by step process of learning was called *assimilation* by Piaget; the much less comfortable process of adopting a new idea that requires the re-organization of one's previous notions, Piaget called *accommodation*. A deductive presentation by the lecturer, with subsequent development of meaning by the student, is more likely to require something like *accommodation* than a presentation in which meaning is foremost, and the deductions serve to justify the understanding.

It is normal practice in school to justify mathematical ideas by means of several examples. From the point of view of university mathematicians, this is a betrayal of the notion of mathematical justification, for it substitutes the notion of plausibility for that of proof, and students are deprived of convincing arguments of full generality. Yes, students at school are rarely given and rarely formulate arguments of great generality, but the special cases they have been given provide meaning, and are in fact, an appropriate basis, not for theorems, but for conjectures.

One of the distinctive steps that can be taken at university is to let students experience and recognize the difference between plausibility and proof, by means of the generation of conjectures. The various fates of possible conjectures – some true, some false, some in need of refinement – clarifies the need for general justifying argument, however many favourable cases may have been generated. Pólya's two volumes on *Mathematics and Plausible Reasoning* (1954) have the intention of demonstrating the importance of guessing in undergraduate mathematics. Guessing has two roles, in formulating conjectures and in devising methods of proof.

There are many examples in Pólya's book, but it has become important today to clarify the distinction between plausibility and proof. (Pólya's concern had been the recognition of the importance of plausibility: the need for proof was not problematic in the way it has become for many students today.) Of course this is best done within a mathematics course in terms of the conjectures and theorems peculiar to the course, but it may be worth offering some examples that would be comprehensible to any university student. Each example here builds on the most obvious source of conjectures, namely pattern recognition.

Table 2.2 Making and resolving conjectures

Context (special cases)	Conjecture (generalization)	Resolution: T/F
$2^3 - 2 = 6, 3^3 - 3 = 24,$ $4^3 - 4 = 60, 5^3 - 5 = 120,$ $6^3 - 6 = 210, 7^3 - 7 = 336$	all numbers of the form $n^3 - n$ have a factor 6	
Join 2, 3, 4 and 5 points on a circle and count regions	joining n points on a circle can make a maximum of 2^{n-1} regions in the circle	
1 2 3 4	the fourth column contains no primes	
5 6 7 8 9 10 11 12	the second column contains one prime	
13 14 15 16 17 18 19 20 21 22 23 24 25 26 27 28	every pair $(4n - 1, 4n + 1)$ contains at least one prime	

Consider the three contexts given in the first column of Table 2.2. In the first example, the invitation is to look for common factors. The second column identifies a plausible conjecture from the computed data; this is the student's suggestion following scrutiny of the data. The third column may be completed after sharing various justifications in class.

In the second example, the invitation is to count the regions within a circle into which it has been divided by the chords joining a certain number of points on the circumference. For up to five points on the circle, the counting can be done easily and convincingly. With six points on the circle, the counting is a little harder, and, what appears to be the obviously emerging pattern of powers of 2, breaks down. The correct formula is in fact $n^4/24 - n^3/4 + 23n^2/24 - 3n/4 + 1$. The conjecture that students suggest can be shown to be false by a counter-example.

In the third example, a search for prime numbers in the table may lead to various conjectures, of which three possibilities are stated in the second column. The search for justifying reasons or for counter-examples then comes to the fore again.

Each of the collections of data here invites an initial conjecture, which then needs to be tested by exploring further. Either a counter-example can be identified, showing the conjecture to be false, or, in the other cases, a proof of the conjecture converts the conjecture into a theorem.

The act of pattern-recognition that is crucial in all the examples above is central to much of the genesis of learning. 'Spot the pattern' is a challenge of great universality. Most students want to do it. But there is more to it than that. The very act of responding is an attempt at generalization. When that generalization is the student's own, the matter under discussion has meaning that undergirds subsequent deductions. 'Spot the pattern' leads to a conjecture and thus to a potential theorem. When the conjecture has meaning for the student, the student has a stake in its justification or the location of counter-examples. When committed to a proposition, it is deeply satisfying to find a justification that can withstand the fiercest criticism. Moreover, the description of a pattern is a step from the concrete to the abstract. Pattern-spotting and pattern-description are central processes in the genesis of mathematics.

To illustrate a didactic approach at a more detailed level, which seeks to support the genesis of the ideas, we provide in Figure 2.1 an illustration derived from material used in a workshop at ICME-8 in Seville in 1996.

Exercises like this are commonly given *after* giving the proof of the dimension theorem in a lecture or a book, but the exercises themselves are accessible without the theorem and provide the genetic background for the generality and abstraction of the full theorem.

We have shown the relation of pattern-spotting to conjectures and thus to theorem formulation, and mentioned how pattern-spotting involves the student in generalization and abstraction. But we shall claim more. Pólya heads chapter 5 of *Mathematics and Plausible Reasoning* with the declaration, 'When you have satisfied yourself that the theorem is true, you start proving it' (Pólya, 1954).

A student's ownership of a conjecture is the basis of proof-construction. Examples will have given the conjecture meaning, counter-examples may have led to the refining of the conjecture. It may be that the generation of data has thrown up examples that are *generic*, that is to say, so typical of the claim being made, that the general structure is immediately evident. How does a generic example suggest a proof? In the first example of Table 2.2: $9^3 - 9 = 9(9^2 - 1) = 9(9 - 1)(9 + 1)$, an example that indicates why any number of the form $n^3 - n$ is equal to the product of three consecutive numbers (at least one of which is divisible by 2 and one by 3).

Figure 2.1   Preparing for the dimension theorem: a worksheet

We presume that the students are already familiar with the notion of a basis of a vector space and how a basis determines the dimension of a finite-dimensional space. We also assume that students know what the kernel of a linear transformation is and that the kernel is a subspace of the domain.

The first exercise is intended to provoke the theorem in the form of a conjecture. The second exercise has two intentions, one is to generate some generic examples, and the other is to dissociate the dimension of the codomain from the pattern.

1. Identify the kernal and the dimension of the image space of each of the following transformations of a real vector space. Add the dimension of the kernel to the dimension of the image space. Is there a pattern?

(a) $(x, y) \rightarrow (0, 0)$;

(b) $(x, y) \rightarrow (x + y, x + y)$;

(c) $(x, y) \rightarrow (y, x)$.

(d) $(x, y, z) \rightarrow (0, 0, 0)$;

(e) $(x, y, z) \rightarrow (x + y + z, x + y + z, x + y + z)$;

(f) $(x, y, z) \rightarrow (x + y, x + 2y, x + 3y)$;

(g) $(x, y, z) \rightarrow (y, z, x)$.

2. Identify the kernel and the dimension of the image space of each of the following linear transformations of a real vector space.

(a) $T:(x, y) \rightarrow (y, y)$;

(b) $T:(x, y) \rightarrow (y, y, y)$;

(c) $T:(x, y) \rightarrow y$.

For each of these transformations, find a basis $\{\mathbf{a}, \mathbf{b}\}$ of the domain for which $\{\mathbf{a}\}$ is a basis of the kernel and $\{T(\mathbf{b})\}$ is a basis of the image space. There are many correct answers to this question. Be satisfied with a simple answer.

(d) $T:(x, y, z) \rightarrow (y, z)$;

(e) $T:(x, y, z) \rightarrow (y, y, z)$;

(f) $T:(x, y, z) \rightarrow (y, y, z, z)$;

(g) $T:(x, y, z) \rightarrow (y + z, y - z)$.

For each of these transformations, find a basis $\{\mathbf{a}, \mathbf{b}, \mathbf{c}\}$ of the domain for which $\{\mathbf{a}\}$ is a basis of the kernel and $\{T(\mathbf{b}), T(\mathbf{c})\}$ is a basis of the image space.

(h) $T:(x, y, z) \rightarrow z$;

(i) $T:(x, y, z) \rightarrow (z, 2z)$;

(j) $T:(x, y, z) \rightarrow (y + z, 2y + 2z)$.

For each of these transformations, find a basis $\{\mathbf{a}, \mathbf{b}, \mathbf{c}\}$ of the domain for which $\{\mathbf{a}, \mathbf{b}\}$ is a basis of the kernel and $\{T(\mathbf{c})\}$ is a basis of the image space.

In the exercises leading to the dimension theorem of Figure 2.1, there is no one generic example, but a sequence of examples that together indicate the structure of the proof. A generic example is the way used in school to justify methods of subtraction, and in college to explain how to solve linear differential equations. Generic examples were often used in the justification of European mathematics before the 19th century. They were also the standard form of justification in Indian and Chinese mathematics.

Generic examples are not always available. When they are, the translation of numerical mathematics to algebraic generality provides a proof. When a generic example is not available, other methods must be sought. Mathematical induction may be relevant. The proposition may need to be broken down into distinct cases that exhaust the possibilities, or when all else has failed, one may seek a proof by contradiction by examining the consequences of supposing the failure of the conjecture. The devices that may be used in a proof are endless and both of Pólya's books (1954, 1962) are devoted to the process of finding proofs. But the motivation for all this is a student's belief in the truth of the theorem.

Special cases

The idea of a generic example is of great significance. So far we have claimed it only as a possible source of the structure of a proof. But special cases are the ordinary source of meaning for all mathematical structures, ideas and applications. Even logic itself gains its meaning from special cases: **if** it is raining, **then** I will take my umbrella when I go out; **if** two triangles are congruent, **then** they are similar; or the less familiar, **if** $a < b$, **then** $a \leq b$. The ordinary understanding of the distinction between an implication and its converse develops from special cases like this.

Let us listen to some outstanding scholars.

> I can't understand anything in general unless I'm carrying along in my mind a specific example and watching it go.
>
> (Feynman, 1986: 244)

> If you want to solve a problem, first strip the problem of everything that is not essential. Simplify it, specialize it as much as you can without sacrificing its core. Thus it becomes simple, as simple as it can be made, without losing any of its punch, and then you solve it. The generalization is a triviality which you don't have to pay much attention to.
>
> (Richard Courant, talking about David Hilbert's consciously used principle. Courant, 1981: 161)

> I look for an example that captures the quintessence of a whole branch of mathematics, that you can constantly refer back to fruitfully as you go deeper into that subject. Each example should naturally generate a few theorems

around itself to prove its key properties. But even before you do this, it should be sufficiently intriguing to capture the attention.

(Professor Christopher Zeeman, 1995, private communication)

For the development of group theory, Zeeman's key examples are S_3, S_4, A_5 and $SO(3)$. For the development of algebraic topology his examples are the Möbius strip, the real projective plane, the trefoil knot, the utilities problem, Borromean rings and Dodecahedral space. For differential equations his first four examples are $\ddot{x} + x = 0$; Mock van der Pol $\dot{r} = r(1 - r^2)$, $\dot{\theta} = 1$; Hopf bifurcation $\dot{r} = r(\varepsilon - r^2)$, $\dot{\theta} = 1$; and coupled oscillators $\ddot{x} = -x + \varepsilon y$, $\ddot{y} = \varepsilon x - y$. It is a fine challenge to pick on any subject you know well, and to identify a handful of examples around which the central theory may be developed. For some courses, the number of key examples will be larger. For a real analysis course, one needs particular sequences, particular series, particular functions and particular integrals. Of course one's preferred special case changes according to context. In particular what is general at one level of thinking becomes special at a higher level of concept development, as is excellently explained by Richard R Skemp in Chapter 1 of *The Psychology of Learning Mathematics* (1986). The process by which a student shifts his or her attention from the properties of particular examples to the properties themselves, which are then defined in their own right and given a name of their own, is called *encapsulation*. Encapsulation is identified clearly and helpfully in an article by Tony Barnard (2000).

The genetic phenomenon in context

Concept development: the rule of three

The development of concept upon concept, and the encapsulation of concepts are of the essence of mathematical maturity. Just how this encapsulation and development takes place is not clear, but it is certainly assisted by meeting the same mathematical notions in different guise. We have already seen the importance of meeting the same ideas in different examples, but it also seems to be important to meet the ideas in different *representations*. This may be because different forms of awareness are associated with different parts of the brain, and the experience of different representations brings more of the brain into play in relation to a mathematical idea. The 'rule of three' was something of a slogan in the calculus reform movement in the United States in the late 1980s. This amounted to a principle that any mathematical notion in the calculus should be met in
numerical,
graphical and
symbolic form. Those students who could interpret mathematical ideas in all three forms had facility and competence with the idea.

Just to make clear what this 'rule of three' means, we illustrate in Figure 2.2 a particular sequence in all three representations.

Figure 2.2   Three representations of a sequence

numerical

n	1	2	3	4	5	6	7	8
a_n	1/2	2/3	3/4	4/5	5/6	6/7	7/8	8/9

graphical

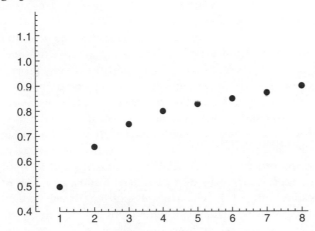

symbolic

$$a_n = \frac{n}{n+1}$$

A numerical representation must usually be looked at sequentially. A graphical representation exhibits the idea all at once, but parts may be focused on at will. A symbolic representation, which will always have to figure in a proof, is generally the tightest encapsulation.

Just how effective visual representations can be is demonstrated quite dramatically by Nelsen (1993) (for a general discussion of the 'rule of three' see Hughes-Hallett, 1991).

Axioms and definitions: examples of historical genesis

In an ordinary deductive treatment of mathematics, axioms and definitions arrive without rationale, and their value has to emerge as theorems are developed from them. It is normal to introduce axioms and definitions with examples and counter-examples to clarify their meaning and to promise that their significance will emerge. Because Euclid used axioms it is possible to get the erroneous impression that stated axioms are a condition of doing any rigorous mathematics. This impression is false. Most of the axioms systems in use today, whether in algebra or analysis, were developed late in the 19th century *after* significant developments in the concerned subject areas.

Group theory, for example, started with the study of permutations of roots of polynomial equations (by Lagrange in 1770 and Galois in 1831). Group theory was extended to the study of geometrical symmetry (by Hessel in 1830, Bravais in 1849 and Jordan in 1868) and developed further with the study of linear transformations (by Jordan in 1870). All the group-theoretic theorems available *before* the proposal of the group axioms in 1882 concerned the transformations of a finite set to itself. But this context was rich enough to allow the formulation of any proposition concerning finite groups. The group axioms, when formulated, summarized common properties of all those systems that had been seen to provide examples of groups in the older sense. Any theorem developed from the axioms would necessarily apply to every one of the previously known examples, thus it is obviously efficient to work from the axioms. But the newly-stated axioms, because they were abstract, would apply in many other contexts, including contexts quite different from those from which the subject originally developed. The historical genesis of abstract group theory has something of the character of 'spot the pattern', which we have seen to be the source of many mathematical theorems.

A much more detailed discussion showing how group theory arose out of the study of special cases is given by Hans Freudenthal (1973). Of course, for students today, the special cases chosen for study must be sufficiently interesting in their own right, and for this purpose geometric symmetry is more immediately accessible than algebraic symmetry. But with well-chosen special cases the theorems developed will transfer readily, when the time comes, into theorems in the more abstract system.

The conventional logical presentation of mathematics comes in the sequence: definition, theorem, proof, corollary. The research mathematician may come to his results starting from some special cases, which will appear as corollaries in the final version, from which he gets the idea, which is worked with until he has a proof. Then the theorem is what has been proved. At this point, he formulates his definitions so as to make the theorem and proof as neat as possible. The genetic sequence is again the reverse of the logical sequence. To quote Hans Freudenthal again:

> Fundamental definitions do not arise at the start but at the end of the exploration, because in order to define a thing you must know what it is and what it is good for.
>
> (Freudenthal, 1973: 107)

This runs counter to the ordinary conventions of exposition so the notion deserves some illustration, first from group theory, then from analysis. The term 'coset' appears in the literature from 1910. However, the theorem attributed to Lagrange, that the order of a subgroup divides the order of the group, was proved in much the way it appears in texts today, from 1866, but without the cosets, which structure the proof, being named as such. Put together with Hölder's notion of 'factor group' (from 1889), the need for a definition and a name became compelling.

The definition of 'limit' is normally attributed to Cauchy in his *Analyse Algébrique* (1821). But in his 'Preliminaries' he writes:

> When the values successively attributed to the same variable approach a fixed value indefinitely, in such a way as to end up by differing from it by as little as one could wish, the last value is called the *limit* of all the others.

> (Cauchy, 1821: 4; translation from Fauvel and Gray, 1987)

This definition has a 17th-century ring about it. One looks in vain for ε, N, or ε, δ. The first hint of an ε appears in the book in the course of a proof that:

$$\text{if } f(x + 1) - f(x) \to k \text{ as } x \to \infty, \text{ then } f(x)/x \to k$$

[The result assumes some condition on the function f such as its continuity on R.]

(Cauchy, 1821: 49; translation from Fauvel and Gray, 1987)

Cauchy writes:
Let ε denote a number as small as one may wish. One can give the number h a sufficiently large value so that when $x \geq h$,

$$k - \varepsilon \leq f(x + 1) - f(x) \leq k + \varepsilon$$

(Cauchy, 1821;. translation from Fauvel and Gray, 1987)

The proof proceeds much as a modern proof would. What was for Cauchy a method of proof has been turned by his successors (ie us) into the standard definition of the limit of a sequence.

Cauchy's definition of limit cited above (1821:4), is repeated verbatim on page 1 of his *Résumé des Leçons sur le Calcul infinitésimal* (1823). In his third lesson he defines the derivative of f as the limit of:

$$\frac{f(x + i) - f(x)}{i}, \text{ as } i \to 0$$

(Cauchy, 1823: 8)

But only in his seventh lesson, when he is about to prove the Mean Value Theorem, do we meet ε, δ for the first time:

Denote by δ, ε two very small numbers, the first being chosen in such a way that for $i \leq \delta$, and for any value of x between x_0 and X,

$$f'(x) - \varepsilon < \frac{f(x + i) - f(x)}{i} < f'(x) + \varepsilon, [i \text{ is presumed positive}]$$

(Cauchy, 1823: 27)

Again, Cauchy's proof-method has been turned by his successors into the standard definition of the limit of a function.

There are steps in undergraduate mathematics that are notorious for the widespread discomfort that they cause. Proof by contradiction is one such; the definition of limit is another. In some cases, further psychological research seems the only way to understand the difficulty. But in many other cases an historical study can expose the genesis of the idea.

Sets

The final context for the genetic phenomenon that we will consider is the concept of a set. Sets became part of the undergraduate curriculum only during the 20th century. Since many of the ideas in a modern undergraduate course in mathematics arose during the 19th century it is possible to see in 19th-century texts what these ideas look like, shorn of set-theoretic language. In many cases, the language of sets has introduced a helpful clarity into the exposition of mathematics. One thinks, for example, of the sets $\mathbf{N}, \mathbf{Z}, \mathbf{Q}, \mathbf{R}, \mathbf{C}$, of the notation $\{x \mid f(x) < 0\}$, of the symbols $\in$, $\cap, \cup, \subset$, and of the empty set $\varnothing$. And the discovery that all of mathematics could be expressed in set-theoretic terms was a remarkable unifying achievement. But the reduction of all mathematical notions to those in the set-theoretic axioms gives familiar notions a strange form. $\{\varnothing, \{\varnothing\}, \{\varnothing, \{\varnothing\}\}\}$ does not *look* like the definition of a number. The Bourbaki definition of a function from A to B as a subset of the Cartesian product $A \times B$ has caused considerable difficulties to students, as witnessed to by the massive compilation, *The Concept of Function: Aspects of epistemology and pedagogy* (Dubinsky and Harel, 1992). This study does not recognize the Bourbaki definition as a generalization that incorporates formulae, mappings, transformations, symmetries, permutations, operations, functionals, operators, sequences, morphisms and machines. To reach the general notion of function there are two stages of going from special case to generality: from particular functions to particular types of functions, and then to functions in general. The very simplicity of the Bourbaki definition of function may beguile the teacher into believing that the genesis of the idea is trivial. The psychological evidence shows that the idea causes widespread difficulty. As with axioms and definitions, when mathematical ideas formulated in a set-theoretic fashion appear to be difficult for students to engage with, it may be possible to look at their historical genesis and to see what a non-set-theoretic presentation looks like.

Conclusion

The process of solving problems, gaining insight and forming generalizations is the way of growth in mathematics. Students, however, cannot usually be expected to recreate the genetic process without support. Lecturers need to find ways to expose the genetic phenomena for their students rather than simply present them with deductive or formal products. Lecturers also need to find ways to help ensure that students themselves engage in generating their own understanding of mathematical products.

References

Barnard, T (2000) Why are proofs difficult? *Mathematical Gazette*, **84**(501), pp 415–22

Cauchy, A L (1821) *Cours d'Analyse de l'École Royale Polytechnique: Analyse Algébrique* (Debure), reprinted 1989, Jacques Gabay, Paris

Cauchy, A L (1823) *Résumé des Leçons sur le Calcul Infinitésimal* (Debure), reprinted 1994, Edition Marketing, Paris

Courant, R (1981) Reminiscences of Hilbert's Göttingen, *The Mathematical Intelligencer*, **3**(4), p 161

Dubinsky, E and Harel, G (eds) (1992) *The Concept of Function: Aspects of epistemology and pedagogy*, Mathematical Association of America, Washington, DC

Fauvel, J and Gray, J (eds) (1987) *The History of Mathematics: A reader*, Open University Press, Buckingham

Feynman, R P (1986) *Surely You're Joking Mr Feynman*, Unwin, London

Freudenthal, H (1973) What groups mean in mathematics and what they should mean in mathematical education, in *Developments in Mathematical Education*, ed A G Howson, Cambridge University Press, Cambridge

Freudenthal, H (1983) *Didactical Phenomenology of Mathematical Structures*, Reidel, Dordrecht

Howson, A G (ed) (1973) *Developments in Mathematics Education*, Cambridge University Press, Cambridge

Hughes-Hallett, D, 1991, Visualisation and Calculus reform, in *Visualisation in Teaching and Learning Mathematics, Mathematical Association of America (MAA) Notes 19*, eds W Zimmermann and S Cunningham, MAA, Washington, DC

Lakatos, I (1976) *Proofs and Refutations*, Cambridge University Press, Cambridge

Nelsen, R B (1993) *Proofs Without Words*, MAA, Washington, DC

Pólya, G (1954) *Mathematics and Plausible Reasoning*, Princeton University Press, Cambridge, Mass

Pólya, G (1962) *Mathematical Discovery*, John Wiley, Chichester

Skemp, R R (1986) *The Psychology of Learning Mathematics*, Penguin, London

3

Developing active learners

Afzal Ahmed, Derek Holton and Honor Williams

Mathematical scientists typically address educational issues exclusively in terms of subject matter content and technical skills, with the 'solution' taking the form of new curriculum materials. Curriculum is, indeed, a crucial aspect of the problem, and one to which mathematically trained professionals have a great deal of value to offer. But taken alone it can, and often does, ignore issues of cognition and learning, of multiple strategies for active engagement of students with the mathematics, and of assessing their learning and understanding. (Hyman Bass, 1997)

Introduction

In this chapter, we discuss ways of developing active learners of mathematics within the higher education context. This discussion is necessarily condensed but we have provided references to supplement our arguments. We believe that active learning enables a greater number of people to learn mathematics successfully as well as providing opportunities for more people to study mathematics at a deeper level. Hence active learning can help teachers to respond positively to the current Learning and Teaching and Widening Participation agendas within the higher education sector. Similarly, active learning may also help deal with some of the difficulties posed by the transition to higher education that were raised in Chapter 1. Further major outcomes of adopting this approach can be to engender excitement, enthusiasm, motivation and a sustained love of mathematics both for teachers and students.

Consider the following example. In order to understand later work related to Jordan canonical forms and generalized eigenvectors, students in advanced linear algebra courses need to know the concept of nilpotent matrices. Using experimentation, students can gain a good background for this material. Hillel (2001) uses the following approach with the 'drudgery' of matrix manipulation being removed by using *Maple*. The stimulus below, comes from a worksheet used in a computer laboratory exercise. The non-standard language is used deliberately:

The 'life span of v under A'

Starting with a matrix A, a non-zero vector v may not 'survive' the first application of the matrix A in the sense that $Av = 0$. It might survive the first application of A, so $Av \neq 0$ but not the second, so we get that $A^2v = 0$, and so on.

Let v_k be the kth iterate of A on v, so $v_k := A^k v$, with $v_0 = v$. If $v_0 \neq 0$, but $v_1 = 0$, we can say that 'v has 1-life span under A'. If $v_1 \neq 0$ but $v_2 = 0$ then v has '2-life span under A', and so on. In general, the *life span of v under A*, is k if $v_{k-1} \neq 0$ but $v_k = 0$. The zero vector is basically 'lifeless', so we can say that it has 0-life span under A.

We say that v has *finite-life* span under A if $v_k = 0$ for some $k \geq 0$. Otherwise, v has *infinite-life span* under A.

The students then have to consider the life span of some specific examples such as the following.

$$
\text{Let } N := \begin{bmatrix} 8 & 8 & -5 & 4 & -3 & -2 \\ -5 & -5 & 8 & 4 & -3 & -2 \\ 3 & 3 & 3 & 8 & -6 & -4 \\ -2 & -2 & -2 & -1 & -4 & -6 \\ 2 & 3 & 2 & -1 & -7 & 7 \\ -1 & -1 & -1 & -7 & -11 & 3 \end{bmatrix}
$$

- What is the life span under N of the column vectors $[1,2,1,2,-1,1]$, $[-3,0,-3,2,-1,1]$, and $[1,1,1,1,1,1]$?
- Pick several other vectors of your own choosing and find their life span under N.

After the students have completed this experimentation, they are given more theoretical questions relating this new idea to eigenvectors, nullspace and nilpotent matrices. The lecturer then has a foundation on which to base work on the concept of minimal polynomials of a vector under A, etc. This example is a manifestation of an active learning approach currently used in an undergraduate mathematics course.

We now consider several different perspectives on the way in which mathematical knowledge is constructed. This will provide a basis for the more practical suggestions that follow later in the chapter on how to develop active learners of mathematics.

Construction of knowledge

Mathematical research

We have already seen in Chapter 2 that there is a divergence between formal mathematical structures and their genesis. A similar divergence was also noted between the process by which mathematical ideas are created or discovered and the style in which they are written up for publication in appropriate journals.

It is worth emphasizing here that the genesis of mathematical ideas proceeds in an active fashion. For instance, research begins with a problem that is frequently tackled experimentally with the researcher casting about for patterns. Similarly, expert readers of a research paper will need to stop from time to time to generate their own examples in an effort to understand particular steps. In addition they may also need to draw diagrams as an aid to understanding what the author of the paper is trying to convey. Generally speaking, reading a mathematics research paper is not as easy as reading a novel. Research papers invariably require a great deal of effort on the part of the reader before understanding is obtained.

When it comes to lecturing and writing textbooks we have traditionally taken a more structured view of the subject. This is justified because we wish to convey a certain body of knowledge and to do so in a way that shows the highlights of that body of knowledge and possibly the links between them. Hence we have tended to adopt a more prescribed form of presentation that moves from definitions to theorems to possibly facts or properties or techniques. The important results are illustrated with examples. The student may be left on his/her own at this point to learn the lecture material as well as is possible. There may be exercise sheets to enable the techniques to be practiced and these examples may be extended to word problems where the technique is hidden in a 'real world' situation. Extensions of the main theorems may also be asked for to help the student assimilate the material of the course.

This traditional style of teaching is closely related to the style of research papers but with more examples and words of explanation and it is delivered in a transmission style. It is subject-centred. As with research papers it is left to the student to interpret it either alone, in a group, or with the aid of the lecturer or tutor. However, a mainly transmission style of teaching can exclude a large proportion of students who are not able to recognize and use the implicit connections of structures and thinking processes that have become second nature for their teachers.

Procepts and APOS theory

Two closely related theories in tertiary mathematics education seek to explain the way that students learn new material. These are the concept of procepts (see Gray and Tall, 1992) and APOS theory (Asiala *et al*, 1996). A further discussion of APOS theory can be found in Chapter 14. Gray and Tall (1992) see mathematical entities as potentially being both objects and procedures. They say that 'Whilst mental objects are easily manipulated, procedures occur in time'. They define 'a procept to be a combined mental object consisting of a process, a concept produced by the process, and a symbol which may be used to denote either or both'. For example, 4 + 3 is either the process of addition or the concept of sum:

> If number is seen as a flexible procept, evolving a mental object, or a counting process, whichever is the more fruitful at the time, then children are likely to build up known facts in a meaningful way. Thus the 'fact' that 4 + 3 is 7 becomes a flexible way of interchanging the notion 4 + 3 for the number 7. …In this way, seeing addition as a flexible procept leads to subtraction being viewed as another way of formulating addition. Successful children learn how to derive new facts from old in a flexible way.
>
> (Gray and Tall, 1992)

They propose that those students who do not see an object as more than a procedure may well be good at performing computations and succeed in the short term but in the long term they may lack the flexibility that will give them greater success. Precise definitions of mathematical concepts that are given in lectures focus on the object at the cost of the inner process. This prevents a large number of students, who do not sense the flexible power of the symbolization, from succeeding in mathematics. Although Department of Education and Science (1985) and Tall (1991) predate Gray and Tall, they contain practical expositions that complement their work.

APOS theory (Action, Process, Object and Schema) is an extension of the work of Piaget (it is discussed in full in Asiala *et al*, 1996). An *action* is at the lower end of this quadruple. It is an essentially external operation on a mathematical entity. For instance, finding the value of a given function $f(x)$ for a particular value of x, and finding a particular right coset of a given subgroup, are both actions.

After an action has been performed several times it becomes internalized to the extent that the action can be thought of without using specific examples. At this point it has become a *process*. Hence being able to think of finding $f(x)$ for all x and being able to think about finding cosets are processes.

At the *object* stage, the process has become a totality and the student is aware that it can be operated on. So function has become an object when there is the realization that two functions can be added, or that functions can be differentiated. Cosets become an object when the person is able to compare two cosets or think of them in certain circumstances as forming a group.

A *schema* for a given mathematical concept is the student's collection of actions, processes and objects. The student's collection of schemas are linked by various overlying principles to form a framework in the student's mind. When solving problems the student is able to use the different schema as appropriate.

Although APOS theory as it has been presented here appears to be nicely linear, it has to be realized that, in practice, things are more haphazard. As Dubinsky and

McDonald (2001) say, 'the construction of these various conceptions of a particular mathematical idea is more of a dialectic than a linear sequence'.

The two ideas of procept and APOS theory imply that learners play an active role in their own learning and that it requires action on their part to develop to a deep level of mathematical understanding. This, and the notion that intervention by teachers is necessary, is at the heart of much of the content of Chapter 2.

Two orientations

We wish to discuss two common curriculum orientations and their implications for teaching. Miller and Seller (1990) call these transmission and transaction models.

In the *transmission* model, 'the function of education is to transmit facts, skills, and values to students. Specifically, this orientation stresses mastery of traditional school subjects through traditional teaching methodologies' (Miller and Seller, 1990: 5). From this transmission model arises the concept of a teacher as an explainer or presenter. Content is presented for the students to assimilate, often in a typical textbook order of the kind:

- definitions/theorems;
- facts/properties;
- techniques;
- examples;
- practice examples;
- word problems;
- further practice.

While students may be expected to see connections between different areas of mathematics and know the how and why of different ideas, they are passive recipients of *presented* mathematical knowledge. Dossey summarizes this by saying 'This conception of teaching embodies the notion of authority in that there is a presenter with a fixed message to send. Such a position assumes the external existence of a body of knowledge to be transmitted to learners' (Dossey, 1992: 42). In this model, there is little room for autonomy or self-reflection.

We believe that the transmission model of teaching, which has dominated the teaching of mathematics both at school and at tertiary level over a long period, has excluded access to mathematics for a considerable proportion of pupils and students. In the UK and many other countries in recent years there appears to have been a shift away in conviction and in some cases practice, from the transmission model.

The second curriculum orientation is one of *transaction*. Here one of the main functions of education is to develop problem-solving skills in the learner so that these skills can be applied for the benefit of society. The individual in this model is considered to be rational and capable of intelligent problem solving. The theories of Dewey, Piaget and Vygotsky have had considerable influence on this model. In the transaction model, the student is as important as the content. A key difference between the transmission and the transaction models is that, under the latter, knowledge is actively constructed rather than being passively received. This is essentially a fundamental tenet of constructivism (see Von Glasersfeld, 1995). Consequently, the teacher must relate the mathematics that she or he wants the students to master, to the mathematics that the students already know. Learning is achieved by building on students' current knowledge. This is achieved by strategic interaction with the students. Through these interactions the teacher can assess the students' current knowledge and the most fruitful directions to take next.

In advocating this shift from transmission to transaction we suggest a move from a tidy and easily manageable domain of procedural aspects of mathematics and mathematics learning towards a more complex domain of conceptual mathematics and learning. The proposed change concerns raising the level of awareness rather than offering an alternative system. Active learning can take place in a wide range of teaching situations, for example, lectures, tutorials, individual and group study. What is important is that the teacher extends his or her repertoire of questions, assignments, tasks, resources and assessment frameworks which enable him or her to enrich a student's 'connected web' (Hiebert and Lefevre, 1996) of mathematical ideas and topics. The major challenge is to enable students to make a range of connections: the linking and interlinking of mathematical elements and ideas into topics and structures within mathematics.

Our conviction of the power of the transactional approach is based on our experience of teaching mathematics at tertiary level as well as on the projects based at UCC, Flexible Learning Approaches in Sixth Form Mathematics (1989–92) and Flexible Learning Approaches in Mathematics at Higher Education (FLAMHE): 1996 onwards. Note that in the UK, the term flexible learning is used synonymously with active learning.

By 'active learning' we mean learning where the students' minds are actively engaged in creating knowledge in an interaction with their teachers, peers and the subject matter. This, at least initially, requires the creation of a suitable learning environment. So teaching for active learning is necessarily a transactional form of teaching that is based on the notion that learning is constructed by the student.

In some sense active learning involves a scaled-down version of the research process that we have outlined in the last section. This has two important aspects for the learner. One of these is that the teacher models the creative process so that students can internalize it and use it to attack problems that they will meet during their course and even long after graduation. So they develops a learning style. The other is that, in the process, students gain some idea of how new mathematics is created. Certainly in art, students are encouraged both to criticize the works of masters and to create their own works. In the traditional way of teaching mathematics we have only allowed students to 'paint by numbers' over the 'great works'. Through active learning, students have an opportunity to see and experience how researchers tackle problems and the frustrations that they endure. Hence they can experience and appreciate mathematics from both a practical and an aesthetic point of view.

There are three key aspects of developing active learning. The various processes and structures of mathematics that we referred to above (problems, facts, definitions, symbols, theorems, methods of reasoning, proofs, relationships, techniques and so on), occur in a range of orders depending on the topic, the available resources, the students' and the teachers' interests. They occur more often in the order used by a research mathematician.

Second, there is interaction between student and teacher. This implies a two-way discourse of some nature, which may be via the Web or some other means that does not require the two partners to be in direct contact. As part of this interaction, in addition to providing appropriate information, such as where students' methods are inefficient and where there are nicer proofs than the ones they have produced, the teacher will be undertaking continual formative assessment. This is necessary so that he or she can judge what progress has been made and determine which direction should be taken next. On the student's part, the interaction should involve them in both questioning and making suggestions.

The third important aspect is that the students will continue to take an active part in their learning even in the absence of the teacher. This means that the students are not just practising a learnt technique and working through examples of a similar nature to those they have been shown in class. It also means that they will be engaged, through problem solving, etc, in learning new ideas. This is an important aspect of active learning that engenders in students the ability to become independent learners, having the skills at a later stage to learn new material by themselves if necessary.

Subject specific and transferable skills

Active learning approaches can enable students to develop some or all of the skills outlined below, within four domains. These domains formed a basis for an A-level assessment system (Ahmed and Williams, 1996), as well as having an influence on the undergraduate assessment system within FLAMHE.

Domain 1

Knowledge and technical mastery:

- Select and use appropriate mathematical tools and knowledge to solve a breadth of problems independently.
- Develop and apply skills, techniques and systems as appropriate in order to solve multi-stage tasks/problems.
- Explore alternative approaches to problems and check validity of solutions.
- Draw productive links between different areas of mathematical knowledge.

Domain 2

Organization and research skills:

- Extract essential information from books, notes and other resources as appropriate in solving problems.
- Organize and effectively deploy study time.
- Plan and work on extended tasks with autonomy, including consulting experts as appropriate.

Domain 3

Oral and other communication skills:

- Communicate methods and logical arguments both orally and in writing.
- Understand and use precise mathematical notation and analysis.
- Work productively with others in ways that enable groups to solve problems.
- Pose questions and participate usefully in mathematical discussion.

Domain 4

Breadth of application and mathematical insight:

- Understand and appreciate the wider applications of mathematics.
- Make abstractions, develop hypotheses, create and adapt strategies to solve problems; perceive and cultivate elegance in mathematical argument and analysis.
- Formulate problems in response to given circumstances using physical/technical resources appropriately.

From our experience, a focus on the above skills within curriculum as well as assessment has led to:

- learning becoming more interesting and enjoyment of the subject increasing;
- an increase in students' confidence;
- a better learning and understanding;
- students gaining a wider view of mathematics;
- a greater communication between lecturer and students, students and students, and greater cooperation among students;
- the development of independent and lifelong learners.

Strategies for active learning

In this section we provide some strategies for active learning, a brief case study of an active learning approach within an undergraduate level module, and implications for assessment. All the following strategies are flexible in that they can apply to a wide range of topics, situations and students. Many of these have been developed and used in FLAMHE and Flexible Learning approaches in Sixth Form Mathematics Projects.

General strategies

Here we provide some general ideas to promote active learning:

- Involve students in starting points, then try asking how they might vary these or what questions they could think up to answer next. Collect together students' suggestions for variations or questions.
- Ask students to keep a record of questions or other ideas they have not yet attempted to work on at appropriate occasions.
- Try to involve students in comparing their methods in an attempt to find the most efficient. Try to involve students in generalizing for themselves.
- When you want students to practise skills, think whether it would be possible for such practice to emerge through students' own enquiries or through problems that necessitate the use of these skills.
- Think how you might 'twist' tasks and questions described in textbooks, worksheets or test papers so that students can become more involved in making decisions, describing patterns and relationships, and testing conjectures.
- Encourage students to ask themselves questions such as, 'Have I seen something like this before?', 'Is this sensible?', 'Can I check this for myself?', 'Is there a better way of doing this?'
- Offer activities that will involve students in making decisions relating to the 'correctness' of a piece of mathematics.

- Show students examples of mistakes. Ask them to sort out what the mistakes are and to think how they might have arisen.
- Consider how you might incorporate the terms and notations that you want students to learn so that meaning can be readily ascribed to them and that they can be seen as helpful and necessary.
- Encourage students to look for connections between old and new situations, ideas and skills, and to ask themselves whether something they did previously might be of use in solving their new problems.
- When a student comes up with something that appears initially to be off the track, try to stop yourself from immediately implying that that is the case. Perhaps keep it as a 'further idea' for later or follow it through to see where it fails.

Another way of fostering active learning is by using peer tutoring (see Houston, 1998; Evans, Flower and Holton, 2001). Here students learn new material either independently or with the direct help of a teacher, and then teach their peers. This requires a significant amount of student input and processing. It also enhances students' communication.

As active learning requires more interactions between lecturer and students than the more traditional didactic lecturing approach, then it is likely that less content will be covered. But mathematics is more than content and in the non-content areas active learning has much to offer. The contribution of active learning in these other areas outweighs any slight reduction in coverage of content that may occur. Besides, active learning promotes students' ability and confidence to learn new areas of mathematics independently.

Context-specific strategies

Here we outline relatively easy ways in which change can be facilitated in a variety of teaching situations.

Lectures:
- Consider reducing the number of lectures, thus releasing time to make the lectures you do give more inspiring, motivating and memorable for students.
- Encourage students to make a map of their understanding of the lecture topic before you begin the lecture. At the end of the lecture, allow time for the students to add their new knowledge/understanding to the map.
- During the lectures, consider stopping at an appropriate stage and allow time for working in pairs or small groups to discuss your or their questions concerned with the lecture topic.
- Offer notes on lectures in advance and ask students to undertake their own research on aspects of the topic before the lecture.

(See Gibbs, 1992, for further suggestions)

Seminars:

- Identify topics for seminars in conjunction with students and allocate to them a responsibility for chairing, reporting and writing notes.
- Encourage students to prepare for seminars in groups and ask them to allocate responsibilities for choosing examples of practical activities, problems, making presentations, preparing summary notes, etc.

Provide thought-provoking examples and material that enables students to work productively in small groups in solving problems, making and testing hypotheses, analysing, synthesizing, communicating, etc. Also use publications, for example, Burn (1997), Wells (1990) and Williams (1990, 1992), where key ideas are developed by the student reading through and solving a series of problems and questions.

Tutorials:

- Ask students to take responsibilities for determining the agenda for tutorials and let them devise objectives and determine outcomes.
- Use open questions to stimulate discussions.

Assessment:

- Involve students in the formative and summative assessment process by enabling them to interpret the criteria for assessment by allowing them to assess their own work and other students' work. Keep a dialogue sheet where students and tutors make comments on the progress.

Induction:

- During induction week, involve students in a series of mathematical activities and group work that enables them to develop the basis for good work habits required for the active learning process.
- The course handbook could contain mechanisms such as assessment criteria, recording learning outcomes, student/tutor dialogue sheets, etc. Invite experienced students to explain productive uses of these devices.

Learning Agreements:

- These are devices to help students define learning outcomes for a particular piece of work. Teachers can negotiate long- and short-term learning targets that can include human and other resources required to achieve the targets set jointly.

(For more ideas see Stephenson and Laycock, 1993; Legrand, 2001)

A case study : teaching calculus to students scared of calculus

Here we give an example of a calculus module for students on the second year of a four-year undergraduate degree, which also included students undertaking a Primary Teacher Education course. These students felt nervous about their fluency and understanding of calculus beyond straightforward differentiation and integration of functions. The module was designed to overcome this fear of calculus and to strengthen the students' intuitive understanding of the role of calculus in practice.

One of the topics covered was calculating curvature. A common approach to teaching these topics is to employ powerful algebraic analysis from the start, with a scattering of diagrams, seemingly divorced from the algebra, intended to convey an overview of the process.

In the lecturer's experience as a student and as a tutor, responses to such an approach include:

- learning the 'formula' involved, in order to do the required symbolic manipulation to go from this formula to a result in the examination;
- becoming skilled in the particular sequence of algebraic steps required to derive the formula in order to be ready to regurgitate this upon demand in the examination;
- deciding that this calculus module is too hard and giving up!

Only a minority of students seem able to take a page or more of 'ugly algebra', read it on their own, and derive something meaningful and intuitive from it.

The lecturer did not want to leave students, already wary of calculus and algebra, with even less confidence after taking this course. So when she was preparing to teach the module, she first refreshed her memory of some of the topics by looking over her old lecture notes and reading textbooks. This left her with enough understanding to run through a set of worked examples. However, a more constructive understanding was gained by making up her own examples, playing with conjectures and challenging her intuition. She was able to investigate conjectures with three tools:

- her algebra and calculus skills;
- graph-drawing on a graphics calculator, drawing families of graphs, polar functions, functions of more than one variable, etc;
- using dynamic geometry packages to investigate how a function's behaviour changes as parameters undergo continuous change.

The lecturer decided to incorporate these approaches into her teaching of the module, using the students' skills with graphical calculators and dynamic geometry packages (from other modules) to strengthen their fluency and understanding of algebra and calculus. The module also involved a considerable amount of group work and decoding of tough mathematics (see Flower, 2000).

To see how this worked in practice, first look at a calculus formula for curvature. It is totally mysterious. There seems to be no obvious connection between this formula and the shape of the graph of a function. What is more, the algebra required to derive the formula is rather difficult. So, before tackling any algebra, the class looked at diagrams on their graphical calculators and from the dynamic geometry package. As a result a range of questions was asked:

- Is this circle a good fit to the curve?
- We all agree that this circle is too big, and we can see that it meets the curve three times. Does this mean that a circle that meets a curve three times will always be 'too big'?
- Use the dynamic geometry images to estimate the curvature of this function at that point: try a family of functions like ax^2. Can you find a generalization for changes in curvature as a changes?

Eventually the persistent guessing and inability to pin an answer down as right or wrong left students with a real desire to know exactly how curvature is measured. This was a good starting point from which to tackle the algebra. And even during the algebra work, it was possible to introduce stopping points, where the current expressions were given meaning in the overall problem context.

A similar approach, involving conjecturing before delving into the algebra, was taken for many more topics throughout the module. These topics included multiple integration, the reasoning behind substitution rules, numerical approaches to integration and the resultant errors, polar orbits (curvilinear calculus) and Fourier analysis of sequences.

Without an active learning approach, this module could easily have alienated many students and proved a real obstacle to their progression towards being confident teachers of mathematics who are interested and capable of extending knowledge through an 'algebra barrier'.

Assessment

Since active learning has specific objectives that complement knowledge and technical mastery, forms of assessment other than examinations would be more appropriate in encouraging the achievement of the skills within the four domains (see the above section on subject specific and transferable skills). For example, there are a number of variations on the traditional examination that enable different attributes to be assessed:

- Open book exams are closer to a research setting. They provide the opportunity for students to be asked probing questions rather than questions that require regurgitation of material met during the course.
- Seen exams give students questions before the examination so that they can prepare answers. It allows more searching questions to be asked than might be expected in the traditional examination. It also allows students the chance to use a range of resources in the preparation of their answers.

- Computer laboratory exams allow students the use of technology. Hence they can be provided with 'realistic' data that would not be amenable to solution in the normal examination.

Similarly there are several types of project. They all foster organizational and research skills, communication and mathematical insight. Since it was established, Roskilde University has had most of its assessment based on group projects:

- Individual projects allow students to tackle a broad mathematical topic and see its connections with other areas.
- Group projects, where students work together, also foster cooperation and oral communication.
- Essays are a form of project that are valuable for surveys and historical topics.

It is finally worth noting that Niss (1993) and Houston (2001) offer wide-ranging reviews of assessment. Issues of assessment are also taken up at greater length in Chapter 4 and within Part II of this book.

Conclusion

In this chapter we have attempted to identify and discuss some evidence-based, generalizable features of active learning which have been rooted in the authors' practices. We offer these to the reader not as a prescription but as tools for reviewing or reviving their approaches to teaching mathematics. What we present here reinforces much of what has already been said in Chapter 2.

References

Ahmed, A and Williams, H I M (1996) Can assessment maintain fidelity to the curriculum without exposing teaching quality?, in *New Horizons in Learning Assessment*, ed D Ajar, pp 325–34, University of Montreal, Montreal

Asiala, M *et al* (1996) A framework for research and curriculum development in under-graduate mathematics education, Research in Collegiate Mathematics Education II, Conference Board of the Mathematical Sciences (CBMS) *Issues in Mathematics Education*, **6**, pp 1–32

Bass, H (1997) Keynote address: mathematicians as educators, *Notices of the American Mathematical Society*, **44**(1), pp 18–21

Burn, R P (1997) *A Pathway Into Number Theory*, 2nd edn, Cambridge University Press, Cambridge

Department of Education and Science (1985) *Mathematics From 5 to 16*, HMSO, London

Dossey, J A (1992) The nature of mathematics: its role and influence, in *Handbook of Research in Mathematics Learning and Teaching*, ed D A Grouws, Macmillan, New York

Dubinsky, E and McDonald, M (2001) APOS: A Constructivist Theory of Learning in Undergraduate Mathematics Education Research, in *The Teaching and Learning of Mathematics at University Level: An International Commission on Mathematical Instruction (ICMI) study*, ed D Holton, pp 275–82, Kluwer Academic, Dordrecht

Evans, W, Flower, J and Holton, D A (2001) Peer tutoring at the tertiary level, *International Journal of Mathematical Education in Science and Technology* (to appear)

Flower, J (2000) Using seminars to teach calculus to undergraduates, in *Cultural Diversity in Mathematics (Education): Commission internationale pour l'étude et l'amélioration de l'enseignement des mathématiques (CIEAEM) 51*, eds A Ahmed, J M Kraemer and H I M Williams, pp 311–16, Horwood, Chichester

Gibbs, G (1992) *Lecturing to More Students*, Oxford Centre for Staff and Learning Development, Oxford

Gray, E and Tall, D (1992) Success and failures in mathematics: the flexible meaning of symbols as process and concept, *Mathematics Teaching*, **142**, pp 6–10

Hiebert, J and Lefevre, P (1996) Conceptual and procedural knowledge in mathematics: an introductory analysis, in *Conceptual and Procedural Knowledge: The case for mathematics*, ed J Hiebert, pp 1–28, Lawrence Erlbaum, Hillsdale, NJ

Hillel, J (2001) Computer algebra systems in the learning and teaching of linear algebra: some examples, in *The Teaching and Learning of Mathematics at University Level: An ICMI study*, ed D Holton, pp 371–80, Kluwer Academic, Dordrecht

Houston, S K (1998) Get students to do the teaching, in *Mathematical Modelling: Teaching and assessment in a technology-rich world*, ed P Galbraith, pp 45–54, Horwood, Chichester

Houston, S K (2001), Assessing undergraduate mathematics students, in *The Teaching and Learning of Mathematics at University Level: An ICMI study*, ed D Holton, pp 407–22, Kluwer Academic, Dordrecht

Legrand, M (2001), Scientific debate, in *The Teaching and Learning of Mathematics at University Level: An ICMI study*, ed D Holton, pp 127–136, Kluwer Academic, Dordrecht

Miller, T P and Seller, J (1990) *Curriculum Perspectives and Practice*, Cropp Clarke Pitman, Toronto

Niss, M (ed) (1993) *Investigations into Assessment in Mathematics Education: An ICMI study*, Kluwer Academic, Dordrecht

Stephenson, J and Laycock, M (1993) *Using Learning Contracts in Higher Education*, Kogan Page, London

Tall, D (ed) (1991) *Advanced Mathematical Thinking*, Kluwer Academic, Dordrecht

Tomlinson, P and Kilner, S (1991) *Flexible Learning, Flexible Training*, Employment Department, Moorfoot, Sheffield

Von Glasersfeld, E (1995) *Radical Constructivism: A way of knowing and learning*, Falmer Press, London

Wells, D (1990) *Engaging Mathematics I, II and III*, West Sussex Institute of Higher Education, Bognor Regis

Williams, H I M (1990) *Developing and Managing Flexible Learning Approaches in Sixth Form Mathematics*, West Sussex Institute of Higher Education, Bognor Regis, HMSO, London

Williams H I M (ed) (1992), *The Core – and More*, West Sussex Institute of Higher Education, Bognor Regis

4

Assessment in mathematics

Clifford Beevers and Jane Paterson

Introduction

In a recent survey the Learning and Teaching Support Network (LTSN) Generic Centre asked all subject centres to articulate the three most important issues on assessment in their subject. The LTSN Mathematics, Statistics and Operational Research Network at the University of Birmingham responded as follows:

1. Issues in computer-aided assessment, which include reliability, robustness and ease of use. It should also apply to both formative and summative assessment in the forms of diagnostic, continuous and formal testing. There are at least two special issues for mathematics, which are applicable to other numerate disciplines such as science and engineering:
   - display and input of mathematical expressions; for example, with powers and fractions that typically display over several lines; and
   - equivalently right answers; for example, in mathematical terms $x + y$ is the same as $y + x$ and this would cause some difficulty if standard character matching techniques were employed as the only method for comparing answers.
2. The need to match appropriate assessment methods to learning outcomes for knowledge, basic skills, understanding and problem solving. Some outcomes may be tested within group-work or through independent learning.
3. Coursework and assignments make heavy demands on staff time with regard to submission, marking, monitoring and feedback. In Statistics and Operational Research, project work is very extensive and has special assessment issues including comparability between different types of project and linking project work to the remainder of the curriculum. Ways are sought of making these processes more cost-effective.

This chapter seeks to review some of the issues raised with particular focus on 1) and 2) above. It seems appropriate to present the details as a record, in part, of the assessment techniques that the authors have used in careers of over 30 years in mathematics departments.

What assessment is

Assessment can be defined as the measurement of learning. Physicists know that the act of measurement can affect what is being measured. None of this was known to one of the authors (CB) as a student in Manchester where he took part in what can only be described as conventional assessment in his early career – ask a student a question and expect an answer!

Assessment can take many forms but can be described in at least one of the following categories: diagnostic testing; self-testing; formative assessment; summative assessment; continuous assessment and grading assessment. It is useful to be clear about these terms:

- *Diagnostic testing.* A prescribed piece of assessment that determines a student's aptitude and preparedness for a module or course.
- *Self-testing.* Occurs when learners check for themselves their progress against a model prepared by an expert in the field.
- *Formative.* A prescribed piece of assessment that students are required to undertake during the course of a module. It does not contribute to the overall module assessment but rather 'informs' the students and tutor on the progress that the students are making. It provides constructive and meaningful feedback to help the students improve their performance. It supports the teaching and learning process. Formative assessment can include diagnostic assessments, self-testing, activities and exercises. (An activity can be formative if suitable feedback is provided to aid learning.)
- *Summative.* A prescribed piece of assessment required to be completed during or at the end of a module or course. It makes a specific contribution to the overall assessment. It establishes what students have achieved during or at the end of a programme of study and should, in practice, measure student achievement in all learning outcomes of the module or course. It does not normally provide information on how the students could improve their performance. In the days when universities were more relaxed about their teachers returning scripts at the end of a summative piece of work, teachers could comment on the scripts before handing them back to the students. In such cases the summative assessment was also formative.
- *Continuous.* A prescribed piece of assessment of a subdivision of a module or course. It measures achievement in those learning outcomes that students are expected to have attained at the time of the assessment. The result makes a specific contribution to the overall assessment. How it relates to a final award

may vary. Marks awarded in continuous assessments may be aggregated as part of a final mark. Continuous assessment may also be used as an entry requirement allowing access to the final summative test as in the new Scottish Qualifications Authority awards that form part of the Higher Still programme. In these awards a student is asked to perform some simple tasks in order to display minimum competence in the subject before taking a more traditional examination at the end of the course to test extended competence.

- *Grading assessment.* Determines the level of achievement in summative tasks.

The main purposes of assessment are essentially:

- to inform students on their strengths and weaknesses, enabling them to improve;
- to motivate students by providing an opportunity to review and consolidate what they have learnt;
- to develop student confidence;
- to monitor progress;
- to allow students to demonstrate the knowledge, understanding, attitudes and skills acquired in a programme of study;
- to provide evidence for certification/licensing.

Brown and Knight (1994) give a more detailed description of the purposes of assessment and rightly point out that feedback is an essential part of any assessment.

Students have their ability assessed in four general areas: basic skills; knowledge; understanding; and problem solving. Skills can be subdivided into key; subject-specific; and cognitive.

- *Key skills.* These are often described as 'what is left after the facts have been forgotten' and include skills such as communication, numeracy and creative thinking.
- *Subject-specific skills.* These skills involve the ability to execute various subject-specific procedures; such abilities are normally learnt through practice. More complex skills in this category incorporate the capacity to analyse a situation, to synthesize and to evaluate different types of information.
- *Cognitive skills.* These include application, analysis, synthesis and evaluation being displayed through logical reasoning and critical thinking.
- *Knowledge.* Consists of a set of learnt relationships or facts about a subject. It can be acquired through rote learning and memorizing or can be induced empirically from a given situation or example. Knowledge is essential for understanding and hence problem solving.
- *Understanding.* Reflects an appreciation of the conceptual basis of a subject. It allows for concise explanation and reasoning. Understanding is the basis for thinking and involves the application of knowledge to new situations.

- *Problem solving.* This skill brings together some of those mentioned above in a clear and concise manner. It requires some critical thinking and an ability to plan, organize, review and evaluate the strategy chosen to solve a problem.

The criteria against which assessments are set can differ. Minimum competence can be regarded as assessing the simpler mechanistic skills and recall of memorized knowledge. Extended competence questions assess more complex skills and understanding. Such extended competencies might be produced, for example, in questions that integrate across learning outcomes. Although any discussion of assessment normally refers to criterion-referenced assessment (CRA) there are two other forms: norm-referenced and ipsative-referenced. Criterion-referencing seeks to measure a student's achievement against a range of predetermined learning outcomes. It measures absolute attainment against a minimum competence level. As Freeman and Lewis point out:

> The emphasis in CRA is on identifying what the student has achieved and has yet to achieve. It, thus, tends to be more informative than norm-referenced assessment, providing specific information on which the student and others can act.
>
> (Freeman and Lewis, 1998)

Norm-referencing is a competitive approach where the performances of students are compared. It measures relative attainment and assumes that there will be a distribution of ability. Ipsative-referencing measures personal attainment and compares a student's performance with previous efforts. This is a form of self-assessment and can be formative or summative. Formative assessments play an important role in any learning materials and should ensure that:

- sufficient practice is given in the development of measurable mechanistic skills;
- opportunities are provided to test and encourage recall of knowledge;
- problem solving and more complex skills are developed;
- understanding and extended competence in wider contexts are encouraged and applied;
- the full range of learning outcomes/the entire syllabus is covered;
- practice is given in activities that integrate across learning outcomes.

Computer-aided assessment

Since 1985 one of the authors (CB) has directed the CALM Project for Computer Aided Learning in Mathematics (Beevers *et al*, 1991). From the start CALM recognized the additional benefits that automatic assessment brings to the learning process. In those early days the Service Calculus course was divided into four parts on a weekly basis with software for:

- Theory. To summarize the lectures that week.
- Worked examples. To show students how to do typical questions.
- Motivating problems. To bring the subject to life.
- A weekly test.

This recipe has run successfully throughout the first year course at Heriot–Watt University since 1986. Several thousand students have graduated through the CALM Calculus materials spending the majority of their time in the test section. This behaviour surprised the CALM authors but its discovery led them (Beevers *et al*, 1995) to employ the computer beyond the formative role it had played in the original CALM Project.

Students of mathematics can be assessed in a number of ways and the computer can play a role in at least four types of assessment:

- diagnostic tests where the emphasis is on helping students to discover their strengths and weaknesses;
- self-tests where the computer is employed to provide rapid feedback, for example, picking out predictable wrong answers;
- continuous assessment in which tutors and students alike can see how mathematical topics are being absorbed and understood;
- grading assessment in which the computer is used in the setting and marking of questions that count towards an award.

Over the years there has been much work in the area of diagnostic testing by groups like Appleby, Samuels and Treasure-Jones (1997) following an approach that, in part, derives from earlier work by Middleton, Curran and Moscardini (1990, 1991). Diagnostic testing using student profiling has been studied by Brydges and Hibberd (1994). This work is forming the basis of some current work on Web delivery of diagnostic tests from Keele University (Hibberd, Looms and Quinney, forthcoming). During the MARBLE Project funded by SHEFC, Beevers, Scott and Price developed a pearl script version of the Scottish University Council for Entrants (SUCE) diagnostic test (see http://www.marble.ac.uk/maths/public/assessment.htm). The SUCE test originated in 1980 as a paper test for all first-year undergraduates taking mathematics as part of their degree at a Scottish university.

Self-testing is a feature of the work of Harding *et al* (1995) in their projects Renaissance and Nuffield. CALM used this approach too in its Highers units where predictable wrong answers were trapped and fast feedback helped students consolidate their learning. Self-tests are also a feature of the many Mathwise modules developed during the Teaching and Learning Technology Programme (TLTP) initiative by the United Kingdom Courseware Consortium (UKMCC) (for details of Mathwise see Harding and Quinney, 1996 and http://www.bham.ac.uk/mathwise/).

Continuous assessment was the driving force in the first CALM Project with weekly tests helping the students to assess their own progress through the material. Brunel, Portsmouth and Glasgow Caledonian universities have used a similar approach with Questionmark software (for some details see McCabe, 1995) and the CALMAT units (for a review the interested reader should consult Tabor, 1993).

Grading assessment by computer has been pioneered at Heriot-Watt University initially using the Mathwise assessment mechanism (Beevers, Bishop and Quinney, 1998) but latterly with the CALM assessment engine now delivered over the Web (see http://www.calm.hw.ac.uk/ for a demonstration). Napier University under the SUMSMAN Project (Goldfinch, 1999) employed Mathwise to assess their students.

On the practical side the problems of display and input of mathematics on the Web will be familiar to some readers (see point 1a under the Introduction above). The terms 'rendered' and 'string equivalent' are frequently used in dialogue on this subject. In simple terms the rendered version of the mathematics is the conventional format or layout that the user would write on paper. The string version is the format in which the mathematical expression is input to the computer and is similar to the input on calculators. In other words, brackets are used around fractions and arguments to avoid ambiguity, the slash sign (/) is used for division and powers use the hat sign (^).

In some mathematics packages the use of an input tool allows users to input the string equivalent form of an answer and see the rendered version before submitting it to the computer. This is a very useful facility that places the emphasis more on obtaining the correct answer than on being proficient at converting written work into string equivalents. Such an input tool was used in Interactive PastPapers (Beevers *et al*, 1997) and Mathwise.

There are many strands of research into improving the online look of maths on the Web. There is an international standard MathML for mathematics that is intended to facilitate the use and re-use of mathematical and scientific content on the Web, and for other applications such as computer algebra systems, print typesetters and voice synthesizers (for MathML specification see http://www.w3.org/Math/). The Mozilla MathML project (see http://www.mozilla.org/projects/mathml/) was set up to implement these standards for displaying mathematics on the Web through a browser and once this is achieved the current problems such as alignment on the page should be overcome.

In mathematics and other numerate disciplines, there is an added problem in computer assessment of marking equivalently correct answers (see point 1b under the Introduction above). The CALM Project adopted the approach that mathematical answers would be compared with the correct answer through evaluation at a number of points and, if necessary, a tolerance would be included in the process. This method is well described in Beevers *et al* (1991) and has worked well throughout the lifetime of the CALM Project. A number of situations arise with this approach that have to be addressed such as the equivalence of $(a + b)^2$ and $a^2 + 2ab + b^2$. This can partly be overcome by the use of conditions built into the assessment engine. These conditions are then checked when an answer is submitted. Such conditions may take the following forms:

- Minimum length of characters in an answer: this is suitable for answers such as the expansion of an algebraic expression.
- Maximum length of characters in an answer: this is very similar but can be used to ensure that an expression is simplified as far as possible. It can be accompanied with the message 'Your answer is right but is too long. Tidy it up,' which is the kind of helpful comment that a friendly teacher might say.
- 'Must have' condition: this is very useful where, for example, if the answer is required in fraction form, the 'must have' character will be the slash.
- 'Not allowed' condition: this is another way in which the correct format of the answer can be achieved. Here, for example, to ensure that $(x + 2)^2$ is expanded and not typed in as it stands (which is equivalently correct). The condition could be set as 'must have x^2', which ensures that the user types x^2 as part of the answer.

The CUE assessment engine developed at Heriot-Watt uses such conditions to good effect in the SCHOLAR Project (see http://www.calm.hw.ac.uk/).

Matching appropriate assessment to learning outcomes

There are a variety of ways in which students can be assessed. Each has advantages and disadvantages with some more appropriate to certain subjects. In mathematics the more commonly used methods include: closed book examinations; open book examinations; objective tests; reports; essays; project work; presentations; and self/peer assessment. Looking at these briefly in turn:

- Closed book examinations. This is the traditional examination where students are formally tested usually at a specific time and place without access to the learning materials. Such examinations are relatively easy to present and ensure that each student has exactly the same assessment to complete. They are, however, stressful to most students and rarely provide any formative feedback. Within a time-restricted assessment such as this, the questions tend to aim at testing lower order cognitive skills. This was the standard form of mathematics exams until recently.
- Open book examinations. These are becoming more popular. The students still sit a formal examination but may be allowed to take with them handbooks, textbooks or other learning materials. This allows the assessment to test higher order cognitive skills by requiring the students to use the information rather than just recall it. The examiners, however, need to consider the wealth of material that the student may have and whether a restriction has to be placed on what is permissible in the examination. This may lead to scrutiny problems in trying to ensure that the restrictions have not been breached. In mathematics examinations the use of handbooks containing formulae and techniques are

becoming more common. Surprisingly, allowing access to materials does not compromise standards. One of the authors (JP) has taken several examinations in this format and can confirm that such examinations are no easier for the students.

- Objective tests. These assessments are constructed to give reliable marking irrespective of marker. There are a variety of types but perhaps the most common is the multiple-choice format. This type of assessment will give the same results whether marked by a tutor, by an optical reader or by computer, off or online. If this marking is online the student can receive immediate feedback. These tests allow a large range of questions to be collated. They are expensive to construct properly but very cost effective to run. On the other hand, the student might gain marks through guessing and the tutor is unable to see where the student's reasoning is flawed in an incorrect answer.

It is important that multiple-choice questions are not viewed as an easy option, in fact such questions have a terminology of their own. Earl, McConnel and Middleton (1996) and Earl, Land and Wise (1991) give the following definitions:

- Stem. The introductory part of the question.
- Options. The range of possible answers.
- Key. The correct answer.
- Distractors. The incorrect options.
- Non-functioning distractors. Distractors that attract less than 5 per cent of responses because they lack plausibility. These are usually replaced on rewriting.
- Facility value. The measure of difficulty of a multiple choice question based on the number of candidates choosing the key in a given item.
- Discrimination index. A value that indicates the extent to which a multiple choice question distinguishes more able students from less able students.

For more details the interested reader is directed to the review by Bull and McKenna (forthcoming).

There are many sets of guidelines to help with writing multiple-choice questions. One of these was published by SCOTVEC in 1991 and adapted by Earl, Land and Wise (1991). It is set out again here for completeness:

- All distractors should be feasible.
- All the options should be of approximately the same length.
- The options should be grammatically correct and consistent with the stem.
- The stem should be constructed to reflect the level of knowledge specified in the learning outcome.
- The stem should reflect a level of language appropriate to the student.
- None of the options should have the same meaning.
- There should be no ambiguities in the stem or the options.
- There should be only one correct response.

- The stem should contain as much item content as possible.
- Negative statements should be avoided in the stem.
- Options should not include unintended clues.
- A regular pattern of correct responses should be avoided.

However, recent developments have been made in online assessment to provide a much larger range of question types and in computer-adaptive testing where the next question in the test depends upon the answer given to the previous question. These techniques and improvements will remove some of the problems in using objective testing and allow for higher order cognitive skills to be tested more fully than at present. There is considerable interest in this style for mathematics examinations, especially in using computer assessment.

- *Reports.* These are used in many disciplines and are effective in testing core skills such as communication and organizational abilities. Marking tends to be subjective and such an assessment is time consuming for both the student and tutor alike. Statistics courses rely on this method quite heavily as it offers scope for the students to present full analyses of data sets in a structured manner.
- *Project work.* Although not generally common in mathematics until postgraduate level, projects can motivate students by allowing multi-media use. Many of the key skills can be tested and in constructing the project the student can be encouraged into a deeper learning approach. Project work can be undertaken by groups and provides a different learning environment where the students can support one another. Care is needed to ensure that each student contributes to the overall project. Investigations as carried out by mathematics students in senior schools could be considered as a limited form of project.
- *Presentations.* In higher education, presentations are common and allow the student to demonstrate a deep level of learning. In addition to the obvious communication skills required, presentations can show the presence of good analytical and organizational skills and critical thinking. Presentations may also be carried out in small groups. Presentations are common at postgraduate level mathematics but less so at lower levels.
- *Self/peer assessment.* With the emphasis on student-centred active learning, peer assessment can be expected to increase. Using this method the students are encouraged to examine the learning objectives and performance criteria in detail and to make judgements on whether they meet these criteria or not. Peer assessment reduces dependence on the tutor and promotes the development of key skills and deep learning. In some ways the students act as a group encouraging individual improvements to promote the group standing overall.

There have been interesting studies in this field (see Goldfinch and Raeside, 1990; Goldfinch, 1994) but as yet the method is not widely used for assessment in mathematics. Self-assessment projects, however, have been successful in a number of university mathematics departments including Napier and Heriot-Watt.

Effective learning outcomes need to meet the following five criteria (Earl *et al*, 1999). Specific, Measurable, Achievable, Relevant and Time restricted. An easy way of remembering this is: the learning outcomes should be SMART. In testing any learning outcome the assessment method chosen must allow for the assessment to cover five generally agreed criteria: reliability – giving the same results time after time; validity – testing what it should test; practicality – planning to be efficient and cost-effective; usefulness – aiding the learning process; and fairness – reflecting the expectations of the course objectives. As Ellington, Percival and Race (1993) point out, however, reliability and validity are in no way directly linked. They also warn of the dangers of compromise: to be efficient and cost-effective may have an effect on validity.

The learning outcomes given for any course can vary hugely from simply testing a specific technique in, say, mathematics, to examining a technical design and build specification in, perhaps, electronics. In some cases, detailed performance criteria are used to pinpoint the specific tasks or methods that will need assessing. It is not always easy to find the most appropriate assessment method.

Bearing in mind the five criteria for good assessment the following questions are a selection of the issues that should be considered when choosing an assessment method:

- What resources and finances are available?
- What time restraints are there?
- Is the assessment for diagnostic, formative or summative purposes?
- Which cognitive skills are to be assessed?
- At which educational level is the assessment?
- Which of the available resources can assess the outcomes given?

Bloom's taxonomy of educational objectives (Bloom *et al,* 1956, 1964) splits learning into six different levels: knowledge; comprehension; application; analysis; synthesis and evaluation. In mathematics, many questions are designed to test knowledge, comprehension (understanding) and application. Examples are:

- State De Moivre's theorem.
- Identify the imaginary part of the complex number.
- Perform iteration on the function.
- Find the turning points of the function.
- Use the product rule.
- Solve the system of linear equations.

For these lower order levels, learning outcomes are straightforward and precise, making the assessment relatively easy to construct and mark. The answers are definite, making objective testing very useful. As mentioned earlier, computer-aided assessment is one of the objective test methods of assessment and can be used for diagnostic, self-test, grading and continuous purposes. Multiple choice, judged mathematical expressions, word match and hot spot questions cover most of the learning outcomes at this level but, in mathematics, need careful construction to avoid the pitfalls of equivalently right answers.

For the higher order objectives of analysis, synthesis and evaluation the learning outcomes become more complex and open to interpretation. Marking is more subjective. Examples of these include:

- Determine a general formula from the information given.
- Compare and report on the two sets of data provided.
- Justify the answer found earlier.
- Identify the flaws in the given proof.
- Determine a mathematical model to describe the following practical situation.

In mathematics, assessments have to be constructed carefully to ensure that the outcomes are tested using the methods and techniques required. At this level, closed or open book examinations, presentations, projects and reports are used but computer assessment has made progress in producing new question structures that address some of the likely outcomes. Essay questions and information-only steps help to address some of the more awkward assessment areas for computers such as number theory and statistics. Such question types can be found in the online assessment system known as CUE, which is currently providing the formative assessment in biology, chemistry and physics as well as mathematics in the SCHOLAR Project (the interested reader is directed to the demonstration at http://scholar.hw.ac.uk/).

If students have access to the Web there are considerable advantages to using computer assessment where possible. These advantages include: immediate feedback; help in the form of optional steps; randomized parameters in questions; results available; and students can use it in their own time.

Of the five criteria for good assessment, those of reliability, practicality and usefulness are met easily using computer assessment. Validity and fairness depend to some extent on the author who is matching assessment to the learning outcomes.

Looking to the future

Recently SHEFC awarded £560,000 to Beevers, Haywood and McAteer to establish the Scottish Centre for Research into Online Learning and Assessment (SCROLLA). Initially there are three threads to the research programme: ICT policy, computer-aided assessment and network learning. The assessment theme is being led from Heriot-Watt University and early lines of investigation will include:

- Comparative evaluation of current CAA tools available worldwide.
- Specification of range of desirable objective question types and open standards (eg IMS) for describing these.
- Investigation of the effectiveness of different question types, good practice for use and guidelines, including cross-sectoral analysis of portability.
- Design and development of next generation assessment tools.
- Authenticity of submissions/detection and reduction of plagiarism.

The last theme may have some impact on issue 3 identified in the Introduction above.

SCROLLA is in its infancy but already one of the authors (JP), as Research Fellow in Computer Aided Assessment, has begun the comparison of current CAA tools available worldwide and started to specify a range of desirable objective question types. SCROLLA is funded for three years and will report via its Web site at http://www.scrolla.ac.uk from time to time over that period.

References

Appleby, J, Samuels, P and Treasure-Jones, T (1997) Diagnosys: a knowledge based diagnostic test of basic mathematical skills, *Journal of Comp Education*, **28**, pp 113–33

Beevers, C E *et al* (1991) *Software Tools for Computer Aided Learning in Mathematics*, Ashgate Publishers, Godalming

Beevers, C E *et al* (1995) Mathematical ability assessed by computer, *Journal of Comp Educ*, **25**, pp 123–32

Beevers, C E *et al* (1997) *Interactive Past Papers for A Level/Higher Mathematics*, Lander Educational Software, Glasgow

Beevers, C E, Bishop, P and Quinney, D A (1998) Mathwise diagnostic testing and assessment, *Information Services and Use*, **18**, pp 191–205

Bloom, B S *et al* (1956) *Taxonomy of Educational Objectives: The classification of educational goals, vol 1*, Longman, London

Bloom, B S *et al* (1964) *Taxonomy of Educational Objectives: The classification of educational goals, vol 2*, Longman, London

Brown, S and Knight, P (1994) *Assessing Learners in Higher Education*, Kogan Page, London

Brydges, S and Hibberd, S (1994) Construction and implementation of a computer-based diagnostic test, *Maths and Stats CTI newsletter*, **5**, p 13

Bull, J and McKenna, V (forthcoming) Blueprint on CAA [Online] http://www.caacentre/

Earl, S, Land, R and Wise, J (1991) *MSc Computer-Enhanced Mathematics Education Module on Assessment, Evaluation and Support: Adapted list of factors from SCOTVEC (1991)*, Napier University, Edinburgh

Earl, S, McConnel, M and Middleton, I (1996) *Postgraduate Certificate in Tertiary Level Teaching* [Online] http://www.rgu.ac.uk/subj/eds/pgcert/main.htmÿ

Earl, S *et al* (1999) *MSc Computer-Enhanced Mathematics Education Module on Learning Contexts, Styles and Outcomes*, Napier University

Ellington, H, Percival, F and Race, P (1993) *A Handbook of Educational Technology*, 3rd edn, Kogan Page, London

Freeman, R and Lewis, R (1998) *Planning and Implementing Assessment*, Kogan Page, London

Goldfinch, J M (1994) Further developments in peer assessment of group projects, *Assessment and Evaluation in Higher Education*, **19**(1)

Goldfinch, J (1999) The SUMSMAN project and its implications for computer-based assessment, *Teaching Mathematics and its Applications,* **18**(4), pp 150–54

Goldfinch, J M and Raeside, R (1990) Development of a peer assessment technique for obtaining individual marks on a group project, *Assessment and Evaluation in Higher Education*, **15**(3), pp 210–31

Harding, R D and Quinney, D A (1996) Mathwise and the UK Mathematics Courseware Consortium, *Active Learning*, **4**, pp 53 –57

Harding, R D *et al* (1995) A mathematical toolkit for interactive hypertext courseware: part of the mathematics experience with the Renaissance Project, *Journal of Comp Education*, **24**, p 127

Hibberd, S, Looms, A and Quinney D A (forthcoming) Computer-based diagnostic testing and support in mathematics, in *Innovative Teaching Ideas in Mathematics*, ed M H Ahmadi, Department of Mathematics and Computer Science, University of Wisconsin-Whitewater, Wisconsin

McCabe, M (1995) Designer software for mathematics assessment, *CTI Maths and Stats Newsletter*, **6**, pp 11–16

Middleton, W, Curran, D A S and Moscardini, A O (1990) Remedial mathematics in higher education: a computer-based approach, 7th International Conference on Technology and Education, Brussels

Middleton, W, Curran, D A S and Moscardini, A O (1991) Computer-managed learning for remedial mathematics in engineering, East–West Congress on Engineering Education, Cracow

Tabor, J (1993) Review of CALMAT, *CTI Maths and Stats Newsletter*, **4**, pp 14–18

5

The use of computer algebra systems

David Pountney, Carl Leinbach and Terence Etchells

Introduction

The ever-increasing power and ease of access of computer technology continues to have a significant impact on the learning, teaching and assessment of mathematics throughout higher education establishments worldwide. In this chapter we look particularly at the impact of computer algebra systems, by which we mean software systems that can perform symbolic as well as numerical manipulations and which include graphical display capabilities. Examples include *Mathematica*, *Maple*, *Macsyma* and DERIVE, and some of these systems are available not only on PCs but also on hand-held 'super calculators' such as the TI-92 plus and the TI-89. In this chapter, DERIVE is used to illustrate the issues raised, but these issues are generic in nature and the 'translation' to other systems is straightforward.

Much has been spoken and written about the use of a computer algebra system (CAS) in learning and teaching over the last two decades or so (see, for example, International Congress for Mathematics Education (ICME) Proceedings since 1984, and journals such as the *International Journal of Computer Algebra in Mathematics Education* (IJCAME) among others). Yet the *effective* use of a CAS in learning and teaching still appears to be a topic giving rise to a wide variety of views among mathematics educators and practitioners. Certainly, the use of calculator technology has been blamed for 'the mathematics problem in society' and this bad press has contributed to the debate that the use of technology such as a CAS may be linked to falling mathematical standards among graduates.

On the other hand there have been several studies citing students gaining a better conceptual understanding of mathematics with no significant loss in computational skills. For example, Hurley *et al,* (1999) cite a National Science Foundation report that states:

> Approximately 50% of the institutions conducting studies on the impact of technology reported increases in conceptual understanding, greater facility with visualization and graphical understanding, and an ability to solve a wider variety of problems, without any loss of computational skills. Another 40% reported that students in classes with technology had done at least as well as those in traditional classes.

In the rest of the chapter we highlight some of the issues concerning learning, teaching and assessment that are likely to influence both academic programme designers, and lecturers and teachers responsible for individual modules when incorporating a CAS into their delivery. We will then go on to examine more closely the mathematical skills required of our graduates and show by examples from our own experience how the integrated use of a CAS may help to promote such skills.

Learning and teaching issues with a CAS

When it is appropriate to use a CAS

Many educators have pointed out that a CAS can trivialize some areas of mathematics that are routine in nature and require considerable algebraic manipulation. For example, mathematics students and engineering students are commonly required to undertake methods of integration such as by parts or with the use of partial fractions, often without the use of a CAS. If the object were solely to obtain an analytical solution, then the skills developed by performing such mental manipulations would appear to be virtually redundant if a CAS were available. However, there are few educators who would argue against the benefits for students in being able to integrate simple polynomials, trigonometric and exponential functions mentally. Indeed, the methods themselves should be known to students. Similar questions arise in the teaching of many modules on mathematical methods. The question that needs to be addressed is: When is it appropriate to move from a mental calculation to one making use of a tool such as a CAS?

This question is neither new nor is it resolved. Buchberger (1989) discussed this in his paper entitled 'Should students learn integration rules?' and suggested the use of a 'white box/black box' principle for teaching. This suggested that when a subject area is new to the students, basic concepts, theorems, proofs, examples, etc, should be taught using hand (mental) calculations and the CAS used sparingly (a white box approach). When hand (mental) calculations become routine and as examples and applications become more complex, then the use of a CAS should be allowed and encouraged (as a black box). This didactic principle would appear to give a rationale for effective CAS use. In practice, it would seem that the principle is easy to adopt within a module or subject area, but difficult to coordinate across a programme that includes diverse subject areas and a number of instructors with differing teaching strategies.

Procedures versus concepts

Linked to the above discussion is the desire to teach students to perform algebraic procedures and also to instill conceptual understanding. As Dubinsky and Tall (1991) state, 'Knowing how to differentiate symbolically is very different from knowing what a derivative means.' Similarly, deriving an analytical solution to a differential equation may be of limited use if the student cannot visualize and interpret this solution.

As Dreyfus (1991) suggests, we would hope that students would have sufficient conceptual understanding to explain such errors as:

$$\int_{-1}^{1} \frac{1}{x^2} \, dx = -\frac{1}{x} \Big|_{-1}^{1} = -2$$

without first reaching for a CAS to check the answer. In Buchberger's terminology, the contents of the 'white box' must be well thought out before the 'black box' stage is allowed to take over.

We, the authors, believe that with the advent of a CAS, the necessity to spend large amounts of teaching and learning time on the fine points of technical manipulations would be more profitably replaced by time spent on the development of problem-solving skills and a conceptual understanding of mathematics. Tall (1991) expressed similar views in the statement 'computers can be used to carry out the processes so that the user can concentrate on the product'. It is not clear whether this now happens. For some, 'doing mathematics' has reduced to being able to complete procedures with little reasoning ability and programmes are predominantly a collection of 'white boxes'. Again, it would seem that a good balance is needed. As Wu (1998) comments about mathematics education in general and the Calculus Reform movement in the United States in particular, drill exercises and the role of memory cannot completely be disregarded.

Kutzler (2000) has discussed the topic of 'What mathematical skills are necessary in the age of the CAS?' He equates the necessity to do some mental calculations with the necessity of the body to exercise in order to maintain muscle tone and general health. The point is a good one. It is important to exercise our minds.

On the other hand, manipulations should not be limited to those things that students can do by hand or in their head. They need to understand how to use all of the tools of technology effectively. The instructor has an important role to play in developing this understanding.

Teaching and learning strategies

One approach for the use of the CAS that seems to be rather common is in computer laboratory sessions. During these sessions students are given exploratory tasks to perform that 'support' lecture material and the exercises that had previously been performed mentally. Students *may* use the CAS to perform these explorations. It is claimed that this form of teaching and learning does not rely on a CAS but uses a CAS to enhance discovery learning and motivation and to develop mathematical skills such as visualization and problem solving. This is more of a constructivist rather than an instructivist approach to teaching and learning. Results with students using such a strategy are quoted internationally. Some examples are Kutzler (1994), who reports on the use of DERIVE in Austrian schools and colleges; Stephens and Konvalina (1999), who report on CAS/non-CAS teaching experiments in a college in the United States; Connors and Snook (2001), who analyzed exam results after similar experiments again in the United States, and Beaudin (2000) who describes such an approach to the teaching of engineering mathematics in Quebec, Canada.

A less successful approach would appear to be the use of a CAS as an add-on to a conventional lecture/tutorial style of teaching. It is the authors' experience that students need to be convinced of the relevance of CAS use and given a choice will often prefer to solve a problem by hand if possible. Hence the exploration tasks and questions set should beg naturally for CAS use. Also, students expect a consistent approach to CAS use across the whole programme of study. A 'learn how to use a CAS' module carries little weight if students do not use a CAS elsewhere in their programme even when it is appropriate to do so. Programme design should allow for an *integrated* policy on CAS usage, not only in Mathematics degree programmes but also in service teaching in programmes such as engineering where mathematics forms a part.

Assessment

Adopting the principle of 'we assess what we teach', once it is a fact that a CAS is used in teaching, then the use of a CAS in assessment is a logical and necessary next step. This is particularly the case where the use of CAS forms part of the learning outcomes of a course, as considered in the previous chapter. This simple statement raises a number of issues relating to CAS use, particularly the use of a CAS in formal, timed examinations. This topic is debated extensively even among ardent CAS supporters. Much of the debate centres on the mechanics of implementation and equity of CAS use in which, although important issues, are secondary details compared to the main aim of assessing appropriate mathematical knowledge and skills examinations (see, for example, Ruthven, 1997; Taylor, 1995; Etchells and Monaghan, 1994). Once again, an integrated approach covering learning, teaching *and* assessment is needed.

The use of a CAS in the mathematics exam is not completely analogous to an open book examination. In fact, the CAS generally tells the mathematics student less than (say) the open history book may tell the history student. The CAS merely does the numerical or symbolic calculation; the interpretation of the result is beyond its capability. The interpretation is where the student's understanding of the topic comes to light. It merely emphasizes to the student, and possibly to the instructor, that doing calculations is not the sole purpose for studying a topic. Mathematical problem solving is a process that goes far beyond manipulation of symbols. The use of a CAS removes a computational roadblock that can stand between the students and the solution of the problem.

Examination questions that are set for an environment where students are allowed to have access to a CAS should ask them to develop a strategy or recall concepts and ideas, not just to exhibit manipulations and recall formulae. In short, the evaluator needs to look at what the students have really learnt during the course as opposed to what they have memorized or done as drills.

In the rest of the chapter we look at a possible framework, based on a mathematical skills taxonomy, for establishing a coherent strategy for CAS use, bearing in mind the issues discussed in this section. A wider discussion on skills of mathematics graduates can be found in Chapter 6.

Mathematical skills

In their article categorizing mathematical skills, Smith *et al* (1996) developed a Mathematical Teaching Hierarchy Taxonomy (MATH Taxonomy) that divides mathematical skills into three levels that can be summarized in the following table, as already noted in Chapter 1.

Table 5.1 The MATH taxonomy of Smith *et al* (1996)

Group A	Group B	Group C
factual knowledge	information transfer	justifying and interpreting
comprehension	application in new situations	implications, conjectures and comparisons
routine use of procedures		evaluation

Our experience gained through discussions with colleagues within our universities and at international conferences is that as one proceeds from left to right in this taxonomy, ie from Group A skills to Group C skills, the skills are more valued by mathematicians. Often programmes claim the development of skills similar to Group C skills as a major aim. On the other hand, our experience is similar to that of Smith and his colleagues. The majority of students entering formal education at the level of the UK A levels and above possess mainly Group A skills. A small minority have developed Group B skills, and Group C skills are virtually non-existent. Papers by Etchells and Mongahan (1994) and, more recently, by Mongahan *et al* (1998) have shown that National Assessment Tests for A-level Mathematics still ask questions that give many more points for performance of routine, Group A, tasks than Group B tasks, and practically none that could be labelled Group C. Furthermore, the use of CAS or any technology was not allowed on these exams. In the United States, the situation is somewhat different in that the TI-89, which has a CAS built into it, is allowed for the free response portion of the Advanced Placement Examinations.

Certainly one could contest and debate the contents of a skills taxonomy like the MATH taxonomy, although it is interesting to note that a recent taxonomy proposed by Galbraith and Haines (1995) is similarly based on three levels, which they term *mechanistic, interpretive* and *constructivist*. The reader should note also the reference to Bloom's taxonomy of educational objectives and its role in assessment of mathematics discussed in Chapter 4. The point is that taxonomy can serve a useful purpose in identifying the mathematical skills needed to answer assessment questions and hence measure the balance of skills assessed in an assessment.

In the remainder of this section, we aim to illustrate how a CAS can be used to help in the development of mathematical problem-solving skills and other Group C skills, both in the classroom and in examinations, looking at questions from calculus (for other examples based on algebra see Leinbach and Pountney, 1999).

A worksheet on optimization

We present a concrete example of the integrated use of a CAS in Figure 5.1. This figure contains a worksheet that could be given to students to help them develop problem-solving skills and also to exercise some of the skills listed in the MATH Taxonomy. We have constructed the worksheet so that it progresses through a lesson in optimization using the material taught in a standard calculus course. It starts by reinforcing the graphical ideas of optimization and using the CAS to find maxima and minima. It concludes with a sequence of three problems that start with a standard optimization problem and then abstract it to the general situation that requires insight into the meaning of the answer and policy formulation based upon the answer.

In Tables 5.2, 5.3, and 5.4 we examine the skills used in the worksheet and in the light of the MATH Taxonomy. An examination of these tables shows that those tasks that are essential to mathematical analysis and reasoning are still those that are done by the student, with the CAS simply used as a tool. The right hand column has two attributes. The first is that these activities are at the core of the problem solution. The second is that CAS is not able to perform these tasks. It drives home the point that use of a CAS is not just pushing buttons without having to think about or understand the problem. A good problem solver keeps the problem in the forefront. The tools, whether they are the product rule, the quotient rule, the chain rule, or a CAS, are merely a means to accomplish the task at hand.

Figure 5.1   A worksheet on optimization using gradients

Optimization Problems

LOCATING EXTREMA AND DESCRIBING GRAPHS

1. For each of the following functions locate, using information obtained from the derivatives of the function, all of the local extrema.

    a. $f(x) = -2x^5 + x^4 - 4x^3 + 5x + 5$

    b. $f(x) = \dfrac{4x(x+1)}{4x^4 - x^3 + 3x^2 + 5}$

    c. $f(x) = \dfrac{\sin(x)}{x}$ $-15 \le x \le 5$

    d. $f(x) = 5e^{\frac{-x2}{4}} \cos(x)$ $-5 \le x \le 5$

2. For each of the above examples and the information from the derivative, determine:

    a.   Where is the function increasing?
    b.   Where is it decreasing?
    c.   Where is it concave up?
    d.   Where is it concave down?

3. Given an arbitrary function, $f(x)$, which is twice differentiable write a series of steps in your CAS or a program in the CAS that will separately display

    a.   Those portions of the graph where it is increasing and concave up.
    b.   Those portions of the graph where it is increasing and concave down.
    c.   Those portions of the graph where it is decreasing and concave up.
    d.   Those portions of the graph where it is decreasing and concave down.

    Using the steps or program that you wrote, substitute for $f(x)$ a function of your choice from problem 1; display the four parts of the graph for $f(x)$. If your CAS allows you to graph using different colours, it may be instructive to display each of the four parts of the graph in a different colour on the same graph.

SOLVING AN OPTIMIZATION PROBLEM

4. Petrol prices are getting out of control. This especially affects the shippers whose lorries are terribly inefficient in their use of diesel fuel. The average lorry gets about 2 miles per litre of fuel. The price of fuel is £1.45 per litre. A government study concludes that on the average, the fuel consumption of a lorry decreases by .05 mile per litre for each increase in speed of 5 miles per hour over 45 miles per hour. Assuming that a lorry driver earns £10.00 per hour for each hour of an over the road trip, fund the optimal speed to travel during a trip of 150 miles.
5. Show that the optimal speed for an over the road trip is independent of the distance of the trip.
6. Assuming that the average speed of the lorry and the driver's wages are the significant variables in determining the most economical speed of travel for the over the road trip, find the relationship of the speed of the lorry on the trip to the ratio of fuel to wages. In particular, if drivers are granted a £1.50 per hour pay raise, what would be the appropriate cost for fuel that would suggest that the optimal speed for the lorries by 55 miles per hour or less?

Table 5.2 Group A skills used in the worksheet on optimization

Exercise	Skill exercised	CAS activity	Intellectual activity
1 a,b	locating local extrema	find derivatives; solve equations	identify and classify results
1 c, d	locating local extrema	find derivatives; approximate the numerical solution	know what to do when CAS does not give an exact solution
2	describing the graph of a function	find derivatives	be able to translate the language of derivatives into the description of the curve

Table 5.3 Group B skills used in the worksheet on optimization

Exercise	Skill exercised	CAS activity	Intellectual activity
3	understanding the graph of a function	find derivatives; graph functions defined by conditional phrases	be able to translate the graphical description of the derivative into conditional phrases
4	solving max–min problems	find derivatives	set up the model based on verbal description of a situation

Table 5.4 Group C skills used in the worksheet on optimization

Exercise	Skill exercised	CAS activity	Intellectual activity
5	analysis of a result	take derivatives	replace constants with parameters; recognize that a particular parameter does not appear in the derivative; understand the meaning of the above realization
6	solving a max–min problem that has no numerical data	take derivatives; solve equations symbolically	set up the model using only variables and parameters; analyse the solution of the problem; formulate a general strategy based on the information contained in the solution

Formal assessment with a computer algebra system

We now move from classroom activities using a CAS to an example of a formal, timed examination allowing the use of a CAS. The examination shown in Figures 5.2, 5.3 and 5.4 was taken by first-year undergraduate students at Liverpool John Moores University in April 1998. Around 30 students sat for the exam. This 'Mathematical Methods' examination, composed by Terence Etchells, is typical of a number of CAS-based modular examinations used in the course since 1995, although again, we emphasize that the use of a CAS is integrated throughout the delivery and assessment of such modules.

The instructions on the cover page of the examination include:

- The duration of this examination is 2 hours.
- There are two sections A and B.
- You must answer all questions in section A and 3 questions from section B.
- You are advised not to spend more than 40 minutes on section A.
- You have the use of a networked PC and the software DERIVE.
- Any intelligent use of information technology is allowed in this examination.
- You may not print any material during this examination.

The reason for the last instruction is to eliminate confusion in the exam room (ie computer laboratory) from the noise of the printer and the disruption of students trying to retrieve their printed work. It also forces students to examine their output as they transfer results from their computation to their examination booklet. The reader will also note that the results are not merely copied to the examination booklet. Students need to analyse their results as well as use the correct methods for solving the problems.

It is fairly obvious that Section A of this examination (Figure 5.2) requires, at most, Group B level skills and that Group A level skills are the most prevalent. Questions 1, 4, and 5 are testing at the Group A level. Question 1 could almost reduce to button pushing in the CAS except that the student would need to make the notational translation from the test to the CAS. Questions 4 and 5, by virtue of the fact that the students need to do a paper and pencil demonstration of the processes of differentiation and integration, avoid button pushing. The functions are really straightforward, but force the student to demonstrate an understanding of the product rule, implicit differentiation, the substitution rule and integration by parts. It should be noted that there is no prohibition against a student checking an answer with the CAS. The answer alone is not the goal of these problems.

To answer question 2 a student needs to take an algebraic expression and interpret it geometrically. That is, in our opinion, a level B skill. The student can use the CAS to draw both graphs and test hypotheses, if necessary.

Question 3 is intended to require Group B level skills (information transfer) but it is true that a student could possibly memorize the required formula rather than derive it and hence move the solution of the problem to a Group A level skill.

Figure 5.2 Section A of the examination

Section A

Answer all Questions. You are advised not to spend more than 40 minutes on this section.

1. The universal set S is the set of all natural numbers between 1 and 10. You are given that $A = \{1,3,5,8,10\}$ and $B = \{1,4,9\}$. Find

    a) $A \cup B$ (b) $A \cap B$ (c) $\overline{A \cap B}$ [5]

2. Describe transformations of $y = x^3$ that will produce $y = 3(x-2)^3 + 1$ [4]

3. An investment plan returns 6.9% per annum. Write down a function, in terms of n the number of years and I the amount invested, which will give the value of the investment plan after n completed years. Hence, evaluate the value of a £2,800 investment plan after 15 years at a fixed rate of 6.9% p.a.   [6]

4. Using **paper and pencil only**, find $\dfrac{dy}{dx}$ if

    (a) $y = x \sin(x)$ (b) $xy + y^2 = \sin(x)$ [5]

5. Using **paper and pencil only**, find the following integrals

    (a) $\int e^{5x} d$ (b) $\int_{0}^{\pi} x \sin(x\ d)$ [5]

    Total [25]

In Section B of the exam (Figures 5.3 and 5.4), we see that a mixture of all three levels of skill are required to provide successful answers to the questions. Question 1 illustrates this point extremely well. The first part is a Group B skill in that it requires the student to transfer a geometric construction to an algebraic expression. The second part is an application of the standard max–min procedure and requires two DERIVE commands. The third part requires a demonstration of Group B level skills: the translation of numerical information to geometric reality. The fourth part simply requires the evaluation of the function from the first part and also an appropriate derivative test. The solution of this requires Group skills. The fifth part is a different type of question and is more challenging. Assuming that the students have not seen this problem before, as was the case in this examination, this requires them to demonstrate some Group C level sills. They have all of the information, but need to extend their interpretation of the situation to a new problem. This is not as major a challenge as one might require in course work, but it is appropriate for demonstrating this level of skill in a timed exercise. Students could not rely merely upon their memory of technical manipulations to earn full

Figure 5.3 The first two questions from Section B of the examination

Section B

1. An open box is to be made from a rectangular sheet of cardboard 20cm by 18cm, by cutting out 4 equal shares from each corner.

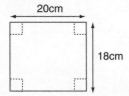

If the length of each side of the square is x cm then show that the volume of the ensuing box is

$$v = x(20 - 2x)(18 - 2x)$$ [5]

Hence find the values for x for which the function v has stationary points.   [4]

Which of these values of x is not applicable to the problem above and why? [3]

Find the value of x that will give the maximum value for the volume and prove that it is a maximum. Find the maximum volume of this box.   [8]

Write down the minimum value of the volume of the box, and which values of x will lead to this minimum.

Find the value of x that will provide the minimum surface area (inside of the box only) of the box.   [5]

Total [25]

2. (a) Find the area enclosed by the functions $y = x^2 - x - 2$ and
        $y = x^3 - 2x^2 - x + 2$ [17]
    (b) Find the length of the curve $y = e^{\sin x}$ between $0 \leq x \leq 1$ correct
        to three decimal places.   [8]

Total [25]

Figure 5.4 The last two questions from Section B of the examination

3. Show that $\int_0^1 x^3\, dx = \dfrac{1}{4}$ by the usual techniques. [5]

Show that if we split the function $y = x^3$, between $x = 0$ and $x = 1$, into n upper Riemann rectangles then the area of the rth rectangle is

$$\frac{1}{n}\left(\frac{r}{n}\right)^3$$

[7]

Hence write down an expression for the area of all n rectangles and evaluate it in terms of n using DERIVE. [8]

Use this result to determine $\int_0^1 x^3\, dx$ [5]

Total   [25]

4. (a) Evaluate $\displaystyle\lim_{x \to 2}\left(\left|\frac{x^4 - 16}{x - 2}\right|\right)$ [3]

(b) Find the coordinates at which the function $y = \left|\dfrac{x^4 - 16}{x - 2}\right|$ is **not** differentiable.

(c) Prove that the function $y = \left|\dfrac{x^4 - 16}{x - 2}\right|$ is **not** differentiable at the point evaluated in part 9b0 by finding the gradient from both sides of this point.

(d) Prove that the function $y = \dfrac{\left|\sin(\pi x) - \dfrac{\sqrt{3}}{2}\right|^3}{\left(\sin(\pi x) - \dfrac{\sqrt{3}}{2}\right)^3}$ is discontinuous at the point

$x = \dfrac{1}{3}$. Find another point on the interval $0 \le x \le 1$ for which the function

$y = \dfrac{\left|\sin(\pi x) - \dfrac{\sqrt{3}}{2}\right|^3}{\left(\sin(\pi x) - \dfrac{\sqrt{3}}{2}\right)^3}$ is not continuous (you need not prove it to be

discontinuous.) [8]

Total   [25]

marks. There was no requirement that the CAS is used for this problem and there were students who did not use it. The availability of the CAS simply removed any computational impediment to the students' demonstration of their knowledge.

Question 2(a) requires Group B level skills. The students need to interpret the graphs that are drawn by the CAS and perform the proper algebraic and calculus manipulations. This includes drawing the graphs in the appropriate window. The roots are easily found even without a CAS and the definite integral is easy to evaluate either by hand or with a CAS. On the other hand, the problem tests the students' understanding of the area between two curves. The solution to 2(b) is made to go beyond button pressing by the specification that the numerical answer is required to be correct to three decimal places. Setting up the integral to find the length of the curve is, at most, a Group B skill. The students' knowledge of numerical techniques is tested by the request for three decimal places of accuracy. The integrand is not a monotonic function over the interval $0 < x < 1$. Thus, if the student has chosen a rectangular or trapezoidal rule to estimate the value of the integral, there is a need to use Group C level skills to guarantee that the desired accuracy is attained.

In question 3, the role of the CAS, if the student chooses to use it, is to help in 'seeing' his or her way through the argument and develop the proof. The student needs to recognize the need to pass to the limit in the last part and not perform a numerical approximation. We believe this problem requires Group B to Group C levels of skills.

Question 4 at first glance looks like it would be trivial using a CAS. Indeed the answer to the first part can be a simple type and read the answer. But then the question starts to really test the student's understanding of the meaning of differentiability and continuity. For example, in the second part the student has to realize that even though the limit existed at $x = 2$, the function is not defined there. The student really needs to study the graph of the function. Part (c) tests understanding of the meaning of the derivative. In part (d) seeing the graph is not enough! The trace of the graph can, at best, identify the point up to the precision that has been set on individual calculators. The point of the problem is for the student to recognize where the jump discontinuity will appear and to find those points. The second part of this process can be done with the CAS.

Student performance in such examinations

The first question that is asked by many people is of the type: 'Does using a CAS in teaching and assessment increase the percentage of students that pass the module?' The students taking this exam found the group C skills taxing, and pass rates and mean marks were similar to their scores in other non-CAS examinations. In fact in an appropriate assessment there is no significant change, either positive or negative, in the number of students who pass. Nor is there a significant change in the overall grade distribution. It is unreasonable to expect that the CAS will change these factors; it will not suddenly make all students into mathematicians. That is a function of student desire and ability coupled with the teacher's skill. What the CAS does bring to our teaching is the ability to teach and assess the mathematics that we profess to be our goal.

It is noted that learning to do mathematics using a CAS is initially a harder skill than most students have developed in their more traditional courses in secondary school. If the importance of the CAS were not stressed throughout the course and in all assessment activities, students would revert to their more comfortable mode of doing mathematics. It is our opinion that in that case, the goals of the course would be lost and the Group C level skills would be overlooked or played down because of a student preoccupation with the manipulative end of the spectrum. As a result of the initial time that the student needs to become comfortable with the CAS, experience has shown that the instructor needs to write exams that do not contain as many questions as on traditional examinations, but which still cover the major ideas of the module. Thus, exam writing at this level requires careful thought about the issues of student capacity as well as the capabilities and role of the CAS in learning the subject matter and answering the examination questions.

Discussion: the role of the CAS in mathematics skills development

A CAS is simply a mathematical tool. Mathematicians and users of mathematics have been developing tools from the very beginning. Why are we in a situation where we hear so many protests because we are using modern technology? The fact is that there should be none. If the CAS is used in an appropriate fashion as illustrated in the above worksheet and examination, not only are students doing mathematical thinking, they are doing better thinking at a higher level. They are dealing with the essence of problems, not working around the fringes by doing complicated manipulations.

The answer to the question of why there is protest to the use of a CAS lies partly in the fact that the ability to do complicated manipulations has been mistakenly labelled as 'doing mathematics'. In the optimization exercises, the CAS did all of the work for finding derivatives. Some teachers believe that this is a fundamental skill that will be lost. Our reply is that this fear is irrelevant to the question of using a CAS. Yes, some students will not be facile at finding derivatives. Others will still be able to find derivatives and enjoy the task. So be it! The fact remains that 'doing mathematics' is about reasoning and problem solving. The 'doing of calculations' is only a means to an end. This holds true whether the calculations are numerical or algebraic.

Undoubtedly, the impact of a CAS will be most significant if allowed in formal examinations. Assessment may not drive teaching but it certainly drives students' learning and a CAS will become used significantly if students perceive it gives them an advantage in assessed work. Yet we have suggested that the use of a CAS in assessed work, including formal examinations, is likely to result in a change of emphasis from successful manipulative work to problem solving and other skills. As a result, we must consider the following question(s): Is it the case that mathematics course work and examinations will only be manageable by students who are accomplished problem solvers? Will the students who only possess manipulative skills or the ability to do straightforward, well-defined applications be unable to pass our courses?

If this is the case then mathematics runs the risk of becoming an elitist subject and may very well be ignored by other disciplines. We believe that the examples given show that it is possible to construct examinations that require the students to use and demonstrate manipulative as well as problem-solving skills.

Conclusion

The authors firmly believe that mathematics courses at all levels need to be taught with an emphasis on developing the skills highlighted in the MATH Taxonomy level C. We also believe that the CAS provides an excellent opportunity to achieve this goal. This means that we, as teachers of mathematics, need to incorporate the use of this tool into our teaching. The CAS does not make our teaching redundant or trivial. It allows us to set our students on the path to mathematical discovery and problem solving. Far from creating an artificial environment in the classroom, we will be preparing them for their futures as either consumers of mathematics or as professional mathematicians. As we stated earlier, doing mathematics and doing mathematical manipulations are two different activities altogether.

In a survey of recent Mathematics graduates working as mathematicians that appeared in the magazine, *Math Horizons* (Moylan, 1995) a two-part question was asked, 'Which of the courses and skills that you took as an undergraduate Mathematics Major best prepared you for your present career? Which prepared you the least?' The respondents replied that the most useful courses where those that involved modelling and problem solving, ie differential equations, finite mathematics, operations (or operational) research, statistics, etc. On the other hand, while they did not identify whole courses as useless, they did, in an almost unanimous manner, condemn the part of their undergraduate training that emphasized manipulative and hand calculation of numerical and technical algorithms. Examples included differentiation problems, time spent on technique after technique of symbolic integration, multiplication and manipulation of large matrices, and closed form solutions of differential equations. They said that their employers had placed packages that did these things on their desktops. They needed to spend more time on developing problem solving and analysis skills.

Many students who go to graduate school in the sciences or mathematics use computer packages as a part of their research work. This practice is just regarded as a basic technique of conducting modern research. No one doubts that the research they are doing is invalid because of a reliance on the computer.

We believe that we have shown how meaningful exercises and examinations can be constructed for use in a CAS laboratory or in a situation where every student has access to a CAS. Far from trivializing mathematics teaching and learning, we believe that we have enhanced it. More time can be spent on problems requiring students to develop the level C skills of the MATH Taxonomy.

We conclude by restating our assertion that mathematics instruction that fails to include the use of the CAS stands the risk of becoming redundant. A CAS is available in relatively inexpensive calculators. It is embedded in at least one word processor (Scientific Notebook). It has been incorporated in some widely used industrial and academic mathematics tools such as MathCAD and MatLab. In both the United States and the United Kingdom there are Engineering schools that are requiring their students to understand how to use CAS in doing their course work. It is time that students in mathematics courses become comfortable with using the tools of the 21st century. The key to this is that the CAS is allowed in all stages of mathematics instruction and assessment.

References

Beaudin, M (2000) Supporting engineering mathematics with the TI-92, *International Journal of Computer Algebra in Mathematics Education*, **7**(2), pp 143–55

Buchberger, B (1989) Should students learn integration rules?, *RISC-LINZ Technical Report series* 89–07.0, Joseph Kepler University, Austria

Connors, M A and Snook, K G (forthcoming 2001) The effects of hand-held CAS on student achievement in a First Year College core calculus course, *International Journal of Computer Algebra in Mathematics Education*

Dubinsky, E, Tall, D (1991) Advanced mathematical thinking and the computer, in *Advanced Mathematical Thinking*, ed D Tall, pp 231–48, Kluwer Academic, Dordrecht

Drefyus, T (1991) Advanced mathematical thinking processes, in *Advanced Mathematical Thinking,* ed D Tall, pp 25–41, Kluwer Academic, Dordrecht

Etchells, T, Monaghan, J (1994) Hand-held technology – assessment issues, *Acta Didactica Univ. Comenianae Mathemathematics*, **3**, pp 119–30

Galbraith, P L and Haines, C R (1995) *Bulletin of the Institute of Mathematics and its Applications*, **31**, pp 175–79

Hurley, J F, Koehn, U and Gantner, S L (1999) Effects of Calculus Reform: local and national, *American Mathematical Monthly*, **106**(9), pp 800–811

Kutzler, B (1994) *International Journal of Computer Algebra in Mathematics Education* (formerly *International DERIVE Journal*), **3**(1)

Kutzler, B (2000) *Proceedings of the 4th International DERIVE-TI89/92 Conference*, Liverpool, see also [Online] http://series.bk-teachware.com

Leinbach, C, Pountney, D C (1999) Appropriate use of a CAS in teaching mathematics, in *Algebra Across the Grades*, pp 59–72, Pennsylvania Council of Teachers of Mathematics Yearbook

Monaghan, J, Johnson, P, Berry, J and Maull, W (1998) *Proceedings of the Day Conference of the British Society for Research into Learning Mathematics (BSRLM)*, Leeds

Moylan, E (1995) Market your mathskills, *Math Horizons*, September

Ruthven, K (1997). Computer Algebra Systems (CAS) in Advanced-level mathematics, *Report to SCAA*

Smith, G, Wood, L, Coupland, M, Stephenson, B, Crawford, K and Ball, G (1996) *International Journal of Mathematics Education in Science and Technology*, **27**, pp 65–77

Stephens, L J, Konvalina, S (1999) The use of Computer Algebra software in teaching intermediate and college algebra, *International Journal of Mathematics Education in Science and Technology*, **30**(4), pp 483–88

Tall, D (1991) Chapter 15, in *Advanced Mathematical Thinking*, ed D Tall, pp 251–59, Kluwer Academic, Dordrecht

Taylor, M (1995), *Mathematical Gazette*, **79**, pp 68–83

Wu, H (1998) *Notices of the American Mathematical Society*, **45**, pp 77–85

6

Developing transferable skills:
preparation for employment

Neil Challis, Harry Gretton, Ken Houston and Neville Neill

Introduction

Generally speaking, humans develop skills as they mature. They will employ skills when they are competent and comfortable with them and using them will lead to an improvement in their quality of life. Children develop speech and then they can more easily tell their parents what they want; they develop dexterity and then they can more readily enjoy their toys. In this chapter we are concerned with developing certain key skills in mathematics students, skills that we describe as transferable and that will enable students to improve their quality of life.

Professional mathematicians require good transferable skills, such as reading, writing, speaking and working with others, as well as subject-specific knowledge. They may be applied mathematicians, in one or more of a variety of guises such as scientists, engineers, economists or actuaries, and will be working with others, using mathematics and mathematical modelling to solve problems and answer questions that may arise in industry, commerce or a social context. If they are pure mathematicians, they will almost certainly be employed by a university with some requirement to conduct research and to teach. Those mathematics graduates who become schoolteachers will certainly need good interpersonal and leadership skills, along with several other attributes that they may not get through an undergraduate mathematics education! Some mathematics graduates will go into general employment, and they, like their peers will need all of the aforementioned transferable skills.

We advocate that transferable skills be taught and practised in the context of their main study, mathematical sciences. Such an approach is also advocated within Chapter 7. In other words, the development of these skills should be embedded in the mathematics curriculum. It is clear that when people are required to communicate an idea to others, whether specialists or lay, then they will understand the idea more thoroughly themselves. We make the assumption that students are interested in learning mathematics, for its own sake, as a tool to develop the intellect, and as a route to a good degree and satisfying employment.

There is no doubt that the need exists for skilled mathematics graduates. Surveys from 1973 to 1999 and our own observations and experiences confirm this. It is therefore incumbent on us, as teachers, to help our students to learn and develop these skills.

In the rest of this chapter, we shall discuss more fully the skills variously described as transferable, key or 'soft', giving a rationale for their inclusion. We shall attempt to categorize them and to discuss how we might observe them develop as a student progresses from fresher to graduate. We shall further describe the various teaching and assessment methods we have employed to develop skills, and the various assessment tools we have used to measure this development. It is worth noting here that mathematical modelling provides a particularly effective context for developing transferable skills, as evident both within this chapter and in Chapter 12. Finally, we shall provide some evidence in the Evaluation section that our students do, indeed, become progressively more skilful as well as knowledgeable as they move up through their course.

Transferable skills

While degree programmes have been attempting to introduce transferable skills acquisition as an integral part of the teaching process, HND (Higher National Diploma) programmes have had to address this issue for many years. Each Edexcel programme contains a Common Skills element, which permeates both years of the course and each student is assessed under the following headings:

- managing and developing self;
- working with and relating to others;
- communicating;
- managing tasks and solving problems;
- applying numeracy;
- applying technology;
- applying design and creativity.

It was to ensure that degree students obtained the same skills-based training as their sub-degree counterparts that the Enterprise in Higher Education Initiative (Training Employment and Education Directorate (TEED), 1989) was launched.

At both the University of Ulster (UU) and Sheffield Hallam University (SHU), there is at least one module in the first year of each programme that is the main vehicle for addressing these issues. Both mathematics programmes have gone further than this and have ensured that skills acquisition is embedded throughout the curriculum. Accordingly many modules contribute in some way to this end.

This does of course beg the question of what constitutes the appropriate skills list for mathematics graduates. Some discussion on this ensues, although it would not be appropriate to try to produce a definitive list here.

There is evidence of international interest in transferable skills for employability. The Society for Industrial and Applied Mathematics (SIAM) report on *Mathematics in Industry* (SIAM, 1998) contained data from a survey of PhD graduates working in industry. The report indicated that modelling, communication and teamwork skills together with a willingness to be flexible are important traits in employees. However the PhD graduates themselves indicated that they felt inadequately prepared to tackle diverse problems, to use communication effectively and at a variety of levels, or to work in teams. Further recent evidence of activity beyond the UK is to be found, for example, in a paper by Woods *et al* (2000).

Within the UK, the MathSkills project (see http://www.hull.ac.uk/math-skills/) identified similar points. An employer survey suggested that a mathematics graduate is advantaged by being logical, systematic and rigorous, being able to take an abstract and broad approach, and being analytical, clear thinking and fast to understand. On the negative side, mathematics graduates tended to lack presentation and communication skills (including report writing and presentation to a non-technical audience), pragmatism in real problem solving, social skills and commercial awareness.

There is remarkable alignment with the skills list suggested by Dearing (National Committee of Inquiry into Higher Education, 1997) that includes communication and learning how to learn, and with other lists quoted by Dearing, which include problem solving and team working.

In our experience, professional mathematicians in industry will probably be working on problems that require their specialized knowledge and skills, and they will be working with others who have different specialities, or who are managing the project, or have commissioned it. They must converse lucidly with others, who are ignorant of mathematics, and they must know what can, and what cannot, be solved mathematically. They must simplify problems through modelling, and find or create suitable methods of solution. They must then convey their findings persuasively to a wide range of others, in discussion, in writing and through a presentation: with many audiences, a persuasive argument is more convincing than a rigorous proof! In their work they will have spent a considerable time on their own, researching, thinking and calculating, and they will have spent a considerable time in discussion with the others in the team. They will have to use information technology, not only for purposes of communication, but also for calculation, using their own algorithms or some of the large number of software products already on the market.

This analysis must also take account of the fact that most mathematics graduates do not go on to call themselves professional mathematicians, although they still bring their special qualities to their job, be it in finance, management, computing or whatever. It is certainly apparent though that while lists may vary in detail, there is growing agreement on the skills required to make mathematics graduates more employable.

Embedding in the curriculum

The Sheffield Hallam University experience

The mathematics provision at Sheffield Hallam University (SHU) has grown within the context of that institution's history as a former polytechnic and a major provider of sandwich education. It is not surprising then that graduate employability is high on the list of aims of the mathematics degree. The University leads a TLTP (Teaching and Learning Technology Programme) project 'The Key to Key Skills' (SHU, 2000), developing generic material for skills development. Our experience, however, is that projects such as this do not have an impact on practice until the agenda is adopted, adapted and owned by a subject group.

The skills agenda has certainly been developed independently in the mathematics subject group at SHU. The BSc (Hons) Mathematics course is relatively young (having started in 1996), and the increasing recognition of the importance of skills development coincided with its design. The degree has a strong applied mathematics and modelling flavour, embracing the integrated use of technology throughout, and aiming to prepare its graduates both for employment and for further study. It was thus natural and timely to embed and integrate activities into the course that encourage such development. The issue of skills was explicitly addressed during planning, with an attempt to integrate aspects of skills development into as many units/modules as possible, and a skills audit carried out to ensure a coherent coverage that ensured that the development was both progressive and cumulative.

In practice this means that several units have some skills element, with more sophisticated demands as the course progresses. An important point though, is that there are particular opportunities for skills work in the practical mathematical modelling units more than in the underpinning techniques or foundation units. In addition, certain units are designed to provide a focus for skills development.

Some of the development work was supported through the Enterprise in Higher Education project (TEED, 1989). Work on learning outcomes and assessment methodology could have been seen as merely bureaucratic. In fact, this work contributed strongly to making explicit what we were aiming for, ie that students should be able to identify skills as well as making the mathematical content coherent. In addition, appropriate ways of assessing whether they could do that were developed. An associated staff development project created the time necessary for staff to consider these issues.

It was seen as important that the development of skills is assessed in an integrated way alongside more traditional mathematical assessment. Constructive debate continues as to the proportion of marks that should be allocated for skills overall. However, there is general agreement that at a time when students are under severe financial pressure, and many must work for a substantial number of hours each week, then in order to send a strong message about what we really value, we must award credit for it!

Particular elements of the course worthy of mention here include the following:

- The one-year industrial placement is optional but strongly recommended. Many do not take advantage of this for a variety of good reasons (eg mature students wanting to 'get on with it', or those wishing to progress to a teaching qualification), but our experience is that there are benefits in terms of maturity, skills development and attractiveness to employers.
- While skills may be practised throughout the course, some units provide a focus. These units sow seeds that are exploited elsewhere. A year-1 unit develops group working, information and presentational skills, providing opportunities for self and peer assessment, and allowing students to receive feedback on oral presentations, posters and written reports. In the final year sandwich students receive academic credit for developmental reflection on their placement, assessed through a report, poster and portfolio. Non-sandwich students receive credit for a unit that encourages them to research the role and qualities of mathematics graduates in employment, while simultaneously working in such a way as to develop the very skills they identify, for instance communicating a mathematical topic to a non-mathematical audience. They also reflect on their skills in the context of job applications, and form plans to improve them.
- A substantial individual final-year project provides an opportunity for students, under supervision, to take a problem of their own from formulation and specification through to reporting and presentation of conclusions. The best cases address the full range of skills, including time management and information seeking.
- Across units there is variously some group working at all levels and some assignments with a discursive element, particularly mathematical modelling case studies. Some marks are explicitly allocated for demonstration of skills. There is also some requirement to read and reflect upon mathematics, to write for a particular audience (eg to write a popular article) and to integrate appropriate technology.
- An important point is that a wide range of assessment methods is used, including posters, oral presentations, open book and technology-based as well as traditional examinations, written reports with credit for use of language, reflective letters, and portfolio type gathering of evidence. We have found it helpful to continue to develop grids and proformas both to help us to mark

consistently (Challis and Gretton, 1997), and to help students to become aware of their own development (Challis and Gretton, 1998).

- The range of students on the course includes some with both Mathematics and English A levels, but it has still proved necessary to hold additional final-year workshops on written English and report writing in the build-up to final project reports. Through the course some students need persuading of the benefits of good writing. Broadly, though, when the philosophy is explained to them, starting during recruitment, the message is well taken.

Before concluding this section, it is perhaps also worth briefly mentioning some lessons learnt when trying to incorporate general skills work into 'service' mathematics courses such as those taught to engineers. For example, use of a learning diary was piloted with first year engineering students (Challis and Gretton, 1998), raising the dilemma of whether to assess it (seen as perverse by both students and engineering staff in a mathematics unit), or not (when very few took the exercise seriously). Some aspects of this kind of approach may be relevant as the idea of a student progress file develops within the UK as part of the QAA (Quality Assurance Agency for Higher Education) agenda. Other broader key skills work with engineering students (Challis and Gretton, 1997) has raised cultural issues with engineering colleagues, concerning their view of the role of a mathematics module in engineering.

The University of Ulster experience

The University of Ulster offers an honours degree in Mathematics, Statistics and Computing and HND in Mathematical Studies. The degree programme includes a compulsory placement year. Upon successful completion of the HND, diplomates may proceed to the second year of the honours course. The curricula are designed to incorporate the principles outlined above, namely, to introduce students to the way of life of a professional mathematician and to provide progressive and cumulative embedded learning opportunities for students to develop the transferable skills of communication, teamwork and learning how to learn.

On the HND the Common Skills Workshop is a coursework-only module, the first half of which introduces new entrants to those IT packages (Microsoft Office, e-mail, Internet, computer algebra systems) that underpin the rest of the course. Students can learn much from observing others and, during the module, each person gives a short presentation on, and demonstration of, a Web site they have produced. The rest of the cohort assess the speaker against the criteria published in Haines and Dunthorne (1996) for oral presentations and hence hopefully can improve their own personal performance accordingly. This exercise not only acts as an icebreaker but also provides an opportunity to assess the Edexcel skill of applying design and creativity, something which is not always easily done on mathematics courses.

The second half deals with oral and written communication skills, presentation techniques and team working. The class is split into, preferably, groups of four that work on a topic under the supervision of a member of staff. At the end of the semester each group submits a written report and presents its findings in front of an invited audience, often including the Edexcel external examiner. An important part of this task is the confidential self and peer assessment element, the students marking themselves and their peers against criteria they themselves drew up at the outset of the work: the 'learning contract'. At the end of the module, as part of the debriefing, students reflect on the skills they have used and refined during the module. This is a useful element of all skills-based teaching as often skills are being acquired implicitly and students need to be prompted to reflect on what they have learnt.

The Tools for Mathematics module on the first year of the degree course is of similar structure but all the group tasks are initiated by the module tutor and no written report is required. Presentations are at three levels: poster sessions, group and individual. Here also self and peer assessment is employed to help students reflect on their own performance and those of their colleagues.

First-year degree students and second-year HND students also take the module Mathematical Modelling I. This is where they begin to apply their subject-specific knowledge and their communication and problem-solving skills to investigations. Again working in small groups, which are largely student selected, they carry out a number of tasks, each designed to help develop one or more transferable skill. First they investigate a particular topic that involves the modelling of some interesting phenomenon such as the behaviour of a projectile or the dynamics of population growth. They are directed to read sections of books or papers, and they have to try to understand what the author is saying. They then prepare both a written résumé and an oral presentation of their investigation with the objective of helping their peers in the class learn this topic. For the oral presentation, they may prepare overhead transparencies or an electronic slide show. They have to explain the background, how the models were created and how they were used to solve problems, and answer questions about the phenomenon. The résumés are made available in electronic form to the class via the university intranet. The seminar presentations are videotaped and played back to the presenting group as part of the feedback process. Both the presentation and résumé are assessed against previously published criteria (see Haines and Dunthorne, 1996, for examples), which had been discussed in class and which they were encouraged to use for the self-assessment of their work before submitting it. There is a week between submitting the draft résumé and the seminar, so students have an opportunity to react to criticism of their résumé by the lecturer.

Students also undertake an investigation of a topic they probably have not encountered before. They have to create their own model and use it to solve the problem. Their work is submitted in a written report and at a poster session.

Staff require students to submit a confidential peer assessment of the overall contributions made by the others in their group, and, where this provides evidence of different levels of contribution, the common group assessment mark is modified for individuals.

Finally, the class has to prepare for an unseen, written comprehension test. They are given a fairly lengthy article to study and they answer questions about this in a timed written test. The questions are designed to test their understanding of the situation described, the modelling processes followed by the author and the mathematics used.

As well as this modelling module, second-year students on both HND and BSc courses undertake a group assignment in the Operational Research I module, which constitutes one third of the coursework. Second-year HND students, in the Computer Systems and Operating Systems module, become involved in peer tutoring in order to further develop their communication skills. The class is divided into groups, each of which is presented with a possible hardware upgrade option. A group investigates the option, carries out the work and evaluates the result. They then teach two more groups that then carry out the task. The tasks are shared so that each group acts in each role and submits a report on tasks undertaken.

In the second year of the degree, the Mathematics Modelling II module has been specifically designed to improve problem solving and research skills. It is entirely coursework based and in it students develop further their formal report writing and oral presentation skills. The module consists of two six-week group investigations with the groups changing for the second assignments. The first set of tasks is based on deterministic problems while the second deals mainly with probabilistic models. Each group submits a substantial report after each investigation and during oral presentations the group must substantiate their findings.

The industrial placement year provides unrivalled opportunities for students to practise and refine their transferable skills. At Ulster placement is compulsory for all degree students and in preparation for this the cohort receives instruction in CV production, interview techniques, professional issues, etc. In addition there are invited talks from a number of parties. The Careers Advisor for the Faculty asks the class to match skills that employers require against those they think they currently possess. This is particularly important as this continued reflection will form the basis for their graduate job applications when they return. When industrialists speak to the pre-placement cohort they usually outline their selection procedures, which often consist of an initial series of non-technical group tasks. During these sessions individual performances are scrutinized and used to select those candidates who progress to the final interview stage. This really brings home the importance of team working and interpersonal skills, especially when faced with the prospect of getting to know, and work productively with, several strangers at short notice.

While on placement all students are visited at least twice and, prior to each visit, they produce a short summary of their work to date, together with the types of transferable skills they have used. The final placement report must contain a major reflective section that again helps to provide evidence of how and where interpersonal and other skills were used. Employers have always rated the transferable skills of our placement students very highly, thus vindicating the amount of time spent refining them in the two taught years of the course that precede placement. It is gratifying, during the talks from post-placement students to the second-year cohort, to hear the final-year students repeatedly stressing the importance of such basic skills as teamwork and time management in the workplace.

During the final year of the degree course, each student undertakes an individual project that draws together many of the skills developed during the preceding three and a half years. To produce a substantial piece of work within a 12-week period requires excellent time management and the ability to work independently as well as utilizing modern techniques of information retrieval. The final report must be coherently and lucidly written and defended during a *viva voce* examination. A critical evaluation of the work by the student is an important part of the final report.

To assist finalists on both HND and BSc programmes with the transition from university to the workplace, a module on Career Management Skills is timetabled during semester one and delivered by the Careers Advisor with responsibility for Informatics. A key element of this module is requiring each person to assess and demonstrate the transferable skills he or she has acquired during the courses. Being able to discuss and provide evidence of transferable skills acquisition is a crucial aspect of the application and interview processes.

Evaluation

In this section we present some evidence that the innovative teaching methods described do enhance students' transferable skills.

A research study of the modelling activities in year 1 of the honours degree and year 2 of the HND at University of Ulster over several years has been published (Houston and Lazenbatt, 1999; Houston, 1998. Note that due to publication delays, the former paper reports the earlier study). These papers report both quantitative and qualitative data. For example, students were presented with a list of transferable skills and were asked which skills did they consider to be enhanced by taking the module. The responses in the surveys, conducted in 1995 and in 1997, are from Houston (1998) and are given in Table 6.1.

It is clear from this that students themselves believe that many transferable skills have been enhanced through studying this module. This self-belief is confirmed through the standard of the written reports and seminars they presented for assessment.

Several studies on the use of comprehension tests at UU have been published (see, for example, Houston, 1993). Comprehension tests are intended to develop critical reading skills in students and to encourage discussion and an enquiring attitude. Student performance in the tests, and other, qualitative, evidence suggests that the strategy works.

Table 6.1 Percentages of students in 1995 and 1997 who believed that these transferable skills have been enhanced

	Skills	1995	1997
i	problem-solving skills	62	86
ii	leadership skills	41	26
iii	followership skills	38	31
iv	research skills	76	94
v	study skills	35	60
vi	writing skills	31	51
vii	reading skills	35	49
viii	talking skills	69	69
ix	listening skills	55	51
x	teaching skills	52	60
xi	modelling skills	48	89
xii	mathematical skills	55	71
xiii	teamwork skills	96	77

Concerning the development of transferable skills in the HND at UU, the Edexcel appointed examiner wrote, 'The range of assessment methods shows that the students learn effectively. In addition to the written assessments, which I have sampled during the year, I have also attended the students'Workshop presentations that went well and provided further evidence of effective learning of key skills' (unpublished examiner's report of 24 June 1997).

The placement year at UU is assessed through supervisors' reports, placement visitors' reports and students' own submitted reports and diaries. These reports consistently comment that students have good transferable skills on entry and that they develop these progressively through the placement year. For example, one employer wrote, 'Technical skills have increased as have her transferable skills in team working and liaising with customers', 'Her ability to learn so quickly has benefited this section greatly'; and '[student's name] works well in a team and can manage his time to meet tight deadlines'.

A similar system operates at SHU, where it seems that employers providing placements for SHU students need little persuasion of students' skills development. One employer wrote of one student, '[student's name] has the ability to fit into existing teams and play a full role immediately' and 'I was impressed with his ability to adapt to the environment … better than many other graduates/placement students'. Other quotes from employers about various other students include, 'The basis of both her roles was teamwork … [student's name] was brilliant at this' and 'On oral communications [student's name] was particularly impressive and confident'. Substantial data and trends in eventual graduate employment destinations are yet to emerge, given that the first substantial output of graduates was in 2000.

Regarding the effectiveness of the final-year project at UU, one external examiner wrote (18 June 1998), 'The best of the projects were really very good indeed and should be a source of some considerable satisfaction to both staff and students', while another examiner, commenting on the course overall, wrote (6 June 1998), 'The special mix of skills and knowledge that students acquire on their course .... makes them particularly employable.' This view is sustained by the fact of the high graduate employment rate. Paragraph 27 of the QAA Subject Review Report says, 'Statistics from the last four years show that 92 out of 93 graduates are in employment or further study' and paragraph 28 says, 'and employers expressed great enthusiasm about the abilities of graduates both in terms of highly developed transferable skills, and in terms of subject-specific skills. In particular they referred to the ability of graduates to learn new skills quickly. These statements were confirmed in discussions with both graduates and undergraduates' (QAA, 2000).

Conclusion

There is no doubt that the world of work demands graduates and diplomates who have a sound academic background and who possess the interpersonal skills necessary to use their knowledge effectively. When the BSc was first introduced at Ulster the employer survey of some 190 companies that informed its content revealed that 85 per cent of respondents rated good communication skills and the ability to work with others more highly than any specific area of academic content. Thus, while subject-specific material may become rapidly outdated, eg operating systems or software packages, the skill of knowing how to learn new techniques and being able to apply and convey this knowledge to others becomes increasingly important.

New entrants to third-level education, especially those in a subject such as Mathematics, are often surprised to see the emphasis placed on the acquisition of transferable skills alongside the traditional material they had expected to encounter. The reasons for this emphasis must be clearly explained at the beginning of the course to place the subsequent learning in context. Having done so, there are a few key points that must be addressed to ensure that skill-based learning is successful:

- Transferable skills must be taught explicitly as are all other aspects of the course:
  - It is not sufficient to put students into groups and ask them to undertake tasks. They must be shown that a group can operate much more effectively than an individual. They must also know how to assign roles to group members and how to plan and monitor the work during the course of a group project.
  - Skills such as report writing, oral presentations and self and peer assessment must be introduced and developed via specific examples and appropriate checklists.

- Teaching transferable skills within one or more first-year modules means that a coherent and structured approach can be taken and that these skills can then be placed within the overall ethos of the course.

- Skills must be embedded throughout the programme and their importance constantly stressed:
  - To avoid being seen as an 'add on', skills-based assignments and tasks must permeate most modules on the course. This requires a unified approach from the teaching team thus reinforcing the message that transferable skills are an integral part of a mathematician's life.
  - An industrial placement year is the ideal vehicle for the consolidation and refinement of transferable skills. If placement is not a mandatory part of the course, students must be strongly advised to undertake it, especially as many employers now treat the placement year as part of their graduate recruitment process.
  - Having input from post-placement students and external sources such as industrialists and careers staff is crucial and helps emphasize the importance of transferable skills in the workplace.

- Skills must be assessed just as the academic elements of the course are assessed:
  - It is important to assign marks for the skills elements of coursework hence showing students the value attached to them by staff.
  - Self and peer assessment are vital elements and force students to evaluate their performance and those of their colleagues against explicit criteria they themselves have agreed upon.
  - Reflection on how their transferable skills have developed must be encouraged as students need to provide evidence to potential employers on how and where they have used interpersonal and other skills during their time at university.

It is clear that there must be firm support at institutional level for the development of the skills agenda, with specific questions, which require the strategy for skills development to be made explicit, being asked at validation events. There can be no short cuts taken if skills training is to be taken seriously by staff and students alike. The effort involved in teaching, embedding and assessing them is considerable but cannot be avoided if the modern graduate is to be properly prepared for the workplace.

(Parts of this chapter were published previously in *Capability* (Challis and Houston, 2000) and appear here by kind permission of the editor)

References

Challis, N V and Gretton, H W (1997) Technology, key skills and the engineering mathematics curriculum, in *Proceedings Second Institute of Mathematics and its Applications (IMA) Conference on Mathematical Education of Engineers*, pp 145–50, IMA, Southend-on-Sea

Challis, N V and Gretton, H W (1998) Learning diaries and technology: their impact on student learning, in *Proceedings of the International Conference on Technology in Mathematics Teaching (ICTMT) 3*, Institut fur Mediendidaktik der Universitat in Koblenz, Koblenz, Germany

Challis, N V and Houston, S K (2000) Embedding key skills in the mathematics curriculum, *Capability*, **4**(3), pp 7–10

Haines, C R and Dunthorne, S (eds) (1996) *Mathematics Learning and Assessment: Sharing innovative practices*, Edward Arnold, London

Houston, S K (1993) Comprehension tests in mathematics, *Teaching Mathematics and its Applications*, **12**(2), pp 60–73

Houston, S K (1998) Get students to do the teaching!, in *Mathematical Modelling: Teaching and assessing in a technology rich world*, P Galbraith *et al*, pp 45–54, Horwood, Chichester

Houston, S K and Lazenbatt, A (1999) Peer tutoring in a modelling course, *Innovations in Education and Training International*, **36**(1), pp 71–79

National Committee of Inquiry into Higher Education (1997) *Higher Education in the Learning Society: The report of the national committee (The Dearing Report)*, HMSO, London

Quality Assurance Agency for Higher Education (QAA) (2000), *Subject Review Report Q175/2000*, QAA, Bristol

Sheffield Hallam University (2000) (accessed 5 February 2001) *The Key to Key Skills* [Online] http://www.shu.ac.uk/keytokey/

Society for Industrial and Applied Mathematics (SIAM) (1998) (accessed 5 February 2001) *The SIAM Report on Mathematics in Industry* [online] http://www.siam.org/mii/miihome.htm

Training Employment and Education Directorate (TEED) (1989) *An Introduction to the Enterprise Curriculum*, Department of Employment, Sheffield

Woods, D R *et al* (2000) The future of engineering education III: developing critical skills, *Chemical Engineering Education*, **34**(2), pp 108–17

7

Designing courses with a sense of purpose

Peter Kahn

Introduction

Courses in mathematics and its applications are currently facing considerable pressures to change. Increasing competition for students, for example, means that particular attention must be paid to attracting and retaining students. Indeed, recent evidence from assessment of teaching quality in the UK has highlighted problems with retaining mathematics students (Quality Assurance Agency for Higher Education, 2000). The extent to which students are adequately prepared for existing programmes of study is a related issue and has been the subject of much debate in the UK (see, for example, Sutherland, 2000). Other pressures for change are also evident, whether stemming from technology, an improved understanding of student learning or new applications of mathematics (see, for example, Haines and Dunthorne, 1996).

An important challenge, then, in the face of such pressures is to design courses that open up mathematics to students in ways that both attract them and serve their needs. In a system of mass higher education, for example, concern will need to be paid to preparing students for employment (Scott, 1995). Thus, while it is essential that courses are built around mathematical considerations, course designers also need to take account of wider considerations. Without such fully informed course design there is every danger that the study of mathematics and its applications will become sidelined in the face of growing competition from other disciplines. And given the way in which mathematics matters to modern societies, as noted in Tikly and Wolf (2000), then poor provision in this area can only be a cause for concern.

This chapter outlines a widely adopted approach to the design of individual courses within a programme of study. The approach is based around carefully chosen goals for student learning, often called intended learning outcomes or simply outcomes (Toohey, 1999: 140). A set of outcomes for a course comprises a concise statement of what it is intended that the students learn during the course. It is possible to view an individual course as consisting of several elements, the first of which is a set of such outcomes. The remaining elements of a course concern the way in which the course is structured, the methods of teaching and learning that are employed and the assessment. In the relatively simplified approach to course design taken in this chapter, each of these elements is designed to match the chosen learning outcomes, as indicated in Figure 7.1. In exploring this approach, we will see how an informed sense of purpose may colour the whole enterprise of designing a course. Such a clarity of purpose, along with the accompanying focus on learning outcomes, is also evident in other chapters of this book as it touches on a range of issues in learning, teaching and assessment.

Of course, it should at the same time be recognized that a set of learning outcomes will never fully characterize a student's understanding of the body of mathematics concerned, particularly for more advanced students. Mathematical understanding relies upon the development of a rich network of connections between ideas. This will only develop depth with sustained study. Learning outcomes from an individual course should therefore always be seen in this longer-term context. A focus on learning outcomes does, however, allow the lecturer to make clear choices about where to guide student learning.

The rest of this chapter will look at each of the elements of a course noted above. In doing so we will cover the main options that are open to the course designer. In addition, we will illustrate how these elements might be shaped in the

Figure 7.1   Designing a course around learning outcomes

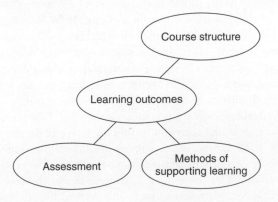

light of such factors as research into learning, good practice and some of the pressures for change outlined above. A number of case studies are also included to illustrate how the approach might be applied in practice. Two of these case studies focus on approaches that draw on problem-based learning. Finally, the conclusion to the chapter will further seek to draw out some of the wider considerations that impact on course design.

Intentions for student learning

Central to this process of course design, then, is an awareness of purpose. What do you want the students on the course to learn? In making any choice of outcomes, it is important to have a clear understanding of the available options. Such understanding will allow the course designer to make the most appropriate selection of outcomes.

The first category of outcomes that we consider here relates to subject knowledge. Students will usually be expected to master a given set of concepts, examples, theorems, applications and so on. A traditional syllabus can be adapted to provide just such a set of outcomes for the student. As noted in Chapters 1 and 5 it will be possible to spell out such mastery at a variety of levels, ranging, for example, from factual knowledge to application in new situation and justification (see Smith *et al*, 1996). But which concepts, examples, theorems and applications are relevant? It will of course be important to ensure that ideas are chosen in a way that respects the cumulative nature of mathematical knowledge. But other factors such as the importance of choosing a coherent set of significant ideas, the students' existing mathematical experience, your own understanding of which ideas are significant and the extent to which the ideas will appeal to the students are also relevant. On this latter point, for example, an appreciation of the interests of your students might influence you to emphasize applications of mathematics at the expense of the proof of certain theorems or vice versa. It is considerations like these that ultimately determine the choice of content.

However, as was evident in the introduction, courses have to meet a wide range of needs. And many of these needs cannot be met simply by helping students to understand selected ideas from given mathematical areas. We can first of all consider what we might term wider mathematical outcomes. Alternatively, one might regard these wider outcomes as simply adding depth of understanding. Take, for example, the issue of helping students appreciate which concepts are significant in the given area of mathematics or its applications. Recent research suggests that students are failing to develop such appreciation (Kahn *et al*, 1998). Indeed, unless this becomes an explicit goal of a course it is difficult to see in practice how most students will develop such appreciation. Similar considerations apply to developing in students a sense of aesthetic appreciation. Finally it is worth noting here the overlap between these wider mathematical outcomes and the Domain 4 skills noted in Chapter 3. This domain refers to such skills as breadth of application and mathematical insight. Outcomes such as these tap into powerful sources of motivation for students that courses cannot easily ignore if they are to attract them.

Also in this category of wider mathematical outcomes are the skills needed to complete a variety of mathematical tasks and to make sense of ideas from mathematics and its applications. The ability to solve extended problems, for example, is particularly relevant. Where students possess gaps in this ability, as has already been noted in the context of the UK (London Mathematical Society, 1995), then programmes will need to take explicit steps to help them develop their ability in this area. However, the completion of other tasks, such as mathematical modelling of the real world and the construction of proofs, are also underpinned by mastery of a range of strategies, approaches and attitudes (see, for example, Schoenfield, 1992; Kahn, 2001). To expect students to acquire such tacit knowledge on their own is unrealistic in a system of mass higher education. Hence the need to include such outcomes at least within courses that fall in the early stages of programmes of study, particularly if problems of student retention are to be addressed.

We can also consider more general outcomes for student learning. While not strictly outcomes that are directly related to mathematics, they can easily be developed within the context of the study of mathematics and its applications. They may also support the achievement of mathematical outcomes. Foremost among these outcomes are those related to transferable skills, such as the ability to work as part of a team or give presentations, as considered in Chapter 6. Outcomes such as these are particularly geared towards preparation for employment and to students' personal development.

Finally, more general intellectual outcomes are also relevant. The ability to analyse complex phenomena, for example, is a valuable skill that can be developed through the study of mathematics and its applications. Similar considerations will apply to the ability to synthesize ideas to form a consistent whole, to solve complex problems and to engage in enquiry. All of these skills are relevant to employment in an economy increasingly driven by the creation of knowledge. Courses in which the development of such skills is explicitly considered are likely to be at an advantage in a competitive market, as indicated in the surveys of employers also cited in the section entitled 'Transferable skills' in Chapter 6 (see, for example, Society for Industrial and Applied Mathematics, 1998).

Aligning course structures with outcomes

Once the outcomes have been set for a course, the next element that needs to be considered is the course structure. When the structure is considered alongside the outcomes we have a curriculum for the course. Traditionally, courses have been structured on the basis of a systematic ordering of the given body of mathematical and other ideas. The ordering typically respects the cumulative nature of knowledge in mathematics and its applications but other principles can also be drawn upon. It may be that the entire content of the course is organized around one or more theorems, applications or problems that provide suitable mathematical highpoints. In such a structure, all of the intervening ideas that lead up to these highpoints are also clearly laid out. This approach clearly provides a reasonable way of addressing the mathematical outcomes of a course. And indeed, it may also allow students to develop an appreciation of which theorems or applications are regarded as significant within a given domain.

However, we have seen that courses will usually need to consider a wider range of outcomes. And the systematic approach outlined above may not always be suited to the outcomes that have been set for the course. For example, it may be difficult to develop students' skills in this approach. Mathematical principles that are evident in more than one topic area may also be difficult to convey to students. While any given structure will always need to respect the cumulative nature of mathematical knowledge, it will thus be important to consider other course structures.

We begin by considering courses organized on the basis of a series of problems, as occurs when problem-based learning is employed (see, for example, Boud and Feletti, 1991). This type of learning is often employed in preparing students for professional practice. Disciplines such as Medicine and Engineering afford problems that are complex and require the mastery of knowledge drawn from various domains. In problem-based learning students are given help to identify and then master the knowledge needed to solve each of a series of problems.

It is apparent that the structure that underpins problem-based learning can be applied directly to the study of applications of mathematics. For example, students might be asked to establish an appropriate mathematical model of some complex phenomenon in the real world. This is likely to involve students drawing on information from the areas of knowledge in which the mathematics is applied. It would also assist students in focusing on the processes of solving a problem and modelling the real world, as well as on constructing their own understanding of the given applications of mathematics.

The modelling of such a phenomenon would typically, however, also require the identification and mastery of relevant mathematical ideas. This, though, is likely to pose difficulties. It is clearly challenging for students to identify the relevance to a complex phenomena of areas of mathematics of which they have no conception. One solution is to use only phenomenon that can be modelled with mathematics that the students have already understood. The outcomes of the course will not then include reference to the initial mastery of the mathematics concerned but only to their application.

However, given the advantages of problem-based learning outlined above, it is worth asking whether we can structure the learning of ideas from mathematics itself in a similar fashion. One such structure is to provide students with a series of clearly articulated mathematical highpoints and require them to identify and master the knowledge needed to understand these highpoints. A highpoint might consist of an important theorem along with its proof, a problem in which the mathematical ideas that need to be mastered are evident or an already well-defined mathematical model. For example, a course on real analysis might take the intermediate value theorem, the mean value theorem and the fundamental theorem on calculus as highpoints. Alternatively, an introductory course on statistics might focus on the normal, binomial and Poisson distributions. The students are asked to provide their own route to these highpoints, rather than the routes being provided within the course. The issue as to how best to support the students when a course is structured on the basis of such enquiry will be addressed later in the chapter.

We can finally consider other structures for courses. It is possible to organize a course on the basis of what might be called a thematic structure (see, for example, Toohey, 1999: 105–10). This would involve organizing content on the basis of a mathematical theme or principle, such as linearity or approximation. Such a structure would not only address traditional mathematical outcomes, but would also address wider mathematical outcomes such an appreciation for the significance of different ideas and help students to make the connections that are needed for genuine mathematical understanding.

We have already noted that skills are difficult to develop within courses structured around a systematic presentation of ideas from a given area of mathematics or its applications. A further option for the structure is to design the course entirely around the development of a given skill. For example, a course on problem solving might focus upon different aspects of a process of solving problems from different areas of mathematics and its applications.

An alternative to structuring a course entirely around a skill, however, is to adopt a hybrid model. Parts of the course may be organized around ideas from mathematics or one of its applications, with the remainder of the course explicitly focusing on the development of the given skill or skills. The methods used to develop the skills would, however, draw on the mathematical ideas used in the other parts of the course. This model is particularly suitable for the development of subject-specific skills. For example, the abilities of specializing, generalizing, visualizing, analysing ideas, making connections and solving problems between ideas could all be developed within the context of material from any area of mathematics or one of its applications. The paper by Kahn (1999) provides an example of how some of these subject-specific skills can be developed alongside material from abstract algebra. Transferable skills, as evident in Chapter 6, as well as more general intellectual skills, can also be developed within hybrid structures.

The final type of structure that we will consider here is one suitable for disciplines that involve the application of mathematics. The course is primarily organized around principles suited to the given discipline. However, when mathematical models of phenomena are required then attention is devoted to ensuring that students have mastered the mathematical ideas involved and the nature of the mathematical models of the phenomena. Such a structure is evident in one of the case studies outlined below.

The different structures considered above are summarized in Table 7.1. While many courses will continue to adopt the traditional structure, the advantages offered by more innovative structures should not be dismissed lightly given their suitability for non-traditional outcomes.

Table 7.1 Course structures

Structure
traditional
problem based
enquiry based
thematic
skills based
hybrid
other discipline based

Supporting the learning of specific outcomes

There is a wide range of methods used to support student learning, as evident in Chapter 3. Lectures provide an opportunity for the tutor to expound a body of knowledge, with scope for varying levels of student activity. Understanding may be developed by requiring students to solve problems, with advice available from a tutor. Students can be assisted in supporting each other in their learning. Technology provides more options, and a variety of other resources can be drawn upon as well. Learning can take place in the workplace. More challenging tasks can be set to extend the more able students. Students can be taught in large groups, small groups or individually. They can be encouraged to discover ideas for themselves or receive already well-defined ideas from their tutors.

The purpose of this section is to provide guidance on how to make an appropriate choice of methods from all those on offer. The chosen methods, for example, will need to help deliver the outcomes that have been set for the course and be suitable to the structure of the course, as well as draw on an understanding of student learning. Rather than seeking a comprehensive answer, given the focus on supporting learning of other chapters within this book, we will illustrate some of the principles at stake by considering two case studies. The first case study involves an innovative selection of methods within the context of a more traditional set of outcomes and structure. The second case study, which is more speculative, considers the methods that might be suited to a more innovative set of outcomes and structure.

Learning 'analysis' through problem-solving

In 1996, Professor David Epstein decided to use the opportunity provided by the text *Numbers and Functions* (Burn, 2000) to design a pilot analysis course for first-year Mathematics undergraduates at the University of Warwick. The course retained a traditional set of learning outcomes, focusing on understanding of specific ideas and processes from 'analysis'. The structure of the course was similarly traditional in that it was based around the systematic coverage of the content from analysis. However, rather than being based around a series of lectures, the course encouraged the students to work in groups of between three and five through the carefully structured and sequenced questions of the text cited above. They had targets of around 35 questions per week, which they could tackle both in the twice-weekly, two-hour sessions (where they could ask for assistance from three helpers – David Epstein, David Tall and Adrian Simpson – in the 40-strong class) and as 'homework' activity. The course built up the formal theory relating to limits of sequences and series entirely through the questions, with occasional whole-group work on particular difficulties (notably, early in the course, inequalities and transformations of graphs). In 1997, the course was scaled up to allow all first-year single honours students, and some joint honours students, to take it.

Clearly the methods adopted ensure both that the students learn mathematics in an active fashion and that they are able to develop their own understanding of the ideas. While these issues have been dealt with at length in Chapters 2 and 3, it is also worth observing here how the methods also tie in with the theory of deep and surface approaches to learning outlined in Table 7.2. Research evidence clearly indicates that a deep approach to learning is far more effective than a surface approach (see Ramsden, 1992: 38–61 for a fuller discussion). By basing the learning on the course around the solution of problems, students are led to make their own connections between the ideas covered by the course. Indeed, informal evidence from the pilot course suggested that students gained much higher grades, appeared to understand the material more thoroughly and were quicker at picking up the fundamental changes in mathematical thinking required than their peers on a standard lecture course. This all points to methods of supporting learning suited to the achievement of a traditional set of learning outcomes.

Table 7.2 Approaches to learning

Deep approach	Surface approach
students seek to understand the material and make connections between ideas	students focus on completing the task and on memorizing unrelated facts

Learning based around a process of enquiry

Earlier in this chapter we raised the possibility of structuring a course, at least in part, on the basis of the students' own enquiries. Clearly such a structure is likely to be particularly well suited to developing students' ability to engage in mathematical enquiry. We would, however, also want such a structure to still allow students to master mathematical ideas. This case study thus explores the kinds of methods of teaching and supporting learning that might be employed to support students on such a course, drawing on ideas from problem-based learning. The aim is to support students in engaging in a process of enquiry designed to complete a given series of learning tasks.

The learning tasks that we will consider here comprise both understanding clearly articulated mathematical ideas, such as theorem and its proof or a model, and solving problems. When seeking to understand a carefully chosen model, for example, students could be required to reconstruct a version of each of the stages of the modelling cycle. When trying to understand a theorem and its proof, students could be asked to explain the theorem itself, provide an outline of the structure of the proof and an explanation for each of the lines of the proof. When solving problems, students might be prompted to follow a process drawn from ideas developed by Pólya (1957) or more recent research (Schoenfield, 1992).

However, each of these processes also needs to be underpinned by the ability to engage in more fundamental mathematical thought processes. Such an ability is termed here an intellectual skill. While research has identified a wide range of such skills (Tall, 1991), the issue here is to focus on skills that students will be able to employ directly in the given learning task. Such a practical focus is evident in the guide for students on how to study mathematics and its applications (Kahn, 2001). This text stresses the fundamental skills of working with examples of an idea, visualizing ideas, analysing concepts, interpreting symbols, drawing on an understanding of logic and making connections between ideas. The application of these skills will further need to be built into the process of enquiry. For example, students would be required at different stages of the learning task to analyse the concepts involved. Where this analysis indicated an idea that the student did not fully understand or had not previously encountered they would then need to seek out an explanation of the idea. Similarly, students might be required to find both the definitions and a varied set of examples for any new ideas.

Induction into such processes of enquiry and the underlying intellectual skills would form an important part of the early stages of the course or programme. It might also be useful to include an introduction to a given computer algebra system, focusing on the role of the system in supporting students ability to employ the skills. Assessment will further form an important part of the methods used to support this process as it does in problem-based learning (Boud and Feletti, 1991). Issues related to assessment will be addressed in the next section. Finally, support will need to be provided to help students engage in the process itself. Following the approach taken by problem-based learning, students would need to work in teams, taking on different roles within the team. The tutor would primarily help students engage in the process, rather than provide knowledge. Students would further need access to a variety of resources and these might include so-called 'fixed resource' sessions involving input from a tutor.

The approach advocated in this case study is summarized in Figure 7.2. The focus is on enabling the students to construct their own understanding of mathematical ideas rather than, for example, on enabling them to discover the ideas. Requiring students to grapple with well-defined ideas and problems allows them to structure their own learning to a greater extent than is possible within the context of a systematic presentation of a body of ideas. Students thus are required to make their own connections between ideas and thereby encouraged to adopt a deep approach to learning.

Matching assessment with outcomes

Various assessment options are again open to the course designer. Examinations can require students to solve problems of varying complexity and recall important information, such as definitions and proofs. Coursework can also require students to solve various types of problems. More widely, assessment may involve students making presentations, working in groups and writing reports and essays. There may be scope for students to assess both their own and each other's work, as well as for assessment by tutors. Assessment can further incorporate various types of feedback. Model solutions may be given for problems, comments can be written on a student's work and feedback can be given verbally to an individual student or

Figure 7.2   Support for learning structured around enquiry

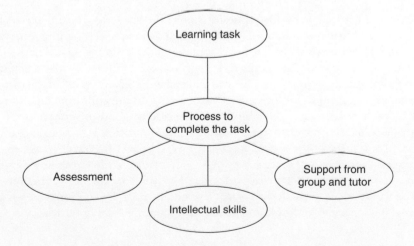

to a group of students. Computer-based assessment offers particular opportunities for extensive feedback on students' work, as evident in Chapter 4. The feedback may relate to the accuracy of the students' work, to their ability to write coherent text, to the approach taken in solving a problem and so on.

Given the way in which assessment drives student learning, it is particularly important to make a careful choice of methods of assessment and feedback. Any choice will seek to ensure that the assessment methods are valid in that they actually test whether students have achieved the outcomes of the course. The methods will also need to be reliable so that they measure student achievement on a consistent basis. Assessment will be conducted that is both formative, focusing on student learning within the teaching process, and summative, providing evidence for decisions about progression or awards. The criteria employed in marking should further explicitly relate to the outcomes. And assessment on one course will need to fit with assessment on other courses in the programme of study. Feedback can target weaknesses in underlying skills so that these can be explicitly addressed, as well as addressing more immediate errors. Students, for example, often find the formal writing of mathematical text a significant challenge and this can be addressed within feedback.

Rather than seeking to provide a detailed view given the focus of Chapter 4 on matching appropriate assessment to learning outcomes, the approach taken in this section is again to use case studies to expose some of the principles at stake within the wider context of course design. The first case study considers the assessment on a course for students who are studying on degree programmes in the biological sciences, while the second case study returns to the more speculative approaches based around student enquiry.

Assessing mathematical knowledge and its application

Quantitative Biology 1 is a first semester course for first-year students on degree programmes within the School of Biological Sciences at the University of Liverpool. The course seeks to ensure that undergraduates in the school have suffi-cient numerical knowledge to support their academic studies. In particular, the course aims to ensure that students can understand a given set of mathematical ideas and apply them to biological problems. Topics on the course include surface area to volume ratios and their biological implications and introduction to the normal distribution, standard errors and Z-tests. The structure is based around a systematic ordering of the subject knowledge covered by the course. In all parts of the course there is an integration between mathematical skills and their biological applications. In terms of the support offered to students on the programme, a lecture component provides a formal presentation of 10 sections, which are covered in a coursework book, and in addition there are weekly tutorials.

The assessment incorporates both formative assessment, in the shape of 10 weekly self-assessment tests, and summative assessment through four multiple-choice question (MCQ) tests. The MCQ tests are worth 95 per cent of the final grade while completion of each self-assessment test contributes 0.5 per cent to the final grade. All of the tests cover basic skills in the mathematical method (eg logarithm rules) and their application to biological problems. Furthermore, the tutorial support is closely integrated with the assessment. Tutors review any general problems that students had in the previous week's test and discuss any other problems that the students are having as determined from computer analysis of the test results.

It is possible briefly to explore some of the principles that may be seen to underpin the design of the assessment, which measures how well students achieve the outcomes of the course, both the understanding of a specific body of numerical knowledge as well as the application to biological problems. It thus validly reflects the integrated nature of the course as a whole. More, however, is evident than simply a match between the assessment and the learning outcomes. The weekly tests tie in with the methods used to support the learning of the students. Again the lectures and tutorials focus on the integration of mathematical skills and their application to biological problems. The assessment and teaching methods are thus mutually supportive.

Assessment of learning based around a process of enquiry

This case study concludes the focus that has run throughout this chapter of drawing on approaches to course design that are based upon a process of enquiry. While it will still be possible to use examinations to assess understanding of mathematical ideas that were mastered by engaging in a process of enquiry, such an approach would clearly be difficult to apply when assessing students' ability to engage in enquiry. Furthermore, questions of validity would also be raised if such an approach were adopted. We will thus consider forms of assessment that tie in more closely with the processes of enquiry.

Students could be asked as a group to document the process by which they carried out the investigation, providing reasons as to why they proceeded as they did. Clearly this would provide students with an opportunity to demonstrate their understanding of the role of the intellectual skills that were outlined in the previous section. However, it would also open up scope for displaying awareness of the significance of ideas or of aesthetic appreciation. Understanding of mathematical material can further be assessed by asking students to produce a statement articulating their understanding of the material. Assessing this by means of individual statements would provide an alternative to group work. The individual statement might, for example, explain each of the steps of the proof of a theorem.

In terms of the marking criteria that might be employed to grade such assessment, grade descriptors could be developed. These descriptors would be based upon such factors as mathematical accuracy, evidence of a rationale for the process and so on. Feedback would then be closely tailored to how well students had performed against the criteria, with evident scope for targeting specific errors of understanding of the relevant mathematical ideas.

Conclusion

This chapter has suggested that course designers should make clear choices about where to focus student learning and that they should implement those choices in a consistent fashion. It is not a question of jettisoning mathematical content in order to address learning outcomes of dubious value. It is simply that for courses in mathematics and its applications to flourish it is essential that their design is driven by more than mathematical content itself.

It is, however, worth emphasizing that wider considerations are important when designing courses. Courses are often taken as pre-requisites for subsequent courses and this will clearly impact the choice of outcomes. The outcomes will often be tightly laid down where mathematical material is taught to meet the needs of a discipline other than mathematics. It is important to remember that progression from one course to other courses should also be accommodated within this approach so that it is possible to meet longer-term aims. Indeed, the age in which an individual academic can choose the content of his or her course in isolation from colleagues has long since been left behind. Furthermore, patterns of learning quickly become set, so that it may be more difficult to introduce more novel approaches in the later years of a programme. Resource considerations are also important. If particularly novel outcomes are included then significant development time will be required. Finally it is worth emphasizing that the course designer needs to be aware of his or her own attitudes to mathematics and to its study. It is, for example, only too easy when one's own concerns are focused exclusively on mathematics to assume that such a focus is all that is needed when making choices about what students should learn.

The complexity of the issues involved certainly warrants a scholarly approach to course design. Such an approach includes but goes beyond being able to provide a well-thought-out design for the given course. It must also include evaluating the effectiveness of the design and exposing both the design and the evaluation to the critique of colleagues. Effective dissemination to others in the sector is also needed if best practice is to be shared. If the study of mathematics and its applications is to thrive in higher education then such a scholarly approach to course design is essential.

Acknowledgements

I am grateful for assistance with the case study material as follows. The text of the case study on 'Learning "analysis" through problem solving' was adapted from material written by Adrian Simpson, University of Warwick, while the section on 'Assessing mathematical knowledge and its application' was based on text provided by Brian Merry, University of Liverpool.

References

Boud, D and Feletti, G (1991) *The Challenge of Problem Based Learning*, Kogan Page, London

Burn, R (2000) *Numbers and Functions: Steps into Analysis*, 2nd edn, Cambridge University Press, Cambridge

Haines, C and Dunthorne, S (1996) *Sharing Innovative Practices*, Edward Arnold, London

Kahn, P E (2000) Easing the transition to higher education by developing skills of advanced mathematical thinking, in *Proceedings of the Fourth British Congress of Mathematics Education* [Online] http://www.edweb.co.uk/bcme/proceedings/research/kahn.htm

Kahn, P E (2001) *Studying Mathematics and its Applications*, Palgrave Press Ltd, Basingstoke

Kahn, P E *et al* (1998) The significance of ideas in undergraduate mathematics, *Teaching Mathematics and its Applications*, **17**(2), pp 78–85

London Mathematical Society (LMS) (1995) *Tackling the Mathematics Problem*, LMS, London

Quality Assurance Agency for Higher Education (QAA) (2000) *Subject Overview Report: Mathematics, Statistics and Operational Research*, QAA, Bristol

Pólya, G (1957) *How to Solve It*, 2nd edn, Penguin, London

Ramsden, P (1992) *Learning to Teach in Higher Education*, Routledge, London

Schoenfield, A H (1992) Learning to think mathematically, in *Handbook for Research on Mathematics Teaching and Learning*, ed D Gouws, pp 334–370, Macmillan, New York

Scott, P (1995) *The Meaning of Mass Higher Education*, Society for Research into Higher Education and Open University Press, Buckingham

Smith, G *et al* (1996) Constructing mathematical examinations to assess a range of knowledge and skills, *International Journal of Mathematics Education in Science and Technology*, **27**, pp 65–77

Society for Industrial and Applied Mathematics (SIAM) (1998) *The SIAM Report on Mathematics in Industry* [Online] http://www.siam.org/mii/miihome.htm

Sutherland, R (2000) Disjunctions between school and university: the case of mathematics, in *The Maths we Need Now: Demands, deficits and remedies*, eds C Tikly and A Wolf, pp 74–103, Institute of Education, London

Tall, D O (ed) (1991) *Advanced Mathematical Thinking*, Kluwer Academic, Dordrecht

Tikly, C and Wolf, A (2000) The state of mathematics education, in *The Maths we Need Now: Demands, deficits and remedies*, eds C Tikly and A Wolf, pp 1–25, Institute of Education, London

Toohey, S (1999) *Designing Courses for Higher Education*, Society for Research into Higher Education and Open University Press, Buckingham

8

Enhancing the Total Learning Environment for students

Peter Petocz and Anna Reid

Introduction

Developing a learning environment that supports high-quality student learning, covers curriculum that is relevant to students and their future work, caters for diverse student and academic populations and fits into university strategic plans has always been a major challenge for academic staff. In the area of mathematics it is possibly even more problematic, as it may have to counter students' adverse perceptions of a subject that is only one part of their studies, or is not their first choice.

Different solutions to the problem of setting up such a learning environment have been proposed at various times and places. Often, these solutions would focus on single aspects of the learning environment, for example, a curriculum using problem-based learning (Bookman and Friedman, 1994), a modification to assessment tasks for students (Dreyfus, 1999), increasing teaching skills of student tutors (Jacques, 2000) and so on. However, any change made in isolation from other aspects of the learning environment can help for a while, but is often unsustainable for any length of time.

In Chapter 7 we investigated the process of course design with a particular emphasis on student approaches to learning. In this chapter, we describe the notion of the *Total Learning Environment*, in which we consider all participants, curriculum, assessments, evaluations and perceptions as part of the one learning entity. We thus draw together various issues addressed in earlier chapters. We consider that all aspects of the Total Learning Environment play a critical role in the development and maintenance of high-quality student learning and high-quality teaching. Each aspect needs to be supported in a strategic manner to enhance the quality of all aspects of the Total Learning Environment.

In this chapter, we will describe the various components of the Total Learning Environment through the use of a model. Although this model may vary slightly from university to university, it highlights the important issue of improving student learning at all levels. We will further illustrate our ideas using a case study of how one Mathematics department used this model to improve the first-year Mathematics learning environment. We also discuss the students' perceptions of the Total Learning Environment, how a group of academics have recognized their role within this environment, and how they have evaluated and then strategically modified aspects of this environment in order to help students achieve higher-quality learning, to help tutors develop their understanding of teaching and of mathematics, and to help lecturers improve their professional practice.

The Total Learning Environment

Goos, Galbraith and Renshaw (1999) suggest that mathematics learning environments can be developed by challenging beliefs and values within a mathematics classroom. They refer to this as 'establishing a community of practice'. One aspect of the Total Learning Environment that is critical to students is being able to see where and how mathematicians work. Establishing a community of practice that is based on research or work addresses an important student need. Booth *et al* (1999) would support this view as they indicate that there are multiple paths to learning and that encouraging students to work in groups enables them to jointly constitute meaning about mathematics. Both these groups focus on the students' situation: Keitel offers a slightly different solution:

> If we accept that the teaching and learning process consists of an interaction between persons for the purpose of developing and sharing meaning, then the particular means and patterns that show this interaction are crucial if the development of meaning is to occur.
>
> (Keitel, 1999: 248)

This implies that learning interactions are between *persons* and that the focus of this interaction is the development and sharing of meaning.

In our model of the Total Learning Environment students, tutors and teachers all share in the constitution of mathematical meaning, and all three groups are offered support. Indeed, Biggs (1999: 12) suggests that 'meaning is not imposed or transmitted by direct instruction, but is created by the students' learning activities, their approaches to learning'. He maintains that learning is about conceptual change and that such change only takes place when students understand the objectives of the course, feel the need to get there, are able to focus on tasks that help them get there, and are encouraged to work collaboratively with fellow students and teachers. These ideas lead to the development of 'aligned' teaching/learning practices, where students and teachers use strategies that help foster an environment resulting in deep approaches to learning. Prosser and

Trigwell (1999: 4) claim that 'without exception ... deep approaches to learning were more likely to be associated with higher quality learning outcomes' and that there is a relation between students' conceptions of learning, the ways in which they are aware of the learning environment and the approach that they take to learning and their learning outcomes. Such ideas lend theoretical support to the very reasonable notion that the Total Learning Environment is intimately related to the quality of students' learning.

The concept of the Total Learning Environment includes the people involved in the learning situation (the students, student tutors and lecturers), the academic curriculum (taken here to refer to the content, the assessment and the final outcomes) and the relations between them. Of course, the relations between all these components are complex, but a recognition of what can be considered a quality learning environment enables appropriate supports to be developed. Prosser and Trigwell (1999) indicate that, from the students' perspective, the Total Learning Environment can be improved through the development of learning contexts that support high-quality learning. This means that content and assessment objectives need to be set up to encourage students to take a deep approach to their learning. Ramsden (1999) looks at the problem from another perspective, that of the academic staff, in terms of developing the quality of academic leadership. Here, we discuss the Total Learning Environment from several perspectives and suggest that there are similarities between the learning needs of students, and the needs of tutors and lecturers, and that each of these groups requires support if the Total Learning Environment is to change for the better.

It is important to note, as Prosser and Trigwell suggest (1999), that students' *perceptions* of their situation are related to their learning outcomes. It is critical to enhance the Total Learning Environment with the right sorts of structure and support, and also to ensure that students are aware of the existence of this structure and support. Similarly, the academic staff need to ensure that their perceptions of the students and the subjects they are teaching are accurate.

Figure 8.1 illustrates the components of the Total Learning Environment and the relations between the various aspects. In the diagram, we have chosen to include the participants (students, student tutors and lecturers) as a related component for whom support can be provided at a number of levels. These levels are the content of the programme, the assessment and the outcomes.

If we follow through each line on the diagram we can see that the idea of 'outcomes', for example, means different things for the different participants. For cxample, the students are supported in their learning by tutors and lecturers, they experience the content of the course mediated by these others and by their own previous experiences of the content, and they focus on aspects of the assessment tasks that they find important to their learning, and which have been flagged as important by the tutors/lecturers! Finally, the outcome is that their understanding of mathematics changes in some way. The final outcome for the lecturers is quite different. They have engaged in different activities with tutors, students and their

Figure 8.1 The Total Learning Environment in a mathematics course

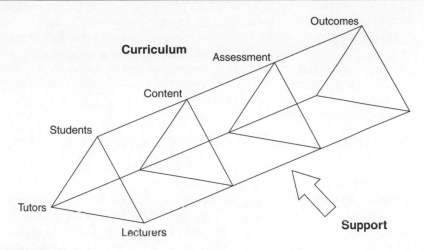

peers, they have developed mathematical contents that they believe are appropriate, and they have developed assessment tasks that they believe will enhance their students' learning. It is very important to understand that the encounters with other participants in the experience, the mathematical knowledge and the ways in which students have responded to the assessment tasks, all contribute to the lecturers' understanding of the course. Their outcomes, then, are an awareness of the strengths and weaknesses of the course materials, the developing quality of their student tutors and the ways in which the students respond to the environment. The student tutors are in an intermediate position. The outcomes for them include some of the outcomes noted by the students, often including a deeper awareness of areas of mathematics that they have studied a few years previously. Additionally, in common with the lecturers, they develop an awareness of how they may learn about teaching and improve their own teaching. This total experience is not a linear progression but is iterative and integrative, and can lead to many different forms of outcomes for all the participants.

An important aspect of the diagram is the role of support. Obviously the immediate support comes from the participants themselves, as lecturers support the tutors (in learning about teaching and mathematics), each other (by focusing on curriculum and teaching development), and students. Tutors support the smooth running of the course, the lecturers (with immediate feedback on problems students are having), the students in their tutorials, and finally each other. Less obvious is the need for support from external areas. For example, in the case study that follows, we indicate that the mathematics lecturers received support from other academics whose focus was on teaching and learning in higher education. Further, an aspect that the Mathematics lecturers knew needed improvement – the assessment – was supported financially. This financial support enabled a developmental focus on assessment (again, through providing support for students, tutors and lecturers) that could be maintained for an extended period of time.

An important feature of the diagram is the implication that improvement and support in a single aspect of the students' environment is unlikely to result in significant change. Rather, this support needs to be provided at all levels, although particularly for the students themselves. A holistic approach is the key to successful enhancement of the Total Learning Environment.

Background to the case study

Before we proceed to describe each component of the Total Learning Environment in detail, it is important to outline the context of the case study that we will draw on to illustrate our argument. The case study focuses on activities established in the Department of Mathematical Sciences at the University of Technology, Sydney (UTS), to help make the students' first-year experience more positive and rewarding, and to enhance their learning outcomes. The needs of the particular students concerned were important in determining the nature of these activities.

Students entering the Department of Mathematical Sciences at UTS in the first year are predominantly recent school leavers, many with English as a second (or later) language, and often do not have a clear idea of the sorts of careers available to them when they finish the course. Many of them have mathematics as their second choice of study at tertiary level, after one of the more popular (and hence harder to enter) choices such as information technology or business. Furthermore, these students enter the department with a variety of mathematical experiences. All of these aspects contribute to the students' perception of the learning environment before they even start the course.

When they do, the students become aware of many other factors. They meet the lecturers and tutors who will be working with them for the next few years, they encounter different ideas and cultures, they find out what is required of them in each subject, they start to organize their own time to fit in study, socializing and work. Fairly soon, they become aware that they will have to think and behave in many different ways in order to achieve successful learning outcomes.

The Department of Mathematical Sciences at UTS has been evaluating the educational experience of their first-year students for a number of years. The focus of these evaluations has been to inform the development of a positive learning environment. Previous successful developments include the establishment of a Mathematics Study Centre – a drop-in resource centre staffed by academics and student tutors – the implementation of a first-year subject, *Mathematical Practice*, which examines the nature of mathematical thinking and mathematical communication, an orientation programme before the start of classes in first year, a shift away from traditional lectures towards student-centred laboratory classes and the appointment of honours-year students as tutors in many first-year subjects.

An evaluation in mid-1999 suggested that students were generally happy with their first-year experience but indicated that further improvement was possible in the area of assessment and teaching quality. In November 1999, the teachers of the first-year programme successfully bid for an (internal) Assessment Improvement Grant to fund a coherent developmental programme. The major part of this funding paid for the liaison services of a part-time lecturer throughout the semester. At the same time, a university-wide developmental programme for part-time teachers provided a way in which the tutors involved in the first-year programme could participate in a series of developmental teaching workshops. These two initiatives, supported by the services of a lecturer from the university's Centre for Learning and Teaching, paved the way for the development of a comprehensive programme aimed at supporting the development of a particular realization of the Total Learning Environment with a specific focus on assessment.

Mathematics departments in other universities will be familiar with aspects of this specific context. However, each individual department will also have different experiences and developmental needs. The case study material illustrates the experience of UTS but the *model* described above may be used as a framework to enhance the quality of learning within any institution.

Participants in the Total Learning Environment

The most important participants in the Total Learning Environment are the individual students. Prosser and Trigwell (1999: 17) suggest that 'Each student will have a unique perception of his or her situation ... [and] that an individual student's perception is related to that student's prior experience of other situations, and to his or her approach to learning and their learning outcome.' In their constitutionalist model of student learning they suggest that the students' prior experience, their perceptions of their situation, their approaches to learning and their learning outcomes are bounded by the learning and teaching context. It will therefore be valuable to consider how the Total Learning Environment supported student learning in this particular realization in the case study.

As the prior mathematical and learning experiences of its students are so varied at entry level, the Department of Mathematical Sciences instigated a series of strategies to help students develop their understanding of mathematics and learning prior to the commencement of the course, during all stages of the first year, and beyond. Mathematics bridging courses are run prior to the start of first year, giving students an opportunity to refresh their understanding of the mathematics usually covered in secondary schools. This form of support is focused on the students' understanding of mathematical principles and uses learning strategies that support active student learning, such as teaching and learning in small groups, discovering mathematics using problem-solving strategies, applying mathematical principles to real-life situations and so on.

Many students have levels of English proficiency that can inhibit their ability to communicate mathematically. There is a perception among some of our entering students that mathematics requires less language fluency than other courses. In the case of the Department of Mathematical Sciences, a large proportion of the students enter the course with English as their second language (one student indicated that English was his sixth language!). Clearly, students with different language backgrounds (and some of the students with an English language background) need support to develop their linguistic and communication skills in preparation for the diverse nature of the workplace. This support is provided by the English Language Study Skills Assistance, a university-wide support centre, by the inclusion of the subject *Mathematical Practice* (described in more detail later) in the first-year course, and by setting up group learning situations, in, for example, computer laboratories, and group assignments for first-year subjects.

The commencement of the course is supported by a first-year orientation programme, where subjects are introduced, study skills are discussed and students are given an opportunity to meet each other and the staff. They are also introduced to the Mathematics Study Centre, opened in 1994 in response to students' need for a mathematics 'drop in' centre. Academics are always available in the centre for any students to ask advice and help on any topic from their first-year course. Students are encouraged to work in groups to solve problems, and tutorial classes focusing on specific common needs are run. In addition, students are encouraged to meet with their individual lecturers from time to time, and this particular aspect is supported by the staff, who publish times of availability prominently.

The diagram of the Total Learning Environment given above includes the student tutors as participants. At UTS a decision was made in 1999 to start using students in their honours (fourth) year as tutors in first-year subjects. In other universities these tutors, where they exist, will often be graduate students. Despite initial opposition from some full-time academic staff, this has been a great success. First-year students generally find the honours students accessible and helpful, and seem to be motivated by contact with them. This group of tutors is often neglected in the discussion of learning and teaching development, although they can play a key role in helping students come to an understanding of mathematics.

The student tutors are successful mathematics students, but very much beginners in the role of 'teachers'. They participated in a university-wide developmental programme for part-time teachers, forming one complete group. In the workshops they attended, they discussed basic techniques for communicating with students, for encouraging them to engage with their studies, and for running effective tutorial classes. These formal workshops were supplemented by regular informal meetings with the lecturers of their courses, usually over morning coffee or lunch, at which specific teaching and learning problems were discussed.

The lecturers make up the third group of participants in the Total Learning Environment. In the case study these included full-time and part-time staff, all with many years' experience in the academic setting. The lecturers were supported by sharing and discussing their subject outlines, and discussing the benefits of using alternative learning strategies (such as small-group work in laboratory classes, flexible learning) and alternative modes of assessment (such as group presentations or projects). The Assessment Improvement Grant funded one of the part-time lecturers to organize regular meetings with students and staff to support assessment processes, prepare materials specific to the learning environment, and survey students regularly about various aspects of their studies. This turned out to be a key to the overall success of the project.

The curriculum in the Total Learning Environment

The curriculum plays a crucial role in the Total Learning Environment. A good curriculum will enable students to perceive the importance of each subject in their overall programme of study, and the relationships between these subjects. Evaluation of our previous curriculum showed that students needed to develop more generic mathematical skills such as communicating mathematical ideas. As a result, the Department of Mathematical Sciences designed a subject called Mathematical Practice to develop communication skills, research skills and group working skills. The content and approach of the subject can be seen clearly from the purpose-written textbook by Wood and Perrett (1997), and other learning materials that have been developed, such as the video package Pattern and Proof – The Art of Mathematical Thinking by Petocz and Petocz (1994). In this very practical subject, students use mathematical content as a vehicle to examine the nature of mathematical thinking and to 'practise' mathematical communications. Ramsden (1992) suggests that students understand the importance of aspects of a course through the assessment requirements. In this case the assessment tasks are focused around the development of a 'mini-conference', organized completely by the students themselves, and involving them submitting abstracts, writing papers, making presentations and answering questions on them. This subject is also used as a vehicle to integrate mathematical concepts – such as the notion of proof – that are important to other mathematics subjects.

The students involved in the case study indicated that they wanted the course to have more coherent and integrated learning/teaching strategies, particularly in the area of assessment. This was addressed in the first instance at meetings of all the teachers of the first-year subjects, at which the overall assessment aims and schedules, and their description in the subject outlines, were debated and modified. The scheduling of assessment tasks was addressed. Some lecturers were of the view that all assessment should take place in a few specified weeks to avoid the problem of students missing classes when assessment tasks were due in other classes. Other lecturers maintained that it was better to spread the load over a wider time and let the students determine their own priorities, and this view was eventually agreed to by all the staff. Discussion also highlighted the benefits of a graded criterion-referenced assessment system linked to the standard university grades of high distinction, distinction, credit, pass and fail, as opposed to a system that tried to distinguish between quality of work on a percentage scale. Meetings were also arranged with the students to suggest to them efficient ways of working, balancing the demands of their studies, and the other aspects of their lives, such as socializing and even sleeping! One of our guiding principles was matching assessment with learning outcomes, in the same way as was earlier exemplified in the case studies in Chapter 7. This kind of support is critical in underpinning the students' approaches to assessment in the programme.

One very important outcome of these meetings was the recognition by staff that their assessment requirements had to be very clearly articulated (even more than they previously had been) to address students' prevalent concerns about assessment. For example, students who were surveyed about how they felt they were coping with their studies during first semester wrote that:

> There are a lot of weekly assignments which need to be handed in. From worrying about completing the weekly tasks there has not been enough time to study. And from this, with assessments creeping up together, I find it hard to catch up. I would prefer to have less weekly assignments that are counted towards my final grade, but more time in class to practice work.

> It's been ok so far.

> A bit slow in adjusting to doing work again, but nothing that hard work won't fix.

Evidence of this type suggests that the students want to learn and that workload related to assignments was encroaching on their ability to learn. It also countered rather cynical views from one of the academics that the students were not really interested in learning. Other comments mentioned problems caused by imbalance in workload between subjects, and highlighted the fact that some students just didn't know how to start some of their assessment tasks. Students were given the opportunity to tell the teachers about issues surrounding assessment through a formal survey and through informal channels such as conversations with tutors. Assessment issues that came up were discussed with the students throughout the semester. For example, when students indicated they were having difficulty organizing their time, the next session of Mathematical Practice included a workshop on time management and ways of going about researching in mathematics.

Enhancing quality

The Total Learning Environment provides a convenient framework within which to analyze student learning, curriculum and the quality of teaching in any given programme. This enables a focus on enhancing different aspects of the support offered to students, tutors and lecturers. We can again illustrate how such enhancement might be effected by returning to the case study. There, each component of the Total Learning Environment was examined with the aim of determining whether learning had been enhanced. The resulting improvements had an effect on all participants involved in first-year Mathematics: students, student tutors and lecturers.

The Total Learning Environment was improved for students in several ways. Their assessment requirements were more carefully designed, and were communicated to them in a clearer way. Their workload was set at a level that was better balanced between the subjects that competed for their time and effort. They were introduced to effective techniques for balancing their academic work with the demands of the other aspects of their lives.

The tutors – who were also students – benefited in a number of ways. They had opportunities to discuss and practise methods and techniques for running effective tutorials, they developed their appreciation of how important it was to communicate requirements clearly to students, and (not insignificantly) they improved their own understanding of learning by being part of a quality learning environment for their own students.

The lecturers also indicated that enhancing the Total Learning Environment led to significant benefits for them. They carefully considered the aims and objectives of their own and other subjects, and refined their assessment and the communication of assessment requirements to reflect this. Overall, there was an increase in the level of communication between lecturers, tutors and their students. Lecturers benefited from an increased awareness of student problems – real or imagined – increased understanding of students' modes of working and increased awareness of the context of the whole first-year course.

The comprehensive programme that we have described was only made possible through the university's support with the assessment grant and part-time teachers' workshops. The supporting role provided by the part-time academic who had oversight of the programme was invaluable. This whole programme appears to have had a significant impact on the experience of students in first-year Mathematics. We think that an important development will be the establishment of similar programmes for all years of the course.

Conclusion

We have argued in this chapter that in order to foster high-quality student learning it is important to pay attention to the wider environment in which students learn. The notion of the Total Learning Environment provides a means of addressing different aspects of this environment. Although the model has been illustrated by a single case study in a university Mathematics department, we believe that it is applicable, with appropriate modification, to any Mathematics department (or, in fact, to any university department).

It is also important to pay attention to participants' *perceptions* of their situation. Ramsden writes:

There is a strong relationship between perceptions of effective teaching, approaches to learning, and learning outcomes. If it is possible to change students' experiences of courses and teaching, we can enhance the productivity of higher education by ensuring that more students develop the qualities of lifelong learning and of high disciplinary competence.

(Ramsden, 1999: 48)

For each of the participant groups, the Total Learning Environment may be perceived in different ways, and the clear communication of expectations and limitations, problems and solutions, is a key component of successful change.

What is most apparent from the case study that underpins this chapter is that support for learning needs to be provided appropriately on multiple levels. When this occurs, the Total Learning Environment is significantly enhanced and all participants benefit.

References

Biggs, J (1999) *Teaching for Quality Learning at University*, Society for Research in Higher Education/Open University Press, Buckingham

Bookman, J and Friedman, C P (1994) A comparison of the problem solving performance of students in lab based and traditional calculus, in *Research in Collegiate Mathematics Education I*, eds E Dubinsky, A H Schoenfeld and J Kaput, American Mathematical Society, Rhode Island

Booth, S *et al* (1999) Paths of learning: the joint constitution of insights, in *Learning Mathematics*, ed L Burton, Falmer Press, London

Dreyfus, T (1999) Why Johnny can't prove, in *Forms of Mathematical Knowledge: Learning and teaching with understanding*, ed D Tirosh, Kluwer Academic, Dordrecht

Goos, M, Galbraith, P and Renshaw, P (1999) Establishing a community of practice in a secondary mathematics classroom, in *Learning Mathematics*, ed L Burton, Falmer Press, London.

Jacques, D (2000) *Learning in Groups*, 3rd edn, Kogan Page, London

Keitel, C (1999) Teaching and learning mathematics, in *Learning Mathematics*, ed L Burton, Falmer Press, London

Petocz, P and Petocz, D (1994) *Pattern and Proof: The art of mathematical thinking* [video and booklet of exercises] Open Training and Education Network and University of Technology, Sydney

Prosser, M and Trigwell, K (1999) *Understanding Learning and Teaching*, Society for Research in Higher Education/Open University Press, Buckingham

Ramsden, P (1992) *Learning to Teach in Higher Education*, Routledge, London

Ramsden, P (1999) *Learning to Lead in Higher Education*, Routledge, London

Wood, L N and Perrett, G (1997) *Advanced Mathematical Discourse*, University of Technology, Sydney

9

Reflection in and on practice

John Mason

Introduction

> One thing we do not seem to learn from experience, is that we seldom learn from experience alone.

To study mathematics is one thing; to learn how to study more effectively and efficiently is quite another. Similarly, to teach mathematics is one thing, but to learn to teach mathematics more effectively and efficiently is also quite another. Neither studying nor teaching is improved simply through experience alone. Both require active intention and directed attention (Eraut, 1994; Moon, 1999). True, habits such as preferences for doing things in a particular order or in a particular manner are picked up along the way, simply through studying or teaching. But habits are not always useful, and if useful for a time, may not continue to be maximally efficient ways of deploying attention or energy. More positively, both studying and teaching can be rich sources of pleasure and fulfilment as domains for lifelong enquiry and development.

This chapter concentrates on the role of reflection in learning from experience as a lecturer or tutor. After considering some reasons *for* engaging in active reflection in the first section, some suggestions are made concerning effective ways to use memories of incidents as the basis for methodical reflection with a view to improving student and tutor experience. This then raises the question of how you know that things are improving, and for whom. Such a focus on improvement is important given the encouragement evident in other chapters to introduce new practices.

One important consequence of such reflection is that it is possible and valuable to assist students in becoming more efficient and effective learners, and one of the ways of doing this is by engaging them in a similar process of reflection. Furthermore, you can get support for your own reflection by getting students to reflect, so that a cycle of mutual benefit ensues.

Why reflect? Why work at improving teaching?

Many colleagues shy away at the thought of spending 'even more time' on their teaching, as this is bound to detract from the time they spend on researching, which is their true love. However, segmenting 'duties' into teaching and researching misses a wonderful opportunity for mutual interaction between and mutual improvement in both. I shall attempt to justify the claim that integrating teaching and research can lead to even greater personal satisfaction. Indeed, working on teaching can actually improve research.

Enhancing research through working on teaching

At a trivial level, you learn an enormous amount about a topic when you try to teach it to someone else. The reason? Because in order to expound a topic to someone else you have to stand outside the intimate relation you have with that topic. Intimacy with a mathematical domain is a 'dwelling-in' knowing, enjoying the way that ideas and associations, links and connections, techniques and theorems come to mind when needed. But when students enter the scene there is impetus for both 'dwelling-in' and 'being aware-of' knowing. As well as enjoying the knowing, there is stimulus to become aware *of* that knowing, of *how* ideas come to mind, etc. The presence of students enhances the possibilities of considering the structure from outside as it were, sometimes as if from the students' point of view and sometimes from your own. You are engaged in a process of revealing structure, of finding a 'simple' and coherent way of 'looking at' the topic, of blazing a path through a tangle of ideas. The result is that you clarify your own understanding by organizing what you know, and more importantly, by recognizing *how* you come to know.

Clearly, therefore, teaching advanced courses on topics of interest to you helps you to organize your thoughts, and may even reveal previously unidentified problems for research investigation. Indeed this can happen even with material that is well rehearsed and centuries old. Similarly, students can improve their appreciation of topics if they are engaged in tutoring colleagues.

But research and teaching are much more intimately tied together than simply having teaching raise problems worthy of research. In order to explain something effectively, you have to enter the world of the student (note the contrast with expounding, where you entice the student into your world). In explaining, you are engaged in a process of recognizing your own experience through being sensitive to the difficulties of students and vice versa; of using your awareness of yourself to become more sensitive to student difficulties. When you start to pay attention to what students are thinking; to what they are making of exposition and explanations to which they are exposed. When you try to enter their experience, you begin to make contact with your own thinking in a new and fruitful way. Becoming more aware of your own thinking patterns can actually be of benefit to both teaching and research.

Now, creative artists are often frightened of discussing how they work, where they get their inspiration, what drives them and how they develop their ideas. Their fear is based on the assumption that the process is so delicate that any interference, any intrusion or extra degree of self-awareness may frighten the muse away, loosening contact with creativity. It is a reasonable fear, because who has not experienced fallow periods when no ideas will come, and nothing seems to work, whether as artist or as mathematician? But this fear is irrational and is not helpful to development as a mathematician. Fallow periods are not due to self-awareness. Quite the contrary. Being stuck is entirely natural and something can often (though not always) be done about it.

The claim made in this chapter is that becoming aware of how you think about mathematics, about how you locate and pose problems, and about how you come up with ideas, actually makes it possible to improve these processes. Furthermore, working with students, even in topics unrelated to your research interests, provides an opportunity for you to become more aware of how you think, as well as to increase your sensitivity to noticing opportunities to use that mathematical thinking intentionally. This enhanced awareness can also inform your research.

These assertions are only conjectures. They have to be tested in your own experience, for it is not possible to 'prove' them within any axiomatic system. But even if you do not accept my conjecture, there are other reasons for paying attention to your teaching.

Dealing with disappointment

Sometimes at the end of a lecture or a tutorial, you come out with a sense of sadness or mild depression that things 'did not go as well as you imagined'. Sometimes even in the midst of a session, you suddenly become aware of 'things not going well'. Perhaps you begin to catch yourself asking 'ok?' repeatedly, or some other phrase with the same intent. Perhaps you detect a blank gaze, a fog of confusion rolling forward from the students. It is entirely natural to become aware that something is not going well in a session and to find oneself reacting to this, either by sticking doggedly to the plan, or by pausing and trying to recover the situation by talking about it with the students. This sort of 'awareness-in-the-moment' is triggered by a sense of things 'not going well'.

Usually it takes only a few moments to recover equilibrium. A few sentences into the next topic, a few steps out of the room, and you are your old self again.

Perhaps you tell yourself a story about students not working hard enough, or being under-prepared before they came to college. Perhaps you find one of your research questions coming back to mind and you rush off to try out a new idea. Sometimes though, the unease resonates with a residual discomfort, and concern begins to grow.

Another source of dissatisfaction comes with marking examinations. Each year you expect that this time students will show that they have understood and each year there are significant numbers of students who seem not to have grasped the main ideas. It seems such a waste of time and human energy.

These sorts of experiences are entirely natural. They involve an ebb and flow of energy, and that energy can be used to greater effect by using it to transform the situation rather than simply tolerating things as they are, by simply using the energy to return to equilibrium.

How then do we learn from experience? How do we make use of these energies to improve our practice, whether as researcher, lecturer or tutor? The proposal made in the next section is that we learn most effectively and efficiently from experience by reflecting upon that experience. But there is much more to 'reflection' than simply 'looking back over what happened', as Pólya (1945) advised. As in any discipline, it pays to be disciplined, to be systematic.

Systematic enquiry

It is one thing to feel some dissatisfaction or disappointment with sessions. It is quite another to do something about it. Although there are distinctive differences between research in mathematical sciences and educational enquiry, there are some significant similarities.

In mathematics, it is vital to formulate and reformulate a question until eventually it becomes tractable. The same is true in education. The first question that occurs to you (eg 'Why do students not remember what I tell them or what they studied last year?', 'Why do they keep on making the same mistakes?', 'Why do they not do better on assignments?') may not actually get to the heart of the matter. In fact they may serve only to preserve the status quo by focusing attention on surface phenomena. So working at reformulating questions is essential. And just as in mathematics, the way you formulate a question is guided by the tools and techniques, the perspective with which you are most familiar.

In mathematics you make conjectures and the same is true in education. But in neither case is it wise to believe your conjecture (Pólya, 1945). The whole point about formulating a conjecture is to externalize it so that you can inspect and study it dispassionately. It is necessary in both mathematics and education to watch out for hidden assumptions. In education these sometimes take the form of opinions or prejudices, which may surface as certainties. The more certain you are about something in education, the less likely you are to appreciate what is going on, which is perhaps opposite to work in mathematics.

In mathematics you either start with some particular cases or examples and try to work out 'what is going on', or, if you start from a conjecture, you quickly try to find a generic example through which to try to see what is going on, as Hilbert advised (Courant, 1981; see also Michener, 1978). So too in education. What constitutes an example in education? Since it is incidents in sessions that make you feel despondent (sometimes), the most useful data consist of brief-but-vivid descriptions of incidents that for some reason won't go away, which come back to mind perhaps all too readily. Just as with mathematics, instead of allowing ideas and possibilities to tumble around in your mind, it helps to make a record of incidents that strike you in some way. The important feature of brief-but-vivid accounts is that they remove as much of the explaining-away, the judging, the if-onlys, the self-criticism and the justifications as possible. A brief-but-vivid description works when colleagues immediately recognize what you are describing and are even tempted to offer a similar one of their own. A moment such as:

I said a rather technical sentence, and suddenly I knew that few if any students were still with me. What to do? Do I stop and go back or do I plough on?

I knew I could carry on anyway; I could stop and go over the ideas again; I could try to find another way to explain it.

This account can be of value only if you recognize it in your own experience. You cannot verify that it actually happened or that it happened like that. You cannot decide whether any theorizing I might be tempted into is relevant, since you cannot know enough of the details. If I had described my frustration with the students, or with myself, or my despair, I might easily not have resonated so strongly with your experience, because your emotions are different to mine and expressed differently as well. If I had justified what I did ('I had to finish the topic in that session', 'I had to go over it again because I know it is vital to the coming work', 'I resorted to my favourite explanation because I knew they had not seen it last year when they encountered this topic': the justifications can go on and on), then I might easily have lost the significance of this event, having explained it away. In any case it would only have reinforced your desire to explain it away. Judgements and explanations smooth disturbances away while at the same time making it difficult for others, who are in no position to agree or disagree with any theorizing since they have too little information to work on.

If you do recognize the incident, in the sense that it brings either particular experiences to mind or it has the taste of familiarity, then you will know what you have chosen to do in similar situations in the past. Has that been effective, in the sense of getting you out of situations in the short term *and* offering you a way of dealing with it in general? You might even wish to eliminate the phenomenon altogether, although if that were achieved, the students would have no struggles, no challenge, and would perhaps not actually be learning anything at all.

The momentary act of asking yourself if you can recall similar incidents, and re-entering those moments, is fundamental to effective reflection. It exercises the basic power of mental imagery, which is how we learn from experience in order prepare for the future. Recall of the past may remind you of a tactic you could use again. It may not, however, so the brief-but-vivid account can be mentioned to colleagues to see whether they recognize it. If they then offer their own brief-but-vivid descriptions of moments, you may find that these include different tactics, some of which may appeal to you when suitably modified to suit your situation. A third source of tactics is through watching others (say at seminars or conferences or even attending their lectures or tutorials) and through reading, as you are at the moment.

For example, the incident described above came from my experience. I can see the room, feel the summer heat, see the students. I can even recall the topic: it suddenly popped into my head to ask the students to try to say to each other the sentence I had just said. It was the first time I had used such a tactic and I was pleased with what happened. They thought about it, tried to say something, then when the buzz died down I asked if anyone could get us started. Well, no one volunteered at first. So I asked what the sticking point was. One of the technical terms was mentioned. So I knew that that was where more work was needed. Off I went.

Since that time I have worked at generating an ethos in which students are willing to struggle to express themselves even when they are unsure or know they are stuck. I call it a 'conjecturing atmosphere': everything said (particularly by me) is a conjecture that has to be tested out, either in experience, if it is an educational assertion, or on examples or by reference to known theorems, if it is mathematical. I have found that pausing after making an assertion and getting students to talk to each other briefly (usually a few seconds is enough) contributes to the conjecturing atmosphere. I am careful not to criticize what is said but to get other students to consider and offer modifications as necessary. If what comes back is nonsense, I praise the fact of a conjecture, which allows me to separate participation in the process from the particular answer. It also contributes to students developing an understanding of the ideas.

Over the years I have found that pausing in a lecture and inviting students to talk in pairs briefly, helps me and them a great deal. Where I can get them to struggle to express themselves, there is extra benefit. Not everyone can address the full group, but everyone can take a moment to write something down having said it to a colleague. Furthermore, I find that students actually ask much better questions as a result. And before you think to yourself that this is fine in a small tutorial but not in a lecture, I have used this successfully with 500 students, and even once with over 2,000 people, though I could not take feedback from them, obviously!

All I am offering here are examples of how you can pick up new tactics. It does not matter if you feel that neither pausing nor talking-in-pairs is helpful to you. The point is that reading people's accounts *can* be a source of inspiration as you take up an idea and modify it for your own use. Many authors (Boud *et al*, 1985;

Tripp, 1993; Carson and Sumara, 1997; Cowan, 1998; Moon, 1999) have written about the use of *critical* incidents (those that come back in your thoughts because of some disturbance and those that serve as turning points in your teaching) as the fundamental data of educational enquiry.

Accounts can be analyzed by getting colleagues to help you look for hidden assumptions, often disguised as 'rules of thumb', which may deserve to be questioned (Tripp, 1993; Brookfield, 1995; Moon, 1999). Looking back over accounts can also serve to reveal habits that, while useful when first employed, may now be blocking you from achieving what you really want to achieve. For example, devices for dealing with unruly students that may be needed early in one's teaching career can develop into habits that block the formation of a deeper and more sensitive relationship with students once you have confidence in presenting the mathematical content. I prefer to think of accounts of incidents merely as triggers to access experience, which for me forms the primary data (Mason, 2001b). Analysing accounts, even justifying or theorizing them, is perfectly possible and frequently done, but the most valuable use of accounts is to strengthen your desire to act in a new chosen way that fits more with your evolving sense of how students can best be supported in learning. The next section elucidates what has to be done and the following section offers some specific techniques.

Reflecting-on to support reflecting-in-action

It would be sensible to pause for a moment and think back to what was being illustrated in the previous subsection. In order to do things differently (presumably to make improvements) three things are absolutely essential:

- An intention to develop your teaching, to be sensitive to students' struggles, difficulties and needs (if you did not have this you would have given up reading this far).
- Recognition in the moment that something needs to be done (eg those moments when it is clear that most students are lost, that a diagram might be useful, or that you are about to present a difficult proof).
- A tactic to employ other than your habitual reaction (eg pausing, talking-in-pairs).

The first is something only you can do anything about, though it becomes more possible when you start to see something that you can actually do. The third requires a collection of tactics, picked up by thinking back to your own past experience, from colleagues or from reading (see, for example, Hubbard, 1991; Angelo and Cross, 1993; Gold *et al*, 1999; Moon, 1999; Mason, 2001).

The second condition you can work at, indeed it forms the essential flip side of reflection as looking back, is what I call *pro-flection* or looking forward. You do it by imagining yourself in some session, imagining yourself as vividly as possible using some chosen tactic in an appropriate situation. It only takes a few seconds, but it pays huge benefits. Having imagined yourself acting in some desired way, you may find that suddenly, in the midst of a session, a possibility comes to mind and you discover yourself using the new tactic. It is like finding yourself filling out a form. More commonly, however, you may find that despite every intention and despite having imagined yourself doing it, you still do not think of it, but only became aware of it as a lost chance retrospectively after the moment has passed. This is usual with working at changing practice. Each moment of recognition, even in retrospect, is a source of energy that can either be thrown away in berating yourself or invested by refreshing your image of yourself acting in the desired manner. If you persevere in using the focus that comes from recognizing to reinforce imagining yourself acting in the future, then you will find that possible tactics do come to mind when they are needed. I enjoy using the term *flection*, poised between reflection and pro-flection, to describe that moment in a session when an idea pops into your head and you choose to follow it. This approach to personal and professional development is developed in Mason 2001b.

A variety of authors have pointed out that the term *reflection* is used in many many different ways, to the extent that the term has almost become meaningless. Schön (1983) popularized a distinction between *reflection-on-action* (thinking back over what happened) and *reflecting-in-action* (exposing to students what you are thinking, your own struggles and ways of working). A third form of reflection has been suggested here and proves to be the essential ingredient if you truly want to learn efficiently from experience: *reflecting-through-action* or *flection* (suddenly changing from being immersed in the details of the moment to also simultaneously being aware of choices you might have). The process described above: of mentally placing yourself in some future event and imagining yourself using some tactic is initiated by reflecting-through-action. Kolb (1984) famously described a cyclic process of learning that has been applied to many situations, including professional development, and developed into a theoretical frame (critiqued by, for example, Letiche, 1988: 22–25). Basically it suggests the natural process of entering into situations as openly as possible, then standing back to reflect upon them, developing a framework or theory to account for them, and using this to inform and take action, resulting in yet further experiences. The critical features of all learning on which most theorists are agreed involve exposure to stimulus that creates some sort of disturbance that draws attention to some feature, aspect or issue not previously salient, which, supported and informed by analysis-logic-analogy, etc, gives rise to conjectures to be tested in experience. These apply equally well to ourselves as teachers, to ourselves as learners and to students as learners as well. General descriptions are of little value unless they are related to specific experiences. The next section describes a few specific techniques for engaging in reflection while involving students in the same process.

Some specific techniques

There are many different ways to trigger and to engage in reflection, taken here as meaning an action in which sense is made of something that has happened. Instead of suggesting things you can do in the quiet of your study, I have chosen to suggest things you can do with students, but which mirror things you could also do by yourself or with colleagues. The reason for involving students is that the presence of the students adds an extra sharpness to help you undertake the reflection with greater intensity, as well as demonstrating that students have a great deal to gain from learning to be reflective learners, so their energy and attention can be harnessed effectively to help you as well.

A few techniques are listed here for reference, as well as to illustrate the process of how you can go about locating ideas through reading. As you consider the following, ask yourself what it is that is stopping you from using something similar yourself: is it lack of time, or lack of clarity as to what might be achieved, or are these seen as mere diversions from expounding content? Is it a deep-seated commitment to demonstrating that what you currently do is already excellent?

Pause in the middle of a session or a few moments before the end and ask students to:

- Write down any question or problem that they currently have, something which seems murky and unclear.
- Say to a colleague nearby what they think you just said.
- Write down on a card (and hand in) what they think was the main or central point of the session for them.
- Write down what was exemplary about a worked example you have just done.
- Construct a more general example like a particular one that you have just exhibited, which satisfies certain constraints.
- Make a note of why they think you just said or something (eg where you have been struck by the presence or absence of a striking response from them, or in the flow of applying a technique, or using a theorem, etc).
- Write down a brief description of something irritating that you do and something they appreciate that you do.

In each case, students will be much more willing to act if they see you doing the same, as they will take this to be part of how a professional acts. If you do something else instead, such as packing your bag, collecting your pens or cleaning the board, they will assume you are not really serious and that you do not really expect them to put in much thought. If you can get colleagues to carry out a similar exercise with their students, then it could be immensely valuable to exchange descriptions of what you did and what you found out. Hearing what others claim they do in similar situations is one of the best ways of picking up practices to draw upon in the future.

Acting differently is one thing, but how do you know it makes any difference to the students? The next section briefly looks at issues in evaluating changes in practices.

Evaluating what you do

There is no point in changing what you do or how you do it unless there is a good reason. Having made a change, how do you know whether it really is an improvement? The difficulty of answering this is compounded by the fact that students are creatures of habit just like their lecturers and their tutors. Change may be resisted simply because the new is unfamiliar. Even if it is accepted, effects may not be immediate, and as a further difficulty what students say may not be the whole story. One consequence is that students need to be involved in or attracted to any proposed changes.

Here we meet a contrast between research results in mathematics and in education. Could not someone do some research and decide which tactics are best, in which situations, and used in which order and with which frequency, and then just tell everyone else the results? The problem is not just that it is rarely possible to locate much less evaluate the effects of the large number of factors that affect lecturing and tutoring. The problem is that teaching and learning are to do with human beings who have their own aims and interests, their own desires and intentions, their own sensitivities and awarenesses. They can choose to act, and they do so. They also spend a lot of time acting through habits. The result is that teaching and learning are fundamentally about choices people make, about what they are attending to and what their intentions are. And these are very hard to externalize accurately, if indeed accuracy is even possible.

All is not lost however: quite the contrary. Developing your teaching is about becoming more aware of *how* you think, of what you stress and what you ignore in different circumstances. For example, you work through an example in front of the students. You are probably thinking about the general but applying it in this particular case. If all the students see is the particular, then they have no access to the general, yet access to the general is presumably why you are going through the particular. As Isaac Newton and many other educators have said many times in different ways, 'craft skills are more easily learnt by example than by precept' (Whiteside, 1983: 429). But students need to know what to do with the example. They even need to recognize it *as* an example of some more general approach, technique, theorem, etc. If you want students to benefit from your working through an example in front of them, you need to make sure that they are with you line by line, that you expose (even write down) what prompts you to make your next move, that they have a moment to consider what you say, and you need to make sure that you are stressing the parts you really intend to stress. Quite often what a lecturer or tutor thinks they are stressing is not what comes across to students.

Apart from talking to the students about their experiences, asking them questions, etc, you can also get assistance from a colleague, perhaps in your institution's equivalent of a 'learning support centre'. What you want is someone who is willing to sit in your session and to do nothing more afterwards than exchange descriptions of moments that stand out for some reason: brief-but-vivid descriptions. If the colleague is judgmental and critical then his or her presence is likely to have a negative effect on you, no matter how open you feel you are. If on the other hand the colleague is friendly and neither judges nor criticizes, then the enhanced awareness you get from his or her presence will be positive. It won't be long before you find that the enhanced awareness you experience when being watched continues even when the colleague is not present. And that enhanced awareness, that inner witness, is part of your inner monitor who warns you when you are making errors on the board or in your research, the one who asks you why you are doing this when it is time to pause and look back.

Reflection is really about awakening this inner witness who comments but does not criticize, who monitors your behaviour and wakes you out of movements of identification when it would be helpful to stand back.

Feeling good yourself is not definitive, because it is easy to misread a situation and think that students are happy when they are not. But student opinion is unfortunately rather fickle and not usually very well informed. They are busy trying to grasp the content, and so not very often aware of things you could have done but didn't. They are also relatively easily swayed by the overall relationship you establish with them, so that their comments on details of your practices may for the most part reflect how they think they are getting on in the course. In the final analysis, what matters is that student performance improves, and that you feel better about what you are doing. The temptation to achieve short-term goals (students doing better on tests and in examinations) by taking short cuts, can be resisted if you have confidence in your sensitivity to students, if you can articulate your pedagogical stance, and if you can get students to cooperate with that approach. All of these are enhanced by reflection and by talking with colleagues. All of these are enhanced by exchanging particular incidents, and relating them to your aims and desires.

In other words, starting to work at your teaching can initiate a positive feedback loop, displacing any negative loops that may have developed through frustration with students and hence with teaching.

Reflection

What, if anything, struck you as you were perusing this chapter? Are you fearful that working more on your teaching will take valuable time away from research? Were you surprised at my conjecture that teaching and research can be integrated to some extent, and that working on one could improve the other as well? Did you recognize the dissatisfactions arising from a session or from exam marking? Did you recognize them sufficiently strongly to want to do something about them?

If you noticed the distinction I drew between exposition (inviting students into your world) and explaining (trying to enter the students' world of mathematical experience), could that inform your future actions in lectures and tutorials? Might it be worthwhile using your own experience of being stuck, or struggling with a mathematical idea, to help you predict the sorts of struggles students might be having with topics you are teaching? Can you spend just a few seconds imagining yourself using a tactic that you picked up in this chapter or elsewhere in your next lecture or tutorial? Would it be worth collecting examples of difficulties students have and asking colleagues about ways of circumventing them?

This is the beginning of reflection, of looking back after an event or incident (whether in your teaching or in your research activities) and of looking forward to inform choices in the future.

References

Angelo, T and Cross, K (1993) *Classroom Assessment Techniques*, 2nd edn, Jossey-Bass, San Francisco

Boud, D, Keogh, R and Walker, G (1985) *Reflection: Turning experience into action*, Kogan Page, London

Brookfield, S (1995) *Becoming a Critically Reflective Teacher*, Jossey-Bass, San Francisco

Carson, T and Sumara, D (1997) *Action Research as a Living Practice, Counterpoints, vol 67*, Peter Lang, New York

Courant, R (1981) Reminiscences from Hilbert's Gottingen, *Mathematical Intelligencer*, **3**(4), pp 154-64

Cowan, J (1998) *On Becoming an Innovative University Teacher-in-Action*, Oxford University Press, Oxford

Erant, M (1994) *Developing Professional Knowledge and Competence*, Falmer Press, London

Gold, B, Keith, S and Marion, W (1999) *Assessment Practices in Mathematics*, Mathematical Association of America (MAA) Notes 48, MAA, Washington

Hubbard, R (1991) *53 Interesting Ways to Teach Mathematics*, Technical and Educational Services Ltd, Bristol

Kolb, D (1984) *Experiential Learning: Experience as the source of learning and development*, Prentice Hall, Englewood Cliffs, NJ

Letiche, H (1988) Interactive experiential learning in enquiry courses, in *The Enquiring Teacher: Supporting and sustaining teacher research*, eds J Nias and S Groundwater-Smith, pp 15-39, Falmer Press, London

Mason, J (2001a) *Mathematics Teaching Practice: A guide for university and college lecturers*, Horwood Publishing, Chichester

Mason, J (2001b) *Practitioner Research Using the Discipline of Noticing*, Routledge-Falmer, London

Michener, E (1978) Understanding mathematics, *Cognitive Science*, **2**, pp 361-83

Moon, J (1999) *Reflection in Learning and Professional Development: Theory and practice*, Kogan Page, London

Pólya, G (1945) *How to Solve It*, Princeton University Press, Cambridge, Mass

Schön, D (1983) *The Reflective Practitioner: How professionals think in action*, Temple Smith, London

Tripp, D (1993) *Critical Incidents in Teaching: Developing professional judgement*, Routledge, London

Whiteside, D (1983) *The Mathematical Papers of Isaac Newton, vol II, 1667-1670*, Cambridge University Press, Cambridge

Part B

Learning and teaching in context

10

Numeracy in higher education

Janet Duffin

Introduction

The job was mine until I failed the numeracy test.

The idea of numeracy in higher education has always seemed something of an anomaly. In part this is because numeracy is seen as the concern of the very earliest levels of education and therefore of no moment at the university level. Furthermore, undergraduates normally possess a qualification in mathematics and are thus assumed to be numerate, even though there is no guarantee that a qualification in mathematics will automatically ensure competence in number.

However, the UK government has recently concentrated on the development of numeracy, both as a specific element within the normal mathematics curriculum in the earlier years of schooling through its National Numeracy Strategy (Department for Education and Employment, 1999, 2001) and in the later years as a key skill (Qualifications and Curriculum Authority, 1999). In this context numeracy can be seen to be an entity in itself to be provided for within universities as much as in the earlier sectors of education. Indeed, this was the view taken by the Dearing Report (National Committee of Inquiry into Higher Education, 1997: 9.16–18), which regarded numeracy as one of four skills crucial to the success of all graduates. In spite of this there remains an ambivalence towards its inclusion at the higher education level. In addition there are differences within universities regarding its provision for students, some seeing it as a constituent part of all mathematics support, others providing specific help with numeracy distinct from the mathematics support for undergraduates in their degree courses.

Students also tend to have a somewhat ambivalent attitude to numeracy, assuming as do universities themselves that a qualification in mathematics absolves them from a need to ensure current number fluency, many having thankfully left all mathematics behind them when they made their subject choices at A level. So it can come as a shock to them to discover, on graduating, that their number skills are inadequate for the employers' tests set to graduates seeking employment. Students may be unaware that failure to use number skills leads to a decline in level of numeracy, as suggested by recent evidence in the context of labour market participation (Bynner and Parsons, 2000).

This chapter suggests that numeracy within higher education has always posed something of a problem for the university sector, especially for students studying subjects other than mathematics. The chapter will initially discuss the genesis and development of numeracy support in one university. This will both allow for a detailed consideration of one approach to developing students' numeracy and raise more general issues inherent in offering numeracy support. It concludes by giving a wider picture of the current situation in the UK, using case studies from a selection of other universities to illustrate that situation. These case studies provide a variety of ways of addressing problems raised earlier in the chapter. It is worth emphasizing here that this chapter focuses on dedicated numeracy provision rather than on mathematics support for undergraduates in their degree programmes, which is considered in the next chapter.

A numeracy course for employment

It was during the late seventies that the Director of Careers at the University of Hull became aware of a problem when the need for graduates to have employment skills in addition to their degree qualification was beginning to emerge. Similar awareness was evident at the numeracy session of a bi-annual conference of UK careers officers in 1985.

Plans to meet this need at the University of Hull were set in motion and a skills package of courses, which included a numeracy course, was jointly inaugurated in 1985 by Careers and Adult Education. Student reluctance to admit to any shortcoming in number competence was reflected in the initial charges for the package – which students had to pay for themselves at that time – for these were set at £18 for computer and keyboard skills combined, with only £2 extra if a numeracy element was also included. The numeracy course later came under the auspices of MACS (Mathematics Advisory and Consultative Service) though numeracy was always seen as something different from other mathematics support provided by MACS (Duffin and Simpson, 1996). The course was eventually discontinued in 1998, numeracy support now being provided on an individual basis by the new umbrella organization SAS (Study Advice Service) established in 2001.

Philosophy and expectations of the course

The course was set up with a dual focus in mind: to help students to approach with more confidence and competence not only employers' numerical reasoning tests but also any numeracy requirements in their future employment. To effect this the course had several specific and perhaps unusual features:

- It was organized to foster student independence rather than relying on an external authority to verify answers (independence, not 'tick-dependence').
- It was based on mathematical principles in order to reduce memory load and show the connectedness of much number material (principles, not isolated techniques).
- It was not to be a rehash of methods learnt in primary school but was set at an intellectual level worthy of a university-trained mind.

These three factors required active student participation in the sessions, rather than a mere reception of material. The teaching method used therefore encouraged such participation and involved the challenging of methods learnt at school where these appeared to be based on the practice of techniques rather than on understanding. Principle-based mental strategies were developed with a choice of methods – often drawn from students themselves – produced in order to encourage the kind of flexible mental manipulation of number required in employment.

Content of the course

The course always began with students taking a test, called *Test with a difference*. This test was compiled from a selection of employers' tests in use at the time (1985) taken from that used at the bi-annual conference mentioned above. Students were asked not to carry out the actual calculations required but instead were to read them through very carefully, noting and recording their reactions to each part of every question: easy, panic, anxiety, etc. In addition, they were asked to record with a tick, a cross or a question mark whether or not they could do them or were unsure about them. This procedure gave each student an indication of where their strengths, weaknesses and uncertainties lay and hence what they would be seeking to gain from the course. Students were also asked to repeat the test at the end of the course to determine what they had gained from it. This self-assessment exercise was seen as an important element in their development of confidence and competence.

Following this exercise students themselves chose which of the two versions of the course to follow: either the Refresher or Basic course. The former was for those who felt they had had quite a good grasp of early number when at school but had lost it through lack of recent practice, the latter for those who felt they had more severe difficulties. The content and approach for each were identical, the only difference being in the time taken to complete the course: the Refresher being of 10 sessions, the Basic taking anything between 15 and 20 sessions.

An additional element of the course, also part of the development of independence, was that though work was set after each session, no marking was undertaken. Instead, students were encouraged to self-check by using a variety of methods, including estimating the answer prior to doing the calculation. They were welcome at all times to bring any difficulties encountered to the attention of the course tutor.

The first session was used to explain the aims and philosophy of the course and what it would require of participants. The session ended with an investigation of the subtraction process they had learnt at school. This served to demonstrate that there is more than one recognized way of subtracting, itself a revelation to many, and that, even better, there are a variety of mental methods that students usually turn out to have developed for themselves, but which they believe to be 'not the right way to do it'. This was also an important early lesson: that their own mental methods are to be valued, not seen as unacceptable.

The remaining content of the course fell into three stages: principle-based approaches to the four basic arithmetical operations followed by a bridging session in which the connections between fractions, decimals and percentages were established using the Equivalence of Fractions. Students were encouraged to develop the ability to move easily between the three forms and to choose the appropriate one for any required calculation. The final section involved the study of percentages and their use in the community, using the competencies developed through the earlier two sections.

During this final section students were encouraged to examine examples in the media that demonstrate that misunderstanding of percentages is rife in the community. Examples of such misunderstanding of percentages are seen in often-heard statements such as '30 times less than' and the erroneous belief that decreasing by a given percentage is the inverse of increasing by the same percentage.

At the end of the course students were again asked to redo the *Test with a difference* and were given a self-assessment sheet of media examples showing misconceptions they were invited to analyse. A sheet of useful number facts and helpful procedures developed in the course was also given out as a learning aid and a self-assessment check. No formal assessment of the course was ever introduced and no certificate given, something that reflected the general university ambivalence towards such courses.

Using challenge and participation to develop number competence

One of the ways in which the course claims to be at a level appropriate to the university sector is indicated through its challenge and analysis of many school-acquired procedures. Challenge, by generating interaction between student and teacher, and the subsequent analysis it engenders, can be seen to be similar to the active learning promoted in Chapter 3. One example of such challenge is given below.

Students are asked how they would multiply a number by 10. The usual response is 'add a nought'. They are then asked how to multiply 2.7 (say) by 10, to which the answer is usually 'move the decimal point'. To demonstrate how principles can lighten memory load, 7 is multiplied by 10 to obtain successively 70, 700, etc, followed by successively dividing by 10 to return to 7 and beyond. Students are asked to describe in words what has been happening and from their verbal description Figure 10.1 is produced.

Figure 10.1   A visual *aide-mémoire*

$$\times\ 10 \leftarrow$$
$$\div\ 10 \rightarrow$$

It is significant to note at this point that the vivid mental image evoked by this example of the inverse principle serves to reinforce the course's claim to be appropriate for the university sector by encapsulating within it a 'rule' for both multiplying and dividing by 10 in contrast to the students' school experience of having two distinct procedures for each operation. The rule is then shown to be part of the general principle that inverse operations undo each other. Pairs of such operations are elicited from students' own experience. This principle, together with those of distributivity, commutativity and associativity, is later used to develop alternative calculating methods for the four basic operations of arithmetic, which more perceptive students then see can be reduced to two.

There are two aims here. One is to show the diversity of possible methods available for any calculation. The other is to help them to move away from the view that there is only one right way to do any numerical calculation and that they have to learn this one right way to be successful. It also gives them a means of checking for themselves that the answer they have obtained is the correct one. The importance of estimating is also emphasized at this point.

For the purpose of challenging the common errors about percentages mentioned above students are asked how to divide by a fraction. Responses to this include 'turn it upside down and multiply' and 'multiply by the reciprocal', but no student can ever offer an explanation of this procedure. A mathematical justification is discussed before going on to a full treatment of percentages using the principles already developed. It is at this point that the course provides the greatest and final challenge. Those students who can meet this challenge are empowered by the course. To enhance the confidence that this gives, successful students are encouraged to be alert to common errors in the media.

Evaluation of the course

In order to help expose some of the problems the course encountered, it is important briefly to consider how effective the course proved to be. There was no formal evaluation of it but there were three sources of informal evaluation: from evidence about its content at another university at a time when no other numeracy course existed in higher education; from student comments over a period of years, both on the evaluation sheets handed out to all students completing the course and spontaneous verbal comments; and from comparison of these comments with those on the same course given for members of staff of the university, largely secretarial, library and administrative personnel.

Evidence from another university

A few years after Hull's numeracy initiative Durham University appointed a Numeracy Fellow who established that it was the only position of its kind then in place. A plan to do a piece of joint research into the issue was thwarted from lack of available funds at the time but Durham did a pilot survey of the local position (Cornelius, 1992), which established that the content of the Hull course met the numeracy needs of employment, besides confirming that some graduates were gravely disadvantaged in work because of their lack of facility with number. This at least in part serves to validate what was happening in Hull at the time.

Evidence from student comments on the course

Student reactions to the course may be seen as falling into two categories: those who felt they had benefited greatly from it and those who had not. A selection of comments that illustrates these two categories is given in Table 10.1. While some of the students on the Refresher course appreciated what the course was trying to do, many did not appear to do so and indeed a significant number of these students dropped out at a comparatively early stage. In contrast, more of those on the Basic course felt that it had offered them something new that enabled them to make a radical change to their whole perception of mathematics and their competence with number.

With such a contrast between those for whom the course had been a positive experience going beyond mere improved number competence and those for whom it appeared to have failed, it is worth speculating about possible reasons for the difference. While many of the positive comments came from those who clearly had long-standing problems with number and mathematics, and were therefore from the Basic course, some were not. What is brought out in the adverse comments is that some students, almost all from the Refresher course, failed either to accept or grasp the underlying philosophy of the course even though the first session sought to explain this underlying philosophy.

Two student comments seem to be particularly relevant in exposing possible reasons for this difference. One came from a Refresher course student who saw the value of the course when he reached the end of it:

> You have to go to the end of the course to see how it all slots in. The first few sessions seemed a bit pointless because they were about very basic things we all knew. Now at the end I can see we had to do them because without it the whole thing wouldn't hang together as you can see it does at the end.

(Duffin, 1990: 6)

The other came from someone who did the course twice because she felt she hadn't understood it the first time. Her comment seemed to epitomize the attitude of those who failed to accept the course philosophy: 'People are dropping out of this course. Don't you think that is telling you something?'

So why did some of these students persist after the preliminary session? Was it because they had not understood what was being said, or for some reason ignored it, or was there another factor that might account for their inability to accept the

Table 10.1   Student comments on the course

Positive comments	Negative comments
Absolutely marvellous; I wish I could have attended a course like this years ago.	It was too slow and only about things we already knew.
It was fun; I learnt methods I would never have thought of before.	I learnt more from a friendly scientist in half an hour than I would have got from the whole course.
I found it particularly rewarding that some of the methods I had been doing in my head which I thought were wrong are actually acceptable.	The course was too theoretical; more attention should have been paid to doing exercises and having them marked.
I feel privileged to have had the opportunity of attending this course; it has raised my confidence in my coursework and in relating to my friends.	I wanted to refresh mathematical techniques, not examine concepts and have my approach changed.
I no longer feel blind panic when faced with a page of numbers.	
Numbers have become exciting and less frightening.	
It was somehow liberating; I don't feel so much to blame for being bad at maths.	
It seems absolute common sense to be taught principles so that you can understand maths.	

course philosophy? There is research evidence that suggests that a teaching style that is far removed from that to which students are accustomed (Davis and MacKnight, 1976) can be counterproductive and not achieve its aims and objectives. However, it is worth exploring another possible explanation of the inability of some students to respond positively to the course, which is suggested by a comparison with a comparable course aimed at members of staff.

A numeracy course for staff

During the nineties the Staff Development team suggested that a course be offered to members of staff who wanted to become more numerate for the jobs they were doing. Significantly, it was revealed that some technical staff were indignant that anybody could think they might not be numerate; perhaps in some way resembling the attitudes of those undergraduates who did not respond well to the course.

In two successive years staff followed the same course as that given for undergraduates, but the outcomes were significantly different:

- The only fallout in numbers, except in one unexplained case, was for personal reasons unconnected with the course.
- All end-of-course comments were positive, including one participant who said how it had enabled her to help her own children with mathematics, which she had previously been unable to do.

These outcomes suggest that work experience may have made these participants more ready to change attitudes because they had actually encountered numeracy demands in their work. This may help to *explain* the difference between students and staff but does not, of itself, offer a solution to the problem. How *do* we enable those not yet in work to appreciate the educational needs that arguably only work experience itself can give?

In the UK the government is attempting to ensure numeracy at all levels of schooling and is implementing plans for ensuring it for prospective teachers (Qualified Teacher Status, 2001). Only if it is also achieved in higher education will we be sure of having a fully numerate society. This requires a full acceptance of the responsibility to ensure it within the university sector. How can this be achieved?

The national picture: a limited survey

Before discussing the national picture regarding numeracy in higher education it is helpful to distinguish two ways in which it has been perceived in the sector and, arising from this, two ways in which it has been developed. These are:

● As an element within the so-called 'skills package' that epitomizes its perception as an addition to the degree studies of any discipline in order to make students employable on graduation.
● As an element within mathematics and its consequent development as part of general mathematics support for other disciplines within the university.

Although in practice the distinction between the two approaches is blurred, it is helpful to be aware of the distinction in attempting to describe and analyse the national picture. In the former case these skills are currently seen to be additions to a degree, required by employers but not intrinsically part of the degree itself. In the latter, while the mathematical component is part of the degree structure of other disciplines and support in it therefore contributes directly to the degree, the numeracy element is rarely seen in this way, largely because it is held to be at a lower level entirely than degree material.

In view of this it may be that, in the future, universities will consider including the skills package as a valid component in their programmes, in which case numeracy might become part of such a programme and hence gain acceptance. On the other hand, if numeracy is merely seen as a minor component within mathematics, it may be lost to a degree programme that concentrates on support for the mathematics within individual disciplines.

An informal survey of universities in the UK reveals a mixed picture of the support offered for numeracy. At least two universities, after incorporating a specific numeracy element in the support they offer students, have recently discontinued such support. Ironically, in another where the mathematics support included a strong numeracy element and where its organizer firmly believed that interest in, and provision of, numeracy was growing in the university sector and would in the future form an intrinsic part of the degree structure, the mathematics department is to be closed down. It is as yet not known whether mathematics support for other disciplines, let alone numeracy, will continue as an element in its provision for students.

However, the picture is not all of closures and the discontinuing of numeracy help for undergraduates. Some initiatives are meeting with more success. Case studies from four universities contain within them the seeds of possible responses to the challenges raised earlier in this chapter.

The Huddersfield Bridging Course

At Huddersfield numeracy is catered for as part of a Bridging Course in Mathematics put on for applicants to the university whose mathematical competence does not reach entrance requirements. The course runs during the July and August prior to admission and gives prospective students the opportunity to update their mathematical skills in their own time. The university invests £8,000 in the course but it is free to students. The numeracy element in the course includes estimation and rounding, percentages, standard form and squares and square roots.

Students have open access to a computer laboratory where they can use modules that consist of expository material together with tutorial matter and assessments. There are also three one-hour multiple-choice tests. A tutor is available three hours every day to answer any student queries.

The course has proved increasingly popular among aspiring students, attracting around 70 each year (80 in the current year), as a result of which the university was able to recruit 35 students it would otherwise have rejected. Around 15 do not return after their first session. Typical comments from participants include the following: 'The course was excellent', 'I never knew I had a mathematical brain until now', 'Even if I don't pass it has been an enjoyable experience'. The importance of this course is that it is forward-looking in two distinct ways. It makes the acquisition of numeracy competence (as part of an overall mathematical competence) a prerequisite for acceptance at the university, thus offering a possible answer to the problems of students not realizing the need to be number confident for employment, and it puts the responsibility for acquiring that competence and confidence on students' own actions through the way it is managed.

The Loughborough Confidence in Numbers Workshop

Confidence in Numbers is the title of a workshop run by the Mathematics Learning Support Centre (MLSC) at Loughborough University in association with a university central support service known as Learning and Teaching Development. It has run once in each of the last four years (1997–2000) and is aimed specifically at those students wanting to improve their confidence and prepare for employers' numeracy tests.

The workshop begins by explaining why students who are confident with numbers have significant advantages, both in obtaining employment and in being promoted once there. Quotations are given from employers who are on record as stating that they are looking to employ numerate graduates irrespective of their degree discipline.

Students are provided with a list of skills that, while not exhaustive, covers most of the important basic areas. Included are the ability to estimate, having a sense of size and relative importance of numbers, the ability to perform simple mental arithmetic, and specific topics such as percentage, ratio, currency and other conversions, etc.

An overview of the resources available to help students with these topics, within the university and further afield, is given. It includes a book list, Web sites containing practice tests, details of computer packages that can help and so on. Finally, students are given the opportunity to take a practice test that takes under an hour, and they can then discuss their answers and raise questions.

Follow-up support is available through the MLSC for any student wanting to seek further assistance.

In spelling out to students why numeracy is an essential competence for employers' tests the Loughborough workshop quotes from employers themselves, something that may well be more effective in persuading undergraduates of the importance of number competence before they seek employment than any exhortations from within the university. Moreover, by giving students the opportunity to choose for themselves the resources they can use to achieve competence with numbers, they help to create the independence needed for success and promotion in the job itself.

The York Award Numeracy Course

The York Award course 'Numbers at Work' has met with mixed success. It has now been running for four years and in the first year was very popular. In keeping with the rest of the York Award course programme, it is voluntary and accessible to students of all disciplines, although it is clearly indicated that the target audience is those who have not studied mathematics post-GCSE.

Experience suggests that students need more encouragement to attend a course in numeracy than they do some of the other skills training offered outside the curriculum. Consequently, the organizing team have been urging academic departments to refer students to them and this policy is beginning to bear fruit: one department is promoting the course actively to second-year undergraduates as part of its timetabled programme (but does not offer academic credit to those who complete it).

One of the biggest motivators for students to take part seems to be the fact that many graduate recruiters set numeracy tests as part of the selection process. Frustratingly, the course team regularly receive enquiries after running the course from students who have just realized that they need to brush up those skills in preparation for such tests.

The course 'Numbers at Work', which forms part of the York Award initiative, endorses the Hull findings about student reluctance to seek numeracy support and appears to be having greater success than Hull did in persuading academic departments of its use to their students. Nevertheless the university is not yet ready to give it credit-bearing status towards a degree.

The Liverpool Higher Skills Development Programme

In the University of Liverpool, Liverpool John Moores University and Liverpool Hope, opportunities for skill development are acknowledged and catered for through the Higher Skills Development Programme and the associated Higher Skills Development Award.

The programme has been designed for undergraduates to recognize the transferability of their skills to the workplace and to develop those skills to a necessary standard. The award has been introduced to give credit to students for a range of personal and professional skills such as team-working, application of number and problem solving, achieved through academic and extra-curricular activities. Large and small companies support the award for which there is a baseline achievement, the award being tailored to each learner through an individual development plan. Successful students receive a certificate from their own university.

Students work with an HSDP advisor to identify opportunities from inside and outside their curriculum to show evidence of development of key skills. For example, a Liverpool Hope student based her skill development in numeracy on the management of a student budget. Following the guidelines in the HSDP booklet, she produced statistics, graphs and charts based on her monthly spending activities. She produced a weekly budget, and a bills breakdown using Excel, thus also producing evidence of her ICT skills. There is no time pressure on the Award; students typically complete in 12 to 18 months, with meetings being arranged at times convenient to them.

This programme with its award of a certificate perhaps holds a key to successful achievement of numeracy among undergraduates. The participation of employers provides a link with numeracy demands encountered in the workplace, while certification provides official and tangible evidence of achievement.

What does the future hold?

These case studies, together with the Hull experience, contain within them possible ways forward for ensuring numeracy within the university sector. Nevertheless, they do indicate that the situation is as yet unsatisfactory, in that number competence appropriate to current needs is not reflected in its acknowledgement as a necessary part of every graduate's portfolio on leaving university. Providing certification is clearly one way forward, as occurs in the programmes at both Liverpool and York, ensuring that students receive tangible reward for making the effort to improve their number skills. Alternatively, the Huddersfield Bridging Course, which includes a numeracy element, ensures that competence in numeracy is specifically part of the entrance requirements of the university.

The Hull course, with its claim that it is set at an intellectual level appropriate to a university course, offers a further way forward, while the inclusion of numeracy as part of a skills package, provided this can be suitably accredited, is yet another. Unfortunately numeracy seen merely as a part of general mathematics support within the degree programme for other disciplines may not receive the attention it warrants unless specifically catered for. Until these issues are fully resolved within the sector we will never reach a position in which no graduate will ever have to say 'The job was mine until I failed the numeracy test'.

Acknowledgements

I am grateful to Dexter Booth at the University of Huddersfield, Tony Croft at Loughborough University, Robert Partridge at the University of York and Patricia Lunt at the University of Liverpool for the case study material.

References

Bynner, J and Parsons, S (2000) The impact of poor numeracy on employment and career progression, in *The Maths we Need Now: Demands deficits and remedies*, eds C Tikly and A Wolf, pp 26–51, Institute of Education, London

Cornelius, M (1992) *The Numeracy Needs of Graduates in Employment*, University of Durham, Durham

Davis, R B and MacKnight, C (1976) Conceptual, heuristic and S-algorithmic approaches in mathematics teaching, *Journal of Children's Mathematical Behavior*, **1** (Supplement 1)

Department for Education and Employment (DfEE) (1999) *National Numeracy Strategy Framework for Key Stage 1 and Key Stage 2*, DfEE, London

DfEE (2001) *National Numeracy Strategy Framework for Key Stage 3 and Key Stage 4*, DfEE, London

Duffin, J (1990) *Numeracy From an Adult Viewpoint*, unpublished course booklet

Duffin, J M and Simpson, A P (1996) Mathematics across the university: facing the problem, *Journal of Further and Higher Education*, **20** (2), pp 116–24

National Committee of Inquiry into Higher Education (1997) *Higher Education in the Learning Society: The report of the national committee (The Dearing Report)*, HMSO, London

Qualified Teacher Status (2000) Trainee support material

Qualifications and Curriculum Authority (QCA) (1999) *Introduction to Key Skills: Levels 1–3 in communication, applications of number and information technology*, QCA

11

Mathematics: the teaching, learning and support of non-specialists

Tony Croft

Introduction

Mathematics is a hierarchical subject that continually builds upon what has gone before. The assimilation of earlier material is essential if it is going to be possible for students to be taught and learn new mathematical ideas. This indeed is the view adopted by the benchmarking group developing national standards for the teaching of undergraduate programmes in Mathematics, Statistics and Operational Research (MSOR) within the UK. The draft statement from this group makes a very important observation about the learning of mathematics:

> The subjects included in MSOR are largely cumulative: what can be taught and learned depends very heavily and in considerable detail on previously learned material. This applies to MSOR very much more than to many other disciplines. An MSOR programme must be designed to follow a logical progression, with prerequisite knowledge always taken into account. Advanced areas of pure mathematics cannot be treated until corresponding elementary and intermediate areas have been covered. Development of application areas can often be done in parallel with other work, but it is always necessary to ensure that the required methods and techniques have been dealt with.
>
> (Quality Assurance Agency for Higher Education, 2001: 6, Section 2.1.1)

The statement goes on to note that MSOR subjects are unique among all disciplines in the extent to which they necessarily occur in programmes in other areas, particularly engineering, physical sciences, social sciences and management. The MSOR benchmark is unlikely to apply to teaching in these disciplines. Nevertheless, it is the crux of the argument put forward in this chapter that the observation above is a fundamental tenet in the learning of mathematics in whichever sphere this takes place.

So, it is particularly disturbing to read reports that provide evidence that much of current teaching of non-specialist mathematics students within the UK is at odds with this tenet. For example, the report *Mathematics Education Framework for Progression from 16–19 to HE* by Sutherland and Dewhurst states:

> On many of the courses surveyed some students enter with A level mathematics and others with a grade C in GCSE. The gap between these two qualifications is enormous and the resultant mix of students is very difficult to manage from the point of view of learning the mathematics necessary for the course.

> GCSE grade C in mathematics is accepted by some departments as an entrance requirement. There was genuine surprise about how little mathematics undergraduates with this qualification are familiar with. It would appear that universities have not taken on board the difference between GCSE and O level mathematics.
>
> (Sutherland and Dewhurst, 1999: 5)

While in *Measuring the Mathematics Problem*, Hawkes and Savage found that:

> There is an increasing inhomogeneity in the mathematical attainments and knowledge of students entering science and engineering degree programmes.
>
> (Hawkes and Savage, 2000: iii)

There are a number of other reports from professional bodies, learned societies and researchers that provide further evidence to substantiate these findings, including Sutherland and Pozzi (1995) and the Institute of Mathematics and its Applications (IMA) (1995).

So, it is clear that we have a situation in which, at least in some universities, students with A-level mathematics and GCSE mathematics at grade C are taught mathematics together that contradicts the tenet that pre-requisite knowledge should always be taken into account. We have situations where engineering and science students are learning basic mathematical techniques when they come to university, at the same time as (and often *after*) they are required to apply these techniques in their main subjects. Clearly they have not mastered the required methods and techniques. It is no wonder that lecturers frequently find this sort of work dispiriting and as Larcombe (1998) writes, 'mathematicians have no appetite for what they see as unrewarding and often thankless work'. Indeed, questions are being raised as to who are the most appropriate people to teach mathematics in the early stages of a student's university career. Again, from Sutherland and Dewhurst:

> The teaching needs are more akin to school teaching and university lecturers are not the best people to be carrying out this kind of work.

> (Sutherland and Dewhurst, 1999)

Hunt and Lawson (1997) suggest that it would be arrogant and unrealistic of lecturers – many of whom have no formal teaching qualification – to assume that they have the expertise to put right the cumulative failures of school education.

In the light of this situation there are a number of questions that all those involved ought to be asking:

- Why is it the case that specialist students of mathematics can expect a standard of care to be exercised in the design of their curricula (through benchmarking), and particularly that in designing their programme pre-requisite knowledge must be taken into account, whereas non-specialists can find themselves in very mixed groups with little regard paid to their previous mathematical experience?
- Why have so few, if any, recommendations in learned society reports that might lead to an improvement in the situation been implemented?
- Why have around 50 per cent of UK universities now established Mathematics Support Centres as an attempt to deal with some of the problems, instead of tackling the problem by more fundamental root and branch reforms?
- Who are the best people to teach mathematics at this level in universities given the nature of the problem?

There has been an enormous growth in the recent past in the use of mathematics, not only in traditional areas such as engineering and physical sciences, but also more recently in the biological and social sciences. There has been an enormous expansion in the numbers of students in higher education, and as a consequence in the numbers required to study mathematics at university. Unfortunately there has not been, at least until recently, a great deal of research done on mathematics education at university level, although there is an emerging and growing body of material. Policy decisions are not based upon sound research evidence. If the many millions of people who will have to study mathematics in some form at university over the next few years are to find it an enriching and empowering experience, and if the many millions of pounds of public money that are used to educate them is to be well spent, then it is right to ask for answers to these questions.

This chapter will seek to explore both the needs of non-specialist students of mathematics and the ways in which these needs might be met more effectively than is presently the case. In the context of this chapter, *non-specialists* are students who come to university to read subjects other than mathematics (either as single- or joint-honours students), but for whom mathematics is nevertheless a compulsory part of their university experience. These students may be contrasted with the wider body of students considered in the previous chapter, where the focus was on all students in higher education and their subsequent employment-related needs. After an initial consideration of who should teach non-specialists, the chapter goes on to review a number of recent reports that express grave concerns about the state of mathematics education of non-specialists in universities. This is followed by a discussion of practical responses to these concerns. The chapter concludes by mapping a way forward to help ensure that the problems that have been highlighted in this chapter are tackled in a serious way.

The mathematical education of non-specialists: who should do the teaching?

The mathematical education of non-specialists has begun to arouse interest in the past few years. Unfortunately, much of this interest has arisen not because of the realization that mathematics provides a wealth of tools for tackling problems in very diverse areas such as genetics, communications, financial modelling, etc. Rather, it has arisen because of the problems faced by both many of the students attempting to study mathematics as non-specialists and by those charged with teaching them.

The term 'service teaching' is often used in connection with the mathematical education of non-specialists. It usually means the teaching of mathematics to those students outside of a mathematics department in, for example, a business school, or a department of engineering; the teaching being carried out by members of staff from the mathematics department. Such teaching is often a vital source of income for the mathematics department. However, in its discussions of mathematics for non-specialists this chapter would like to embrace a wider group and include mathematical education when this is taught either by mathematicians resident in the students' own department, or when the mathematics is taught by non-mathematicians, as for example when an engineer teaches the mathematical components of an engineering degree course, or when a business school lecturer teaches a module in quantitative methods.

The mathematical education of non-specialist undergraduates has long been a bone of contention. Heads of departments of mathematics often assert that the teaching of mathematics lies within the expertise of their staff and so lay claim to the teaching. Heads of departments of engineering, for example, assert that among their staff number many able 'mathematicians' who can do the job far more effectively and with more authority because they are also engineers. The debate about the ownership of the mathematical education of these students may often be reduced to the level of a playground brawl. Decisions about ownership are not made on sound pedagogical grounds, but are often more to do with financial and political considerations, and sometimes to do with failure-rate control. Mathematics is almost unique in being in this situation. This is particularly unfortunate since it is now well recognized and well documented that, if not in crisis, mathematics education is certainly in ill-health. Many departments of mathematics bemoan the ill-preparedness of students entering university to study mathematics. So much worse, then, will be the situation in which non-specialists find themselves, because many of these will also be ill-prepared, and additionally the group will include the maths anxious and those who dislike mathematics.

It is the hypothesis of this paper that the territorial anxieties mask the real issue. It is to some extent irrelevant that the persons charged with teaching mathematical or statistical tools to non-specialists resides in a mathematics department or elsewhere. For example, there are models of excellent mathematics teaching of physics undergraduates from within their own department. What is crucial is the interest shown by these individuals, the awareness they maintain of both pre-university mathematics education and of developments in mathematics itself, and the encouragement and incentives they receive to develop their teaching, and to develop a relevant and up-to-date curriculum for their students. It is too often the case that university lecturing staff are recruited and rewarded not for their teaching ability but for their success in research. This is particularly unfortunate in the present climate. Wherever the ownership lies there can be dangers. For instance, when mathematics is taught by staff in the students own department:

- There can be insufficient awareness of changes in the pre-university mathematics curriculum that impact upon their students ('They should be able to do all this because I did it at O level'!).
- It may happen that students are taught topics in mathematics only as tools for tackling specific tasks; the utility of mathematics lies in the fact that if properly understood it can be applied in different, and new, situations.

On the other hand, when taught from a mathematics department there can be:

- A lack of appreciation that students need to see real and relevant applications of the mathematics they are studying.
- A lack of appreciation that these students are not *mathematics* students.
- A lack of interest in the prior mathematical experiences of these students.
- A perception among those doing the teaching that it is a 'Cinderella' area that is often looked down upon and under-resourced.

And, there are particular problems faced by those in mathematics departments who must teach such students. These students do not come to university to study mathematics, and very often they have little interest or enthusiasm for doing so. So immediately the lecturer is faced with a group of students, many of whom would rather not be there. The group is likely to include those who are maths anxious, who lack confidence and may have disliked mathematics at school. Recent research on attitudes of engineering students towards mathematics teaching (Shaw, and Shaw, 1999, 1997a, 1997b) indicates that only 9 per cent of students across a wide range of institutions are happy with the teaching, 30 per cent have changed from enjoying it at school to not enjoying it at university, 10 per cent hate mathematics regardless of whether at school or university and 50 per cent are ambivalent to the whole process! Those involved in service teaching usually have no say in which students are recruited and often little say in what must be taught (course content is often defined by external accrediting bodies). The lecturer often works in an environment where the client department, because of internal politics and financial considerations, may well be fighting to have service teaching returned. In such a climate there is little incentive to innovate and to keep up to date with developments.

Furthermore, as has been stated, it is not clear that university lecturers are the best people anyway to be trying to tackle the serious problems faced by mathematics education in universities. So, wherever the teaching resides there are certain to be issues.

Recent reports: a survey

An interesting and useful starting point for anyone wishing to study issues concerning the mathematical education of non-specialists is the previously cited report by Sutherland and Dewhurst (1999). The stated aim of the report is to investigate the mathematical knowledge expected of undergraduates as they enter university across a range of disciplines, in order to produce information that would be relevant to schools, universities and policy makers. This wide range of disciplines includes engineering, biological sciences, business studies and others, and at a number of different levels from an institution that recruits well-qualified students to one that has relatively low entry requirements. The report presents some very bleak findings and in particular notes:

> At least one department from each of the subjects surveyed told us that the mathematical background of their undergraduates is undermining the quality of their degree.
>
> (Sutherland and Dewhurst, 1999: 6)

In 1999 a two-day seminar funded by the Gatsby Foundation focused on the mathematical attainment of young people entering higher education within the UK to study subjects that call for a good grasp of mathematics (eg physics, engineering and mathematics itself.) The resulting report *Measuring the Mathematics Problem* (Hawkes and Savage, 2000) drew attention to the significant and measurable decline over the last decade in students' basic mathematical skills even among those with good A-level grades in mathematics. Evidence is provided from several independent sources that even when universities recruit students who are well qualified, many do not possess the necessary manipulative skills in algebra and calculus. The decline in basic maths skills has been rapid. The performance of A-level grade C students in 1997, in a basic maths test on entry, is no different from that of students with grade E in 1993 and grade N in 1991. It would appear that universities are not only faced with the difficulties arising through widening participation and changes in the school curriculum, but also must grapple with an A-level mathematics regime in which it is very difficult to determine what it is that any particular student can do having achieved any particular grade. The report has three main recommendations:

- First, students on maths-based degree courses (especially engineering, physics and mathematics) should have a diagnostic test on entry.
- Second, prompt support should be available to students who need it.
- Third, a national database should be established to provide diagnostic tests.

In addition to the declining achievement of entrants with A-level qualifications, the situation in the UK is complicated because a significant proportion of entrants to many degree courses have undertaken vocational qualifications leading to BTEC and Advanced GNVQ. Although these qualifications are widely treated as equivalent to A level they are not the same. There is evidence from diagnostic testing upon entry to university that students with Advanced GNVQ perform worse than those with A level grade E (Lawson, 2000).

In Croft (2001) attention is drawn to the fact that the Quality Assurance Agency (QAA), which audits teaching and learning at university level in the UK, has brought a number of concerns to the fore. The QAA assesses the quality and standards of teaching and learning at the subject level in each university within the UK. On completion of each subject assessment cycle, ie when all universities offering that subject have been reviewed, the QAA publishes subject overview reports on their Web site (see http://www.qaa.ac.uk/revreps/subjrev/intro.htm). One advantage of an overview report is that it is one step removed from particular institutions. It represents a distillation of the findings of many reviewers visiting scores of universities. It can thus provide a snapshot of the state of health of teaching and learning throughout England and Northern Ireland in that subject. But a subject overview report looks at a specific discipline or occasionally a group of cognate disciplines. It is useful to taker one further step back and look at the overall picture provided by reports in several disciplines. Such an investigation reveals an interesting and commonly occurring theme in subject overviews of chemical engineering, materials technology, electronic and electrical engineering, mechanical, aeronautical and manufacturing engineering, chemistry, molecular bio-sciences: the ill-preparedness of incoming students for the mathematical demands of university courses. Common threads running through many reports include decline in mathematical expertise, lack of preparedness, diversity of mathematical skills within groups of students, the need for universities to provide additional support, mathematical difficulties cited as reason for failure or withdrawal, increasing pressure on teaching staff and on an already crowded curriculum. Croft (2001) suggests that the interface problem is sufficiently important and affects such a large proportion of the university intake that it ought to be regarded as a generic issue, and its treatment adequately supported and resourced at the generic level.

On the international stage there has been recognition of the problem. The International Congress on Mathematics Education (ICME) has recently recognized emerging interest in mathematics education in universities and has sponsored a number of workshops. Discussions have revealed a variety of serious issues facing university mathematics education including widely reported declines in the number of students choosing to specialize in mathematics, and the challenges posed by new clienteles of non-specialist students. The report of ICME Working Group (see http://www.stolaf.edu/people/steen/WGA/rpt.html) notes:

- Individuals from different countries reported that students now arrive with weaker skills, or at least different skills: less fluency with algebra, but more experience with technology, less maturity in traditional mathematics, but more familiarity with group projects.
- Some participants reported that the client disciplines are reducing requirements for mathematics *per se* in favour of teaching mathematics as embedded aspects of their own disciplines.
- There is a new thoughtfulness about teaching in college and university mathematics departments motivated by the pedagogical challenges posed by students with non-traditional preparation and goals who are now studying mathematics.
- Many participants raised issues relating to transitions that were disturbing the traditional order of university education. One is the increasingly challenging transition students undergo in shifting gears from a secondary school perspective to the independence and rigour of a university context. The difficulty and importance of this transition suggests to some that a genetic, developmental approach to pedagogy in early years of university may be essential to smooth the transition to formal deductive mathematics.
- Departments everywhere struggle with the challenge of maintaining integrity of mathematics programmes and at the same time meeting the needs of diverse client departments.
- As mathematics becomes more pervasive in its applications it is also increasingly dispersed to other departments. ... No longer are mathematics departments the primary locus of mathematics education in universities – indeed most mathematics taught in higher education is now under other auspices. This change creates an immense challenge for university mathematics education.

Reports cited previously have been concerned with a range of disciplines. Concerns with specific subjects have been highlighted elsewhere. In 1997 The Engineering Council, the body charged with the regulation of professional engineers in the UK, produced a document SARTOR3 (*Standards and Routes to Registration*, 3rd edn.) in which it seeks to ensure that engineering qualifications in the UK will continue to compare favourably with the highest standards internationally (The Engineering Council, 1997). In its summary the Council records one of its reasons for revising its guidelines as being the reduced coverage of mathematics in A level in relation to the needs of engineering. It also states that there are limited numbers of school leavers with adequate mathematics and science knowledge to allow them to undertake demanding degrees in engineering. It identifies two distinct types of engineering degree course providing the educational base for those aspiring to become Chartered Engineers (CEng) or Incorporated Engineers (IEng). The Institute of Mathematics and its Applications set up a working group to respond to SARTOR 3 and produced guidelines for the teaching of mathematics to undergraduate engineers, following extensive consultation with the engineering institutions (IMA, 1999). Among the guidelines in this report, we note in particular:

- For IEng programmes it is proposed that there should be a significant reduction in the syllabus content from that traditionally found on most engineering programmes. Students should demonstrate mastery of a range of basic mathematical techniques and develop confidence in the application of these techniques to the solution of engineering problems. They should make appropriate use of modern mathematical technologies. It is important that they see the relevance of the mathematics that they study by setting it within an engineering context.
- Universities must demonstrate that students with mathematical qualifications deemed equivalent to A level for entrance are directed towards an appropriate mathematical education.

This second guideline has been included to make explicit concerns that 'A level equivalent' qualifications do not prepare students adequately as far as mathematics is concerned (see Lawson, 2000).

Turning to physics, Gill notes that in the past most students on physics degree courses had passed two mathematics A levels. Nowadays this is very unusual. Furthermore, A levels were acknowledged as examinations for university entrance; again, this is no longer true. He writes:

Mathematics A level syllabuses and assessment techniques have changed enormously over the last dozen years. Yet the mathematics courses taught to the undergraduate physicists have scarcely changed in living memory. Clearly this mismatch will be significant for many students and to close the gap will take a lot of effort. It would seem that the greatest change will have to be in the HE syllabuses so that they follow more logically from school mathematics.

(Gill, 1999)

There are clearly numerous reports, and several others not cited here, dating back to the mid-1990s, which raise concerns about the state of learning and teaching of mathematics to non-specialists in higher education in the UK. Most of these contain recommendations intended to alleviate the situation and lead to improvements. There is little indication that, to date at least, the problem is being tackled in a systematic way. Often, rather ad hoc and piecemeal, although well-meaning attempts are being made, and some of these are described in the next section.

Tackling the mathematics problem

Clearly, universities are faced with major difficulties. Where there is a climate of widening participation, a government agenda to increase the numbers entering higher education and a competitive need to attract and retain students, as is the case in the UK, the majority of universities are not in a position to require the highest-level entry requirements in mathematics. As a consequence they must take what they can find and put mechanisms in place to do the best possible job with the students they have. Universities and individual departments, and individuals themselves, have not been unaware of these problems and many are developing ways to deal with them.

Among the range of strategies for coping with the difficulties, one option is to reduce syllabus content or to replace some of the harder material with more revision of lower-level work. This may help the weaker students. However, if more advanced material is removed to make space for this revision, it disadvantages the more able, making them less well prepared for the mathematical demands of the more advanced and more analytical parts of their studies. It has a longer-term effect of making these students less able to compete for jobs in the rest of Europe and beyond. Some universities have developed additional units of study (sometimes called bridging courses) for their weaker students. However, this option is not universally adopted and may not be an option for some departments constrained by modular schemes that do not have sufficient flexibility to require (or even permit) students to attend more than a specified number of modules. Furthermore, it is not sensible for students to be learning basic mathematical techniques at the same time as they are supposed to be using more advanced techniques in applications and in problem solving in their other studies. Some universities attempt to cope with diversity by streaming their students and teaching the weaker group separately, sometimes using the services of experienced school teachers rather than university lecturers. In order to cover the same syllabus as the stronger group it may be necessary to increase contact hours for the weaker group. However this practice is not universal.

Many departments now routinely carry out some form of mathematics diagnostic testing upon their new students at entry, as explored in Chapter 1. The report *Measuring the Mathematics Problem* (Hawkes and Savage, 2000) recorded that over 60 departments (of physics, engineering or mathematics) carried out such testing, although the figure now is likely to be much higher than this, particularly if a wider range of disciplines were to be included. There are several reasons why diagnostic testing is useful:

- It can provide information about the cohort as a whole and enable curriculum developers to take account of the changing nature of the intake.
- It can provide individual teaching staff with information about gaps in the prior knowledge of the group and so enable them to take particular care when introducing new topics.
- It can help to identify students who are significantly weaker than the rest of the group and thus be targeted with individual help and attention.
- It can inform the development or acquisition of remedial materials in support centres.

Furthermore, by testing over an extended period of time, trends can be observed (see, for example, Lawson, 1997). Some departments use diagnostic testing as a basis for streaming students into two or more groups, in an attempt to cope with diversity. However, there are many other departments where this does not happen. A shortcoming of the whole process of diagnostic testing is the provision of adequate follow-up support. In situations where students are simply told their test result and advised to revise certain topics on their own, there is little evidence that this happens.

Mathematics support centres are one way of providing follow-up support to diagnostic testing and indeed to offer support more generally. In a Learning and Teaching Support Network (LTSN) funded project *Evaluating and Enhancing the Effectiveness of Mathematics Support Centres*, Lawson, Halpin and Croft (2001a) set out to investigate the extent to which universities have made additional provision in the form of mathematics support centres to support students who are struggling with the mathematical and statistical components of their studies. They found that out of 95 higher education institutions replying to a questionnaire about the extent to which additional mathematics support is provided, some 46 stated that they now make this available.

A handbook that provides guidelines and good practice in mathematics support centre provision will be published by the LTSN (Lawson, Halpin and Croft, 2001b). The authors note that while many students have been helped by such centres, they are not panaceas that will solve every difficulty thrown up by the 'mathematics problem'. When students have weaknesses in many areas a support centre may not be an effective solution. Such students are asked to remedy the deficiencies in their mathematical backgrounds through voluntarily attending the centre, while at the same time studying the same mathematics module as their colleagues. They are hit with a 'double whammy'. On the one hand, they are expected to spend extra time improving their mathematical background, while, on the other hand, work for their modules (not just their mathematics module but others that rely on mathematical knowledge) takes them longer because of the weaknesses in their mathematical background. This can often lead to students taking a superficial approach to remedying gaps in their background knowledge. Rather than seeking to construct a coherent mathematical knowledge base, they simply use the centre to deal with isolated problems they are encountering on their current modules. These students often have a blinkered approach, wanting to be able to answer the particular exercise they have in front of them, rather than to acquire sufficient understanding to answer a range of similar exercises. Another danger is that the provision of a mathematics support centre can be used by curriculum designers as an excuse for not developing curricula that are appropriate for the students they are recruiting. The argument goes along the following lines: 'If students cannot do topic x then they can always go to the mathematics support centre to learn it'. A final danger that is worth highlighting is that some institutions have reported that the presence of a mathematics support centre has encouraged certain serviced departments to either remove mathematics from the explicitly required curriculum or to hide it within one of their modules. The students are then told that if they have problems with mathematics then they should go to the mathematics support centre. Both of these approaches are an abuse of the intention of mathematics support centres, which is to provide extra (not replacement) support for students with difficulties in mathematics.

Clearly many are making efforts to tackle what is a serious problem. Unfortunately, while many perceive the problem to be deep rooted and ubiquitous there has not yet been any national enquiry to try to investigate the causes, extent and solutions. The following recommendation by Sutherland and Dewhurst has not yet been implemented:

> There is an urgent need to investigate claims by universities that undergraduates are not able to tackle difficult mathematics problems, work independently and use mathematics in applied situations.
>
> (Sutherland and Dewhurst, 1999)

The nearest we have at present is the report *Measuring the Mathematics Problem* (Hawkes and Savage, 2000), the value of which lies in the fact that views on the extent of the problem were brought into the public domain and representatives from the full range of universities from the highest seats of learning to the lowliest institutions admitted that they were experiencing problems.

Conclusion

Mathematics education of non-specialists at university level is in a serious state of health. It is subject to many pressures. The consequences of these impact upon so many students that a great deal more needs to be done to improve the situation. The extent of the task ought not to be underestimated and cosmetic, superficial tinkering will not lead to improvement. Specifically, action needs to be taken on a range of fronts:

- Mathematics education of non-specialists at university level ought to be regarded as a specialized discipline in its own right. As such it should receive increased funding for research in order to build a research base so that policy decisions can be made upon sound evidence.
- There needs to be more attention paid to the findings and recommendations of studies that report on the mathematics problem. There is little evidence that such findings and recommendations inform policy decisions.
- University funding mechanisms must be changed so that it is not financial pressure that drives the decisions about ownership of mathematics teaching of non-specialists.
- There should be clearly defined criteria for the selection of staff involved in teaching mathematics to non-specialists that should include a) either a proven interest in the specific application area, or a willingness to develop this, b) an interest in the prior mathematical background of the students admitted to the course, and the ways in which their needs can best be served. The appropriate balance between use of traditional lecturing and a teaching style more akin to that found in schools needs to be investigated.
- There must be substantial and ongoing communication between those charged with teaching mathematics and the subject specialists so that both are aware of the issues, developments and difficulties.
- There needs to be much more awareness in the students' own departments about the importance of providing a well-paced mathematics curriculum that takes full account of the background of incoming students, and which does not expect students to learn and apply new mathematical techniques while they are still trying to grapple with basics.
- If access is going to continue to widen and increasingly inhomogeneous cohorts are the norm then the system needs to become much more flexible so that it can accommodate wide variations in need.
- There needs to be a concerted effort on many fronts to change the culture of learning mathematics so that instead of a chore and a hurdle to be overcome, students see it as valuable, enriching and empowering.

These will only come about with recognition from the highest levels that:

- There is a serious underlying problem.
- The status of teaching mathematics to non-specialists needs to be raised.
- Substantial resources must be made available to start to tackle these problems.

References

Croft, T (2001) Following up QAA subject assessments for non-mathematicians, *MSOR Connections*, **1**(2)

Engineering Council (1997) *Standards and Routes to Registration* (SARTOR) 3rd edn, Engineering Council, London

Gill, P N G (1999) The physics/maths problem again, *Physics Education*, **34**(2), pp 83–87

Hawkes, T and Savage, M D (eds) (2000) *Measuring the Mathematics Problem*, Engineering Council, London

Hunt, D N and Lawson, D A (1997) Common core – common sense?, in *Proceedings of the Institute of Mathematics and its Applications (IMA) Conference on the Mathematical Education of Engineers*, pp 21–25, Institute of Mathematics and its Applications, Southend-on-Sea, Essex

Institute of Mathematics and its Applications (IMA) (1995) *Mathematics Matters in Engineering*, Institute of Mathematics and its Applications, Southend-on-Sea

IMA (1999) *Engineering Mathematics Matters*, Institute of Mathematics and its Applications, Southend-on-Sea

Larcombe, P J (1998) Engineering mathematics: the crisis continues, *Engineering Science and Education Journal*, **7**(6)

Lawson, D A (1997) What can we expect of A level mathematics students?, *Teaching Mathematics and its Applications*, **16**, pp 151–56

Lawson, D A (2000) Vocational education as preparation for university engineering mathematics, *Engineering Science and Education Journal*, **9**, pp 89–92

Lawson, D A, Halpin, M and Croft, A C (2001a) *Evaluating and Enhancing the Effectiveness of Mathematics Support Centres* [Online] http://ltsn.mathstore.ac.uk/

Lawson, D A, Halpin, M and Croft, A C (2001b) *Good practice in the provision of Mathematics Support Centres*, LTSN Mathematics, Statistics and Operational Research Network, Birmingham

Quality Assurance Agency for Higher Education (QAA) (2001) *Draft Benchmarking Document for Mathematics, Statistics and Operational Research*, QAA, Bristol

Shaw, C T and Shaw, V F (1997a) A survey of the attitudes of engineering students to mathematics, in *Proceedings of the 2nd* IMA Conference on the Mathematical Education of Engineers, Loughborough

Shaw, C T and Shaw, V F (1997b) Attitudes of first-year engineering students to mathematics: a case study, *International Journal of Mathematical Education in Science and Technology*, **28**(2), pp 289–301

Shaw, C T and Shaw, V F (1999) Attitudes of engineering students to mathematics – a comparison across universities, *International Journal of Mathematical Education in Science and Technology*, **30**(1), pp 47–63

Sutherland, R and Dewhurst, H (1999) *Mathematics Education Framework for Progression from 16–19 to HE*, Graduate School of Education, University of Bristol, Bristol

Sutherland, R and Pozzi, S (1995) *The Changing Mathematical Background of Undergraduate Engineers*, The Engineering Council, London

12

Mathematical modelling skills

Stephen Hibberd

Introduction

Mathematicians in industry and commerce, and also those entering postgraduate study, are expected to possess a range of mathematical abilities from knowledge and implementation of mathematical and computational techniques to the development of mathematical skills. Within nearly all mathematics degree programmes in the UK the acquisition of subject-specific knowledge, essential IT skills, and the use of mathematical and statistical software, as well as subject-specific skills of logical thought and analysis and problem solving, are well embedded in the curriculum (Quality Assurance Agency for Higher Education, 2000). Typically, these are delivered through formal lectures supported by tutorials and/or seminars, problem classes and practical workshop sessions; while assessment is normally heavily weighted to formal examinations. Increasingly it is recognized that some variety of teaching and learning experience helps students to develop both subject-specific and transferable skills, and in many instances these can be accommodated through activities loosely grouped as 'mathematical modelling'. Associated assessments and feedback designed around project-based work, from more extensive coursework assignments through to substantial reports, can allow students to demonstrate their understanding and problem-solving abilities, and enhance both their mathematical and key skills. Often quoted attributes gained by graduates are the subject-specific, personal and transferable skills gained through a mathematics-rich degree. Increasingly, students are selecting their choice of degree to meet the flexible demands of a changing workplace and well-designed Mathematics, Statistics and Operational Research (MSOR) programmes have the potential to develop a profile of the knowledge, skills abilities and personal attributes integrated alongside the more traditional subject-specific education.

A mathematical model is typically defined as a formulation of a real-world problem phrased in mathematical terms. Application is often embedded in a typical mathematics course through providing well-defined mathematical models that can enhance learning and understanding within individual theory-based modules by adding reality and interest. A common example is in analysing predator–prey scenarios as motivation for studying the complex non-linear nature of solutions to coupled equations within a course on ordinary-differential equations; this may also extend to obtaining numerical solutions as the basis of coursework assignments. Such a model is useful in demonstrating and investigating the nature of real-world problem by giving quantitative insight, evaluation and predictive capabilities.

Other embedded applications of mathematical modelling, particularly within applied mathematics, are based around the formal development of continuum models such as are found, for example, in fluid mechanics, electromagnetism, plasma dynamics or relativity. A marked success in MSOR within recent years has been the integration of mathematics into other less traditional discipline areas of application, particularly in research, and this has naturally lead to an integration of such work into the modern mathematics curriculum through the development of mathematics models. Applied mathematics has always been a strong part of engineering and physical sciences, but now extends to modelling processes in biology, medicine, economics, financial services and many more. In addition, other branches of mathematics have been influential by providing real-world modelling capabilities, such as stochastic processes in studying epidemics, coding and cryptography for financial security, etc. In Chapter 13 we read in detail of such an approach in statistics.

Thus an important element in the mathematical knowledge base is learning how to apply mathematical and associated analytical, numerical and possibly computational techniques in order to obtain a solution to a mathematical problem. A typical goal in implementing a modelling element is to stimulate student motivation in mathematical studies through applying mathematics and demonstrating associated problem-solving capabilities. An additional feature is to provide a synoptic element that brings together mathematical ideas and techniques from differing areas of undergraduate studies, which students often meet only within individual modules. These areas, however, can be used to form the centrepiece of a much more extensive provision that leads students into a more active learning of mathematics, and an appreciation and acquisition of associated key skills. A practical difficulty in this area of study is that it is substantially based on skills (intellectual skills, practical skills and transferable skills) that are not readily taught, in, for example, a lecture/seminar environment, but are best accommodated within student-based learning activities.

This chapter identifies the range of key skills associated with mathematical modelling, together with advice on implementation and assessment aspects. Example is provided from experience of a group modelling module (Vocational Mathematics) introduced at a third-year level.

Modelling

The term 'mathematical modelling' is intimately connected to the concept of a mathematical model, but reflects more closely the higher-level interactive skills of formulating, analysing, evaluating and reporting of physical situations through the use of mathematical models. Furthermore, arising from its broad and pervading nature, the scope of problems that can be considered is enormously large. A start might be made from some simple problems based on geometrical considerations, such as identified in the project brief 'area partitioning' (see section below titled Example 1: outline brief for Area Partitioning) to initiate a discussion on problem solving in a workshop. A more demanding project brief is provided by 'optimal cooking' and would be feasible as a substantial individual final-year project. In the latter case, the level of subject-specific knowledge and maturity in the application of selection and analytic and numerical mathematical techniques is, generally, only available to proficient final-year mathematics students. Within the project 'area partitioning' the level of mathematics required to provide a credible solution technique is available to any first-year mathematics students, but the method of approach, analysis and subsequent communication needed provides a significant challenge. In common with most mathematical topics the above does highlight the fact that different levels exist. The demands and expectations of a first-year course that introduces the general concepts of modelling would be rather less than a final-year provision whose outcomes are graduate-level skills proficiency in abilities relevant to the students' impending career choices or postgraduate studies.

The general topic area of mathematical modelling is served by a wealth of texts, journal publications and reports providing experience in the detailed implementations of modelling. Three sources of particular note that provide direct advice and gateway information to other articles are:

- *Mathematical Modelling Handbook* (Townend *et al*, 1995). A handbook designed to provide initial support and guidance for lecturers new to mathematical modelling.
- *Mathematics Learning and Assessment – Sharing Innovative Practices* (Haines and Dunthorne, 1996). Developed under the HEFCE Effective Learning and Assessment Programme.
- MathSkills. A Discipline Network project aimed at facilitating the dissemination of information; this provides Web links to useful sites covering projects and key skills (see http://www.hull.ac.uk/mathskills).

The modelling process

It is informative to identify the objectives in modelling and the obstacles that may need to be overcome in seeking a solution, although this in itself will be limited by assumptions made in the context of the problem. Mathematical modelling is the process of: translating a real-world problem into a mathematically formulated representation; solving this mathematical formulation, and then interpreting the mathematical solution in a real-world context. The principal processes are about 'how to apply mathematics' and 'how to communicate the findings'. There are, however, many obstacles that can arise:

- A given problem may be complex or not readily well defined mathematically.
- A variety of mathematical formulations may exist.
- A mathematical formulation and interpretation of the mathematical results in terms of real-world quantities may be difficult.
- Solutions to realistic formulations may not exist within the framework of available mathematical techniques.
- Model predictions may not agree with real-world observations.

However, some pre-selection or detailed guidance is advisable to enable students to gain an initial threshold-level of expertise prior to exposure to a realistic real-world challenge. In general, modelling is best viewed as an open-ended, iterative exercise. This can be guided by a framework for developing the skills and expertise required together with the general principle 'solve the simple problems first', which requires some reflection on the student's own mathematical skills and competencies to identify a simple problem.

One widely accepted methodology is reproduced in Figure 12.1 in the form of a flow chart with component stages marked 1–7. Generally the process is initiated by the specification for a real-world problem (termed here a brief); this may be in the form of a detailed written specification with clear objectives or sometimes rather less, perhaps only a physical description of the problem. Almost certainly a time constraint will be relevant.

In the flow chart Stage 7 corresponds to the reporting of the results of the mathematical modelling. Stages 1 to 6 correspond to an iterative loop in which the problem can be systematically developed, starting with identifying the most relevant features of the real-world problem and the requirements of the brief. Stage 2 starts the model refinement process by evaluating the possible simplifications that can be made. This is a key stage; sufficient features must be retained to ensure the model remains relevant, however, less important (and certainly superfluous) features may need to be discarded (and possibly incorporated in the next iteration). In practice it may be useful to rank features in order of importance and start with the bare minimum. Stage 3 is akin to lecture-based applications where variables relevant to the simplified model are defined and a mathematical formulation (eg equations, boundary conditions, constitutive relations, etc) made. Stages 3 and 4 define an area of work confined to mathematical expertise and follow the more subject-specific studies of the modeller. Here advice is more readily obtainable from other mathematicians and mathematical texts. These look to provide a solution to the mathematical problem using suitable analytic, numerical and approximate mathematical techniques. In order then to obtain tractable solutions some further simplifications may be needed.

Figure 12.1   Flow chart for mathematical modelling process

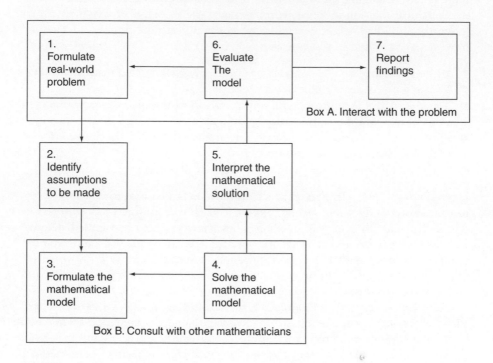

Reinterpretation of the mathematics is needed in Stage 5 to provide a link between the mathematical solutions and the requirements of the brief. This will usually involve an exploration of the results and prediction of the mathematical model checked against known problem characteristics or specified brief data. Stage 6 provides for the current model to be evaluated against the requirement of the brief. A decision can be made here as to whether further model refinement is required, and if so, what additional complexities should be next included. The final stage is the most crucial in that it relates to the measurable outcomes, either in terms of assessment for students or relevance and usefulness to any external user.

Modelling implementation

In general, modelling is a complex, interactive, multi-faceted activity based on applying mathematics. Although reliant on a knowledge of mathematical formulations and mathematical techniques, a major emphasis is typically placed upon the acquisition of other skills areas to complement subject-specific knowledge. Viewed as a skills-based activity, mathematical modelling is thus best learnt by active participation and practice. This does present additional burdens on teaching staff compared with lecture-based teaching. Increased workload in organization, preparation, monitoring, assessment and feedback should not be underestimated. Similarly, such activities are also generally acknowledged as more demanding on students.

Modelling should, ideally, be developed as an integrated activity, progressing through a degree programme in much the same way as, say, design is an integrated theme for any accredited engineering degree. The learning outcomes that can be associated with an extensive modelling provision include:

- knowledge and understanding;
- analysis;
- problem solving;
- creativity/originality;
- communication and presentation;
- evaluation;
- planning and organization;
- interactive and group skills.

Elements of modelling are introduced in many areas of mathematics programmes. The use of mathematical models in a conventional lecture-based or problem-based module provides student with motivation and awareness of the wide application of mathematics. For example, the theory associated with eigenvalues and eigenvectors is well illustrated by applications such as calculating frequencies and modes of vibration in mechanical or electrical systems. Similarly, the requirement to solve common mathematical equations, such as Laplace's equation, can be motivated by models such as those generated from the flow of an inviscid incompressible flow. These are valuable illustrations and add to the richness of applying mathematics, but are restricted in scope for the purposes of incorporating the whole modelling processes.

Undergraduate applied mathematics teaching is predominantly within Box B, as identified in Figure 12.1, in which well-defined mathematical models are formulated and methods of solution can be applied or developed. Appropriately, the emphasis usually lies on problems that can be readily solved, through the careful selection of problem geometry or boundary/initial conditions, in order to focus on the subject-specific knowledge and skills. Correspondingly, within mathematical modelling exercises, it is working within Box B that students are most at ease with, although the realization that all problems may not be as readily solvable as coursework or examination problems is enlightening.

A key requirement for a successful modelling module is that students possess sufficient subject-specific knowledge in which to operate. For a realistic expectation that students will be able to grasp the recursive elements of mathematical modelling and the wider skills base, it is advisable to concentrate on the application of existing mathematical knowledge rather than to expect students to learn new mathematical techniques. Correspondingly the level of the module and the level of projects identified, and of the expectation (deliverables) within the project outcomes, must be well matched. The sophistication of problems that can be addressed and delivered, however, can be increased through making the modelling activities a group activity. This also has the significant advantage of providing a platform for introducing team-working skills.

Modelling skills

A major emphasis in any mathematical modelling provision should be placed on developing skills and on communicating ideas. This accords well with the demands of graduates and their employers. There are innumerable studies that have produced lists of graduate attributes desired by employers and their ranking (see, for example, Harvey, Moon and Geall, 1997; Graduate Employment and Training Report, 1998). A general pattern has emerged that great similarities exist across discipline boundaries, employment sectors and international boundaries. Highly regarded skills are those of communication, teamworking, problem solving, leadership, numeracy, self-confidence, willingness to learn and flexibility. These accord well with the natural outcomes of a significant mathematical modelling provision. A modest survey (Kopp and Higgins, 1997), undertaken to identify the needs of employers who might be expected to employ mathematics graduates with quite high levels of skills, identified the importance of placing a greater emphasis on mathematical modelling. Below are three classifications of skills that may be directly attributed to a significant mathematical modelling provision.

Process skills:

- The understanding, formulation, evaluation and refinement of mathematical models.
- Reading and comprehension of mathematical articles/papers.
- The selection and use of mathematical techniques.
- The physical interpretation of mathematical solutions.

Presentation skills:

- The interpretation and communication of mathematical ideas to peers; oral communication, information selection and presentation.
- Report writing skills.
- Integrated use of IT.

Management/personal skills:

- Group working skills (organization, delegation, etc).
- Time management, project planning.

The range is impressive and demonstrates that much can be going on besides learning an increased base of mathematical knowledge. Of equal importance is that many of these skills are readily transferable to other discipline areas and readily mapped to desirable graduate attributes.

Structuring modelling

The variety of possible demands required to implement a modelling module, and the associated mathematical and non-mathematical skills, mean that the module learning outcomes need to be realistically identified. A pragmatic approach is to consider structuring a provision at more than one level.

An introductory modelling module (Year 1 or 2)

An important element in an introductory module is to provide a basic training in two broad areas. First, to develop modelling skills in mathematics, perhaps by bringing together some of the taught mathematical theory from other modules and providing first-hand experience 'applying' mathematics. Second, to develop the more general key skills, such as an ability to communicate mathematical ideas clearly and effectively. This will be typically implemented through expectation of a written technical report and possibly a short oral presentation. There is also considerable merit in structuring the module to have a strong element of group working activity to facilitate peer-level discussion and sharing expertise and the workload.

A set of learning outcomes for students might be to have an appreciation of:

- The general principles of mathematical modelling.
- Studying open-ended problems that involve model refinement, explanation and reporting.
- Using analytical and numerical techniques and applying them appropriately.
- Evaluating mathematical argument and adapting them to project requirements.
- Working in a team.
- Writing and presenting project reports.

It is important not to expect or demand too much – the above corresponds to a restricted list of mathematical modelling skills – also the mathematical techniques needed should be familiar to the students. Like all skill-based learning, it is practice, support and feedback that are the essential elements, and such a module should provide several projects, tutorial support and provision for detailed feedback. In using then several projects scope exists to provide projects of different complexity (and length) and varying reporting mechanisms, such as written or oral reports either as individuals or as groups.

A main emphasis must be placed on student activity. Supported information relating to communication and presentation of mathematics and of group working skills should be provided together with illustrative examples of example models. It may also be appropriate to encourage IT elements, such as the use of appropriate word-processing package and mathematical software. The latter will help solve mathematical problems analytically or numerically that are too difficult by hand (a realistic expectation), to check answers derived by hand, or to plot graphs to help evaluate the mathematics and to use them in project reports.

Project briefs at a first level are readily available within numerous texts, for example, Townend *et al* (1995), De Mestre (1990) and Bedford and Fowler (1996). Examples at a mathematically straightforward level include projectile flights, ski-jumping, sport throws, growth of a single species, bungee jumping and drug absorption. Topics that require either more proficiency in calculus, linear algebra, etc, or more subtleties in modelling, are provided by projects on coupled oscillators, pursuit curves, predator–prey scenarios, spread of epidemics, sport jumps and population interactions. The majority of these projects tends to be orientated, perhaps naturally, towards physical problems. The provision of non-physical examples tends to be artificial. However, with some ingenuity these can be couched in a real-world context (see section 9). It should be emphasized that the scope to provide any in-depth study, extensive model refinements or key skills attainment at graduate level remains limited.

Advanced modelling module (Year 3 or 4)

Anyone who has been involved with modelling significant real-world problems will know how difficult it is to obtain realistic model solutions to proposed problems in terms of simple tractable mathematics. Modelling of such problems is therefore only approachable to students, following the framework detailed in Figure 12.1, once they have an advanced mathematical capability, typically only attained by Year 3 or 4. The knowledge requirement would typically include a variety of analytical mathematical techniques (advanced calculus, linear algebra, mechanics, probability and statistics), numerical methods and some familiarity with the applications of mathematics to physical situations. Also required are IT skills, including computing, advanced use of mathematical software packages such as Maple, Matlab or Mintab, and presentation aids. Furthermore, the increased maturity of students and their, perhaps, increasing realization of the necessity of securing a career path or route to postgraduate study should be met by anticipating their need to gain an increased facility with enhanced transferable skills.

A target collection of learning outcomes may be based on students reaching towards an enhanced appreciation of a subset of the following:

- the application of mathematical modelling;
- studying open-ended problems that involve model refinement, explanation and reporting;
- defining a strategy for the solution of problem(s) of a non-routine nature;
- selecting analytical and computational techniques and applying them appropriately;
- planning, organizing, directing and controlling project tasks;
- evaluating mathematical argument and adapting them to project requirements;
- writing and presenting project reports;

- working effectively in a team;
- working independently;
- using IT effectively.

Implementation at the higher level can be as an extended development from an earlier introductory modelling module, while scope exists to add additional elements that might include a wider range of assessments, greater student autonomy, etc. One approach adopted for two specialized BSc/MMath courses at Nottingham is to introduce a compulsory group project modelling module in Year 3 (Vocational Mathematics), which is outlined later as a case study. MMath students proceed to take a substantial individual project in Year 4.

At this advanced level, students should be capable of operating within the whole modelling framework. They should be able to cope with an 'open-ended' problem, not readily defined in mathematical terms, and delivery within a specified time-frame. In reality, this will involve gross simplification to provide scope for analytic work, supplemented by computation or advanced use of software packages for less simplistic models. The sophistication of the modelling will be restricted by the analytical and calculational techniques within the student's toolbox of available skills. Any written report should conform to a professional standard with due regard to structure, content, results and adequate discussion and conclusions; it should also be well presented. If an oral presentation is relevant then the selection and display of project material should be appropriate and presented in a professional manner.

Individual project (Year 3 or 4)

A common practice in most mathematics undergraduate courses is that students undertake a substantial project module. This provides a useful framework for students to be involved with modelling activities and to experience an in-depth study of a problem. The project brief is often related to staff research or scholarship interests and builds on the interrelation between research and teaching activities. The specific development of modelling skills, identified above, depends on the detailed implementation of the module, the instruction provided and its modes of assessment. Comprehensive modelling skills are not achievable *de facto* simply because students undertake a project. A poor scenario is that a student is provided with a project brief, over-detailed instructions on the project development, and little guidance on construction and presentation of reporting. This provides little in the way of modelling development and little scope to improve on key skills attainment. More structured ways can be introduced to enable students to learn and practice skills through including the provision of interim reports, learning diaries, inclusion of oral presentations, poster presentations, etc.

Assessment and feedback

The assessment of mathematical modelling work is an integral part of the modelling provision, as the form and criteria for assessment will have a significant impact on the priority of activities undertaken by the students. If assessment is predominantly restricted to assessing the mathematical content of a written report then students will be encouraged to divide their time proportionately and provide an extensive dissertation, with scant regard to the quality of presentation, structure, etc, of the text. In directing the students' activities it is equally important to provide them with explicit assessment criteria and feedback at critical points, as this sets a level of expectation and threshold standards.

Project assessment

The most common form of assessment for modelling is through written and oral project reports. An important aspect is that procedures relevant to the assessment of any component should be transparent to all involved, and that the assessment processes should be fair and unbiased. The transparency of procedures can be realized by providing information to assessors and students. Equitable treatment of students can be derived from independent assessments of each project-related aspect of the student performance, wherever possible.

In assessing the reports consideration can usefully be given to four aspects, as indicated in Table 12.1.

The precise assessment criteria, marking scheme and weighting of components depend upon the chosen module objectives. With reference to suitable criteria templates, items 1–3 can correspond to objective measures agreed by independent assessors. Inevitably, the assessment item 4 requires input predominantly from the project supervisor and has an understandably greater subjective element.

Group assignments

A possible area of anxiety when dealing with group assignments is the necessity to distribute the available marks among members of the group to reflect the contribution each member has made to the overall performance. This can be overcome by requesting students to complete individual written reports and/or oral presentations. This has obvious advantages in ensuring each student has a distinctive outcome, but concerns remain about the practicalities of identifying their 'individual' contribution to the development of the group project. A practical and informative approach is to require each group to indicate (peer assessment) the proportionate size of contribution of each member of the group (scaling factor). The inclusion of peer assessment after the group activity helps to enhance the overall teamwork aspects by enforcing mutual reflection on how the group achieved its outcomes. Decisions may be informed by requiring each group member to keep a log of group activities. Criteria for discriminating that might be borne in mind are given in Table 12.2.

Table 12.1 Criteria for assessment of projects

1. Content (the work)	The formulation of the problem in modelling terms; the formation of mathematical models; the selection and use of mathematical facts, concepts and techniques; the correctness and complexity of the mathematics used; the provision of results; physical interpretation of results and corresponding analysis and conclusions; communication of mathematical ideas; evaluation and self-criticism of the work undertaken; quality and quantity of the work; and relevance to the project objectives.
2. Written report	Clarity and coherence of the structure; quality of the presentation with respect to English, sentence structure, grammar and spelling; use of diagrams, appendices and references; appropriate weighting of relevant sections; and appropriate use of word-processing and graphical utilities.
3. Oral report	Content and structure in relation to the project; method(s) of approach, results and conclusions; choice, coherence and cohesion of topics presented; effective delivery (eg clear slides, well-paced delivery, emphasis of key points, appropriate vocabulary and explanation); and impact and interactivity with the audience
4. The individual (or group)	Planning (eg ability to organize, plan and progress the project work); initiative; and insight and originality

Experience suggests that for most groups the inclusion of peer assessment tends to provide a culture that most group members participate in equitably, and this can be reinforced by provision of suitable self-assessment materials. However, it is inevitable that for a minority of groups, the activity will be compromised by one or more members. Such an outcome is a realistic consequence of group dynamics and therefore part of the experience of group working. Providing a suitable complementary assessment mechanism is in place this should not cause undue concern. As with most project work the spread mark tends to be restricted to a narrower band than for marks from examination. However, the inclusion of peer assessment does promote a greater discrimination. If any submission does not have a full agreement then an arbitrator can subsequently request all group members to complete a confidential peer-assessment evaluation form and may arrange to viva the project group collectively and/or individually.

Feedback

An important element in the enhancement of skills acquisition is the provision of a clear set of assessment and grading criteria, and detailed feedback on each aspect. Feedback can be given effectively in terms of profile grades (eg A–E) and also written comment based on prepared feedback templates. Examples are given below.

Table 12.2 Criteria for assessing group assignments

Effort	How much effective work has each student put into the project (this should not be confused with time spent).
Ability	Proportion of the student's ability in the project, assessed for initiative, decisiveness, ability to distinguish essentials from non-essentials, persistence, determination and judgement.
Mathematical	Assess the student's contribution in providing mathematical and/or computational components.
Management	Assess the student's part in the planning and development of the project.
Presentation	The student's contribution to the production and delivery of reports.
Group skills	Assess the student's ability to work effectively with other members of the group.

Assessment/feedback criteria for a group oral presentation:

- Content: the basic requirements for the presentation is a description of the project, the method(s) of approach, achievements and a discussion of results.
- Structure: assessors will look at the way the presentation has been organized and the choice of an appropriate mode of delivery. The choice, coherence and cohesion of the presentation topics will be scrutinized. An effective report should include well-reasoned arguments and make clear conclusions that are logically derived and can be substantiated.
- Clarity: assessors will wish that the presentation is targeted at a level and with sufficient clarity to be understandable to a general audience, which includes the module participants and possibly external (non-mathematical) guests. Effective delivery would also include clear indications of topic transitions and emphasis of key points. Slides or transparencies should be well set out with clear headings, and diagrams or figures clearly drawn and labelled.
- Impact: assessors will wish to witness an awareness of timing and an appropriately paced delivery together with the appropriate use of visual aids. An effective delivery would include appropriate vocabulary and explanation, varied rhythm and intonation of speech and the use of pauses. Speakers should fully gain the attention of the audience, make good eye-contact with them and exhibit enthusiasm and interest.
- Interactivity: assessors will want to see an appropriate level of interaction between group members and the audience during the presentation, with smooth handovers between speakers. Group members would be expected to respond spontaneously to questions raised in the discussion. Questions should be clearly and concisely answered with appropriate support and/or secondary answers from other group members.

The choice of relatively few criteria is appropriate in the context of a short (10–15 minute) oral presentation. A corresponding grading classification criteria should be associated with each aspect that can be reasonably used within the restricted timeframe of the presentation; more detailed analysis is feasible later if the presentations are videotaped. An example of one aspect is provided for illustration, based on a good performance judged as a grade 'C'. Grades above or /below this should be fully justified in written comments to the student.

Contents:

- Grade C. Provides a clear description of the project objectives. Shows evidence of a clear model development and demonstrates in-depth understanding for some of the results obtained. The content is mathematically sound.
- Grade B. A presentation that excels in at least one attribute and displays most but not all of the attributes of a Grade A.
- Grade A. Develops the project showing an authoritative grasp of the concepts. Demonstrates clear evidence of additional reading and detailed understanding and relevance of the substantial results obtained. Mathematical arguments are well established and developed in a logical and coherent manner.
- Grade D. A presentation that covers the basic requirements of a C grade but which lacks sufficient understanding and interpretation of the concepts expected of a C grade. The presentation demonstrates an informed use of mathematics, but with some errors, uncertainties or omissions.
- Grade E. Displays some knowledge of the project objectives. Offers some kind of model development. The mathematical content may contain serious mathematical errors.

A similar mechanism can be used for assessing and providing useful feedback for written reports, although more in-depth scrutiny of the mathematical detail is possible and subsequently more criteria can give greater objectivity to assessment, reflect the usually greater project assessment and give more helpful feedback to the author. The criteria and grading should be matched to the mathematical modelling provision and should adequately reflect the portfolio of skills and the synoptic use of the mathematics required.

A case study: Vocational Mathematics

A compulsory third-year mathematical modelling module, 'Vocational Mathematics', has been introduced at Nottingham University. Students work in groups of three or four on a succession of three projects to help them develop a strong skills base in applying and communicating mathematical problem solving at a graduate level. Organization of the module is coordinated to include general plenary sessions on communication skills, group skills, and modelling skills within project workshops. Projects briefs are informed by an external industrial consultant who had many years experience of graduate recruitment and project development. As a final-year exercise, student groups are expected to function with less staff-directed study than is normally associated with an individual project, with greater autonomy, within a shorter timeframe, and provide 'professional'-quality oral and written reports.

A major focus is on students interpreting a physical problem from a brief, such as given below, and to progress towards 'deliverables', ie a general description of targets. Each student is required to be involved with three group projects. The focus for the first project is to establish practices for group working and to arrive at a written report and oral presentation within a tight time constraint. Consequently the project briefs are generally based at an elementary mathematical level. The second set of projects looks to extend the modelling capability by increasing the mathematical complexity and to add some element of 'competition' (the same project brief was given to more than one group). The final project introduces a more mathematically demanding problem with expectation of incorporating more activity based around the full modelling cycle.

Each project is assessed as a group and individual marks assigned according to the peer-agreed scaling. A detailed assessment grade profile, together with constructive written comments, is supplied to each group for both the oral and written reports. Oral presentations are videotaped so that each student group can analyse their individual performance later. Groups are encouraged, and do, attend and participate in the oral presentations and are also involved through giving their assessments.

Students are asked at the start of the module to complete a self-assessment questionnaire to gauge perception of their abilities in four key skills areas and to respond to 17 questions on detailed aspects of these skills. The *same* questionnaire is used after the final assessment to monitor changes; students are asked to identify themselves so that a direct comparison can be made student-by-student. A summary of the results for the Session 1999–2000 is given in Table 12.3, corresponding to categories of response 'very confident' or 'fairly confident' (in comparison with categories 'not very confident' or 'not at all confident').

At the start of the module the students' initial perception levels in the keys skills were generally very high even though they had personally experienced few of these elements within their previous studies at Nottingham. The least confidence was associated with making an oral presentation. At the end of the module all students felt confident in three key skills areas and more students felt confident in making oral presentations. Detailed analysis of the changes in perception available from the pairs of questionnaire responses also confirm a significant increase in totals from 'fairly confident' to 'very confident', together with the increases from 'not confident' to 'confident'. Interestingly, some student's responses decreased, highlighting the nature of the module in giving student first-hand experience of these key skills, after which their perception was in better accord with their actual abilities.

Table 12.3 Percentages of cohort self-assessing as 'very confident' or 'fairly confident' for four key skills at the start and end of an academic year

	Start	End
writing a mathematical report	75%	100%
making an oral presentation	55%	72%
contributing to group discussions	95%	100%
working as part of a team	100%	100%

Example 1: outline brief for Area Partitioning

Suppose that you are working for a software house that wishes to develop a range of products for commercial use by various professions. Your brief is to develop a strategy to partition a given area of land into smaller plots of equal area (but not necessarily of equal shape) such that the total length of the boundary between the partitioned areas is a minimum. This application would be of general use to architects and town planners in the allocation of housing plots, to farmers in dividing up fields for crops or grazing, and so on. In order for the software to be of commercial value, it needs to be able to deal with any shape of external boundary. A set of 'deliverables' will be provided as essentially tests to explore your capabilities to address this task.

Example 2: outline brief for Optimal Cooking

A hi-tech company, specializing in providing technical devices for the gastronomy market, wishes to develop a new range of 'intelligent' ovens, in which the heating process acting upon particular items of food is optimized. The ovens incorporate temperature sensors and built-in computers to control the heating process. In each case, the 'chef' has to specify the item of food involved, its weight and how 'well-done' the food is to be cooked. The company has sub-contracted a software house to provide a suite of programs for different purposes. You are required to act as a consultant to the software house by deriving the mathematical solutions for a number of 'test' cases of practical interest, in terms of various parameters that can be specified by the user.

Conclusion

Mathematical modelling comprises a predominantly skills-based activity that majors on problem solving and communication skills, but also links together elements of mathematical theory and techniques. An emphasis on examining problems outside a more standard mathematical formulation and experience in tackling 'open-ended' problems, provides students with a valuable opportunity to consolidate their mathematical understanding and learn the generic skills required in many graduate careers. As a skill-rich activity it is important to provide a supportive framework of instruction, individual support and constructive feedback. Assessment plays a key role in focusing the students' priorities and providing feedback. As a consequence, implementation of modelling activities requires significant planning and resources, but examples of good practice and specimen materials exist. The gains of integrating modelling are, however, important in providing enrichment of the programme curriculum and promoting active learning methods in mathematics. Furthermore, modelling activities typically lead to increased student enthusiasm for mathematics, improved student attainment in mathematical and key skills, and give insight to postgraduate research studies.

References

Bedford, A and Fowler, W (1996) *Dynamics*, Addison-Wesley, Boston, Mass

De Mestre, N (1990) *The Mathematics of Projectiles in Sport*, Cambridge University Press, Cambridge

Graduate Employment and Training (GET) (1998), *Graduate Employment and Training Report*, Hobsons

Haines, C and Dunthorne, S (1996) *Mathematics Learning and Assessment: Sharing innovative practices*, Edward Arnold, London

Harvey, L, Moon, S and Geall, V (1997) *Graduates Work: Organisational change and students' attributes*, Centre for Research into Quality, University of Central England, Birmingham

Kopp, E and Higgins, D (1997) What do employers want? *Mathskills Newsletter* 3

Murray, J D (1989) *Mathematical Biology*, Springer-Verlag, New York

Quality Assurance Agency for Higher Education (QAA) (2000), *Subject Overview Report: Mathematics, Statistics and Operational Research*, Report No. QO7/2000, QAA, Bristol

Townend, M S *et al* (1995) *Mathematical Modelling Handbook – A tutor guide*, Undergraduate Mathematics Teaching Conference (UMTC) Workshop Series, Sheffield Hallam University Press, Sheffield

13

Ideas for improving learning and teaching of statistics

Neville Davies

Introduction

During the year 2000 teachers of statistics in UK higher education (HE) were asked about their needs to enhance their teaching skills so that, in due course, the learning experience of their students could be enhanced. From the results of this information-gathering exercise, and using evidence from elsewhere, I discuss in this chapter some ideas on how learning and teaching standards in statistics could be raised. A summary of the feedback from the statistical community, which can be viewed at the Web site www.mathstore.ac.uk, was reported in Learning and Teaching Support Network (LTSN) Mathematics, Statistics and Operational Research (OR) Newsletter (February 2000).

Experience suggests that it is not a straightforward matter to convince statistical colleagues of the value of new ideas, especially when the proverbial expression 'grandmother sucking eggs' pervades. Indeed, new approaches to convincing users of statistics, namely students and employers, of the value of the subject may be needed as well, especially given the recent decline in the number of students opting to study the subject in the UK, and the number of mathematics departments that have been closed, absorbed and/or 're-profiled' over the last 10 to 15 years.

Paradoxically, statistics is a relatively young subject, and has been at the forefront of embracing technology, especially with the wide availability of software packages that enable very rapid processing of large of amounts of data. However, simply having the use of a software package does not mean that statistical learning takes place.

The role of technology in teaching most subjects in HE has increased in importance, but there is little objective evidence that there is substantial learning gain for
students when this method of communicating or teaching dominates, or even acts
as substitute for more traditional methods of delivery. In my experience the technological side of teaching many subjects in HE has been over-emphasized. Part of
the problem stems from the headlong rush for e-delivery of material, rather than
taking a more considered view of its worth by evaluating the appropriate
e-learning that takes place. Pedagogical research, even in statistics, is not common,
and yet the subject itself is essential for the evaluation of different technological
and traditional approaches to teaching all subjects. The use of the methodology of
statistics to provide evidence for the best balance of the use of technology against
other methods for learning statistics is overdue.

One problem that we face in the statistics profession is that it is well accepted
that learning and researching statistics are scholarly activities, while teaching the
subject has never been regarded in the same way. Indeed, the UK Research
Assessment exercises (RAE) of 1992 and 1996 were never comfortable with the
place of statistical education in the subject of statistics. The creation of 24 subject
centres for higher education in the UK in 2000 under the LTSN initiative was,
perhaps, the first step on the long path to achieving due recognition for teaching
those subjects. The LTSN Mathematics, Statistics and OR Network has, as one of
its aims, the achievement of 'the parity of esteem between research and teaching'.

Related to this, it is clear that teachers of statistics are members of two disciplines, namely their own subject and, more generally, the teaching profession.
Bringing the two closer together has been a difficult task, with publications in the
education area not being highly regarded from the subject-specific RAE point of
view. There are publications that attempt to address the problem. For example, a
relatively new journal *Research and Innovation in Learning and Teaching* publishes
research in the area of scholarship in learning and teaching. Also the Institute for
Learning and Teaching (ILT) National Annual Teaching Fellowship awards give
some recognition to the teaching profession.

The integration of technology into mainstream teaching has not been as fast as
the use of it as an add-on to the activity. Some subjects have embraced the technology for learning wholeheartedly, others less so. For many years in learning and
teaching statistics, increasingly sophisticated software, generally used to ease the
burden of calculation, has been readily available. However, as has already been
alluded to, this technology and software do not necessarily help to optimize the
learning of the subject.

In an important book Laurillard (1993) urged university teachers to develop a
framework for the effective use of technology. The author suggests many practical
ways that teachers in universities can harness technology for the improved learning
of students. Few subjects, apparently, could not benefit from at least some use of
technology in teaching and learning. However, even though Laurillard advocates
formative evaluation of technological and innovative ways of teaching, a scientific
approach, using designed and properly analysed studies, is seen as 'time

consuming'. The author is not concerned with improved performance, but rather with improving performance (Laurillard, 1993: 247).

Since the beginning of 2000 a large number of books have appeared on the market that give advice on a wide range of topics for the improvement of performance in teaching by teachers, and learning by learners. Among the most recent are Fallows and Steven (2000), Cropley (2001), Forsyth (2001) and Jolliffe, Ritter and Stevens (2001). These books are mostly generic, and not subject-specific. In this chapter I take a subject-specific view of some new approaches that teachers of statistics may find useful in trying to improve their delivery of the subject. In particular this chapter proposes that we can improve both learning and teaching statistics by using and extending new ideas originating from:

- Taking on board evidence from research into how students best learn statistics.
- Listening and responding to the statistical community.
- Using real data in innovative ways.
- Using crafted material for teaching developed from simulation methods.
- Engaging more effectively with the main users of statistics, both in universities and the workplace.
- Evaluating the effectiveness of new methods of teaching statistics.
- Attempting to move away from assessment-based teaching to one that helps deeper, longer-lasting learning.
- Being ready to learn from recognized good practice from colleagues and peers.
- Being realistic and pragmatic about the different depth and breadth of knowledge that can be learnt by students with an increased range of mathematical and intellectual ability.

Responding to the UK higher education statistics community

The LTSN Mathematics, Statistics and OR Network has a number of aims and objectives. These include:

- Raising the profile of learning and teaching statistics and OR, eventually to be on a par with traditional research activities as regarded by panels for the Research Assessment Exercise.
- Establishing a UK-wide learning and teaching community in statistics and OR.
- Making a difference in learning and teaching statistics and OR that will benefit students.

Within the area of statistics, the Network (at the end of 2000) invited all teachers of statistics and OR in UK HE institutions to participate in, and contribute, to the debate, by, *inter alia*, asking them what they wanted to see happen. This was achieved through running a series of five regional workshops across the UK. Among a majority of those who responded and attended, the most popular request was for exemplar data-based material for routine use by themselves as teachers and their students. In particular the Network was asked to provide realistic data-driven scenarios, useful to both groups of teachers who need easy access to good practice-type teaching material, and students so that they could benefit from being able to learn more effectively. A Web-based random data selector that we are designing and writing, and which is described in the section below on the innovative use of real data, provides a useful tool to create such learning and teaching material.

Other requests, which will be addressed in due course over the next few years, are reported by Davies (2001). The following is the full list of items identified after the consultation process:

- Identification of champions of good practice.
- Material to improve teaching and learning, especially to make it more dynamic.
- Who does diagnostic testing: where and what is its availability?
- A catalogue of resources, including a list of electronic Web-based resources with comments and gradings, links to books, articles, etc.
- Web-based tutorial-type material, for example the use of Statistical Education through Problem Solving (STEPS) modules in teaching.
- Good practice in the use of remote access-type student learning and teaching.
- Good assessment practice.
- Examples of case studies or projects, including the corresponding data, and use with packages such as Minitab and Excel in service courses.
- 'What is being used in teaching?' A search machine is needed to find individual topics, especially a catalogue of applets.
- Sources of data associated with projects.
- What are the methods that should be used to attract people to want to teach statistics.
- The list of university contacts should be distributed to everyone.
- Connecting and involving the many teachers of statistics who are attached to non-mathematics and statistics departments.
- Reach out and help service teaching.
- How do we deal with:
  - a wide range of mathematical backgrounds for beginning students;
  - large classes with a wide range of ability?
- Need for good service course examples, especially data sets with teaching tips.
- Create graphical explanation of concepts for advanced/honours-level students.
- What can we do about helping staff development for new lecturers?

How students learn statistics

Statistics is often regarded as being difficult to understand, especially by non-specialist students of the subject. However, since society is being increasingly exposed to more and more data across a broad range of disciplines, it is vitally important that people involved in those disciplines get at least a basic understanding of what variability means. For many an appreciation of how that variability within their subject area can be managed is vital for success.

Very often there will be just one opportunity to learn statistics, and this is usually at school or HE level. It is therefore very important for teachers of statistics, whether specialist statisticians or other subject experts who teach it within their own curriculum area, to know how best to approach teaching the subject. Indeed they should recognize that even when teaching a basic level of statistics material students of different subjects could need a different approach to learning such material. Research into the optimal and best-balanced approach to teaching different client groups has not been undertaken, but on a generic level a number of papers have been written. The most influential of these was published just six years ago.

In a wide-ranging paper, Garfield (1995) reported results of a scientific study of how some students best learn statistics. *Inter alia*, she concluded that the following five scenarios needed to be part of the learning environment so that students could get the optimal learning gain for the subject:

- Activity and small group work.
- Testing and feedback on misconceptions.
- Comparing reality with predictions.
- Computer simulations.
- Software that allows interaction.

The above five points are looked at in detail in the paper, but rather than expand on them I shall now discuss how using carefully crafted data sets can bring these key teaching issues together.

When the mathematical foundations of statistics are being studied, it is often necessary to indulge in deep and esoteric theorem-driven aspects of the subject. However, many experienced teachers of statistics have the view that the glue that binds all the above five scenarios together are data, and it is *that* that should be stressed in many statistics courses, especially those delivered to non-specialist students of the subject. Even so, some scholars advocate that, at the same time as teaching data handling, probability concepts must be taught as well, and as early as possible (see, for example, Lindley, 2001, who cogently argues that even at school level, probability concepts should be taught). Others observe that probability is such a difficult and sophisticated topic to teach properly that its treatment should be left until the later stages of a student's statistical education (see, for example, Moore and McCabe, 1998). The pedagogic evidence is scant.

Mathematics can, and often has to be, the tireless tool for some applications, but for motivating students and enhancing understanding of the need for statistics, a data–driven approach to learning is often the key to success. My experience is that non–specialist students of the subject respond to realistic data-based scenarios (see, for example, Bowman *et al*, 1998). Further evidence that teachers of the subject want this approach is provided by many of the requests that we received, following the staff workshops we ran from October to November 2000. Many requests were for easily accessible and relevant data.

There are many Web sites that allow free download of data sets (see www.research.ed.asu.edu/siip/webdata, for example). However, few of them provide 'value-added' to the data they provide. By 'value-added' I mean educational material suitable for learning and teaching over and above the raw data on its own. One book that has been a great success with providing data to teachers of statistics in recent years is Hand *et al* (1994), and although hints on using each data set are given, a good deal of work still needs to be done for specific use in statistics classes. The book by Cox and Snell (1982) also gives a detailed analysis of some data sets, but is rather specialized.

These books, apparently, do not go far enough in providing teachers of statistics with ready-to-use material for teaching the subject to students of statistics at all levels. In the next section I describe our plans to help provide value-added to data sets, using the Internet, from databases of real data, but augmented with easily usable tools that will enable teachers of statistics to generate student worksheets, projects and, where appropriate, teacher solutions to them, crafted and delivered using only a Web browser.

Innovative use of real data

As well as a discipline in its own right, statistics is the science of doing most other subjects and, consequently, at some stage data will need to be collected for and on behalf of each of those subjects. This could comprise primary and/or secondary data. When we consulted the statistics community of teachers in HE institutions, they expressed a need for exemplar data-based material for routine use by themselves and their students. We were asked to provide realistic scenarios, useful to both the teacher for good practice teaching material and students for effective learning material. The Web-based random data selector, described below, provides us with a useful tool to create such learning and teaching material.

We now show how easy it is to cast learning activities into meaningful contexts from a real data set we have collected from a survey of schools in the UK. We have stored the data on a database that can be scrutinized and accessed by anyone with access to a Web browser.

Using the Web-based random data selector

In this section we illustrate how easy it is to access the database, take a random sample of up to 200 responses and carry out simple analyses, either using paper-based methods or standard and widely available computer software. Figure 13.1 shows the entry page to the random data selector, which can be accessed from the results and analysis page on the *CensusAtSchool* Web site (www.censusatschool.ntu.ac.uk).

Figure 13.1   Entry page to random data selector

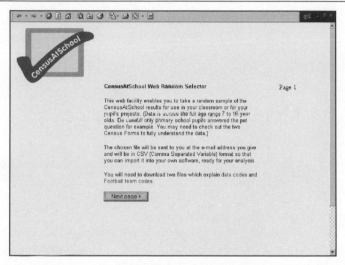

The sequence of instructions on the Web pages that follow allows the user to take a sample from our national database and get the comma separated variable (CSV) file of the data e-mailed back to the user's own address. This file can then be imported into a spreadsheet or specialist statistical software package for analysis.

The diagram in Figure 13.2 is a screen snap of such a CSV file that has been returned as an attachment to an e-mail sent to a user-specified address, after it has been read into an Excel spreadsheet.

The spreadsheet illustrated in Figure 13.2 shows the responses to a simple questionnaire that has been administered to schools in the UK. The data comprise a random sample of size 100 from the East Midlands area in the national database held in the UK. The data can be used at all levels of teaching in school and at different HE levels too. For example, if the learning outcome for a lesson/seminar is knowledge of (linear) relationships between two measured variables, a first step can be to investigate the scatter plot of the data. The following Excel graph of foot size versus height, in centimetres, of the 100 East Midlands pupils has the potential of producing some useful classroom exercises and discussions. For example, at an introductory, or non-specialist level, a student could be asked to interpret the individually produced and unique-to-that-student graph:

Figure 13.2   Typical data sample in spreadsheet form

key stage	gender	dob	year group	place of b	height	foot size	football te	mobile	computer	inter...
2	M	19/01/1990	6	1	144	23		0	1	
3	M	14/10/1988	7	1	132	21	1	0	1	
3	F	18/05/1989	7	1	145	21	49	0	1	
2	F	24/12/1989	6	1	138	20		0	0	0
2	M	12/12/1990	5	2	149	20		0	1	1
2	F	18/04/1991	5	1	137	24		0	1	0
3	M	05/11/1986	9	1	160	24	81	0	1	1
3	F	05/06/1986	10	1	164	22	53	0	1	1
3	F	03/08/1989	7	1	152	25	21	0	1	1
2	F	15/09/1991	4	1	150	20		0	0	0
2	F	26/10/1991	4	1	135	19		1	1	0
3	F	28/01/1989	7	1	154	21	45	1	1	1
3	F	18/08/1986	10	1	157	24	1	1	1	1
2	M	11/02/1990	6	1	154	22		1	1	1
3	F	07/06/1985	11	1	165	22	0	1	1	1
2	F	15/11/1992	3	1	132	21		0	1	0
2	F	20/07/1991	5	1	133	21		0	1	1
3	F	03/03/1986	10	1	160	22	6	1	1	0
3	M	12/05/1985	11	1	190	26.5	49	1	1	1
2	F	08/05/1993	3	1	131	21		0	1	1
2	M	12/03/1993	3	1	124	18		0	1	1
2	M	12/01/1990	6	1	155	24		0	1	1
3	M	06/07/1988	8	1	157	22	53	1	1	1

1. Describe the graph in three simple sentences.
2. Use the Excel spreadsheet, in electronic or paper form, to investigate the other characteristics of the two responses that correspond to: height = 113 cm, foot size = 18 cm; height = 155 cm, foot size = 30 cm.
3. Decide whether the pairs of values in point 2 are typical or a-typical of the whole data set.

To extend the project and exercises associated with data of this kind, further tasks could be to:

● Using primary data, collect similar measurements of both variables from pupils in local schools, and make graphical comparisons with this and other samples of data from the *CensusAtSchool* database.
● Using secondary data, make graphical comparisons between scatter graphs of random samples taken from different regions of the UK (up to 13 regions are defined within the database).

As an extension, for students who need a little more specialism, we might be interested in getting them to understand the concept of modelling the relationship between foot size and height. In this case a good starting point could be, after looking at and interpreting the graph, to carry out a simple linear regression of the former variable on the latter. Even if the basic modelling concepts have been

Figure 13.3 Graphical representation of data

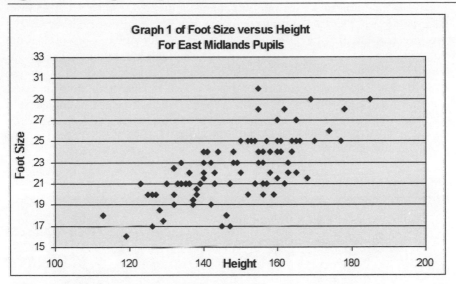

taught, if a computer package were used for the routine calculations the computer output would need to be interpreted. That output would have varying degrees of complexity, depending upon the particular software package used, and the sophistication of the underpinning methods to produce all the output may not have been taught. It is often a challenge for a HE teacher to get the students to filter off and, indeed, sometimes ignore, the more advanced and often irrelevant parts of the output. At a more advanced level again, the census data could be used to exemplify the (negative) correlation between slope and intercept estimates in simple linear regression, or the sampling distribution of these estimates, if results from many different random samples were pooled across a class.

In the next section we describe a Web-based system that we are designing, using the random data selector, to enable teachers of statistics to generate student worksheets, projects and, where appropriate, teacher solutions to them, crafted and delivered using only the Web browser.

Worksheet, project and solution creator

When the UK statistical community was consulted over their needs for enhancing their teaching in the future, a popular request to help to do this was that routine worksheets, using real data, should be made available for teaching at all levels. We have embarked on a long-term project that will help to do this.

We give an example, motivated by the need to teach ideas behind the use of simple linear regression to a wide range of student ability, which uses a version of the Web-based random data selector described in the section on the innovative use of real data. In doing so we demonstrate the flexibility that can be achieved from using random samples from a database of real data. The engine for delivery of the statistics needed to provide differentiation between different levels of a topic is the freely available software 'R' (see, for example, the review by Ripley, 2001). Our plans are to provide a Web-based resource that will enable teachers in school, university and elsewhere to choose material that will enable them to enhance the learning of statistical methodology and the experience of data handling across a wide range of statistical topics for a number of curriculum subjects. An early version of the proposed worksheet tool is shown in Figure 13.4.

Figure 13.4   Sample worksheet

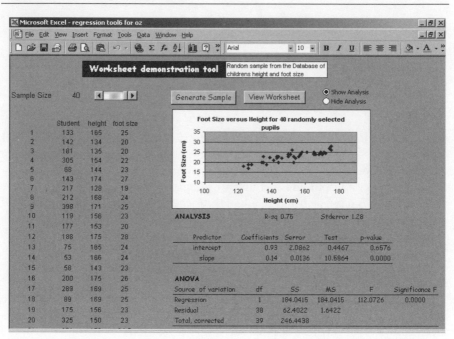

The worksheet shown in Figure 13.4 is designed to use real data, in this case taken from our database of returns from the *CensusAtSchool* project, to generate graphs and linear regression analysis statistics that can be used by teachers and students alike. For example, the display shows the first 20 of 40 randomly generated pairs of values from the variables height and right foot length of pupils' returns in the schools' census project. The scatter plot and typical regression-type output is optionally displayed.

Figure 13.5   Random data from *Census At School*

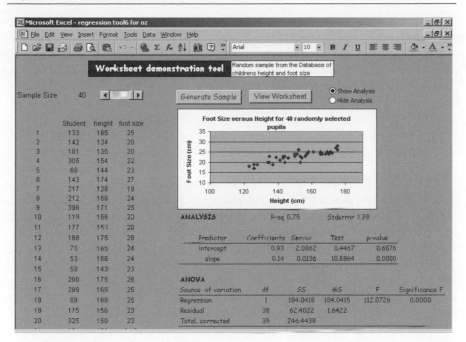

The sample size that is used is controlled by a standard slider-type control that allows integer increase/decrease of that size, dynamically linked to the graph and, if displayed, the analysis output. At each sample size a new sample can be generated and at each stage of the simulation a worksheet, which can be used by teachers to craft ones for students, is dynamically updated, and is shown in the immediately preceding diagram. The final form is yet to be decided, but we intend to build in options about the extent of the solutions to various questions. These questions will depend upon the level of statistics taught, and will be controlled by options within the master Web browser page.

The Web page, which is available at http://worksheet.edev.ntu.ac.uk, gives access to a prototype dynamic worksheet creator, and we would welcome comments from colleagues using the feedback e-mail address there. Using this template, we plan to design and write similar Web-based generated material for other key statistical topics from exploratory data analysis through hypothesis testing to complex modelling problems. These will be for routine use of work-sheets and, eventually, fully flexible projects for use as major contributors to HE programmes for specialists and non-specialists. In the next section we describe the creation of a case study, currently only in paper-based format, which covers a number of topic areas in statistics.

Case study packs for non-specialist students

Another popular request from teachers of statistics is that paper-based case studies should be made available across a wide range of statistical applications. We have a prototype of this kind of material, which we have called 'Statistics in practice, case studies in medicine', in hard-copy format or as pdf Acrobat files with corresponding data files, which may be found at http://science.ntu.ac.uk/rsscse/schools/StatPack/index.html. This is a paper-based teaching and learning pack and is intended to provide a valuable and practical resource for teachers involved in teaching statistical methods as part of service or introductory statistics courses, and also as a learning resource for students.

The hard copy of this pack comprises student cards containing background information and real data sets from medical research. There is also a teacher's guide, containing outline solutions for all problems. The pack contains three case studies and the problems covered include the following commonly used statistical methods: summarizing data, hypothesis testing (Z-test, Chi-squared test, t-test), Wilcoxon rank sum test, scatter plots and box plots, correlation, linear regression and prediction, epidemiology and topics for student projects. However, rather than being driven by these methods, the pack uses them, as and when appropriate, to help produce a solution to a relevant practical problem.

Simulation for learning and teaching

Statisticians have used simulation methods to explore, verify and discover new methodology in statistics for many years. These can be powerful tools and require intellectual effort to generate illustrative data, usually from a computer, in order to communicate different aspects of a curriculum. Recently the pedagogy of using simulation methods to teach statistics has been investigated by, among others, Chance *et al* (1999). Software for creating animated Web-based illustrations of different statistical methods are becoming more and more innovative (see, for example, www.statweb.calpoly.edu/chance/applets/applets.html for the collection of applets).

The key to success appears to depend upon the students being visual learners, able to interact with the software and able to receive feedback as they construct their knowledge. However, evidence suggests that they do not have an intuitive sense for simulation. A recent paper by DelMas *et al* (1999) (available online at http://www.amstat.org/publications/jse/secure/v7n3/delmas.cfm), addresses the issue of using simulation to help students learn statistics.

The following screen snap (Figure 13.6) shows, in the extreme left-hand graph, the shape of a bi-modal distribution from which random samples can be simulated and selected. The mean and standard deviation of the distribution can be specified by the user, as indicated by the dialogue box below the graph. Repeated samples of specified number and size can be taken from this population, and the graph of the sampled distribution is shown in the middle display on the snapped screen. The far right-hand graph displays the distribution of the sample means, corresponding to the sampled distribution just referred to. These graphs are very well presented and could, for example, provide the teacher with a convincing way of demonstrating the central limit theorem. It is of course a challenge to decide whether this rather clever e-delivery of a famous theorem results in a corresponding amount of e-learning.

Figure 13.6 Sampling distributions

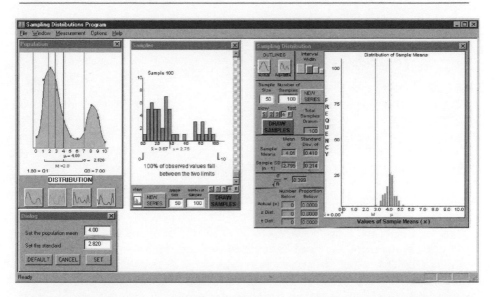

The next display (Figure 13.7) shows, using the same data that was simulated to produce the sampled distribution, the plotted confidence intervals of the 100 samples of size 50. The number of sampled intervals that cover the mean line of 4 are presented, and these can be used to provide an excellent way of explaining the often mistakenly understood concept of statistical confidence intervals.

Non-specialist statisticians: a new way to teach statistics to engineers

In teaching statistics to non-specialists it is the responsibility of statisticians to respond to their needs, especially with regard to their own discipline. However, there may be occasions when vested interests and subject integrity lead to decisions that give the impression that statisticians live in an ivory academic tower.

Figure 13.7   Illustrating confidence intervals

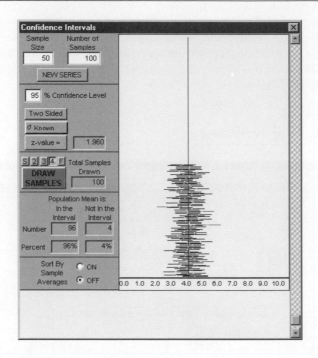

These and other issues are discussed by Greenfield (1993) and has led to suggestions that statisticians may not be the best people to teach statistics within other
subject areas.

A potentially controversial approach to teaching statistics to engineers was
proposed by Parry-Jones (1999). In May of that year, as Group Vice-President
Product Development and Quality, Ford Motor Company, he delivered the Royal
Academy of Engineering Manufacturing Lecture. He covered three themes, namely
customer insight, engineering manufacturing quality, and wealth creation and share-
holder value. Within the second theme he described the importance of taking into
account, while keeping a keen eye on quality, variability in engineering design. The
lecture, comprising nearly 30 pages of typed script and 57 PowerPoint slides, can be
found at http://www.raeng.co.uk. The importance of using statistics and statistical
thinking for managing variability in product design was emphasized time and again
through well-thought-through and illustrated examples. Furthermore he suggested
that the approach to teaching statistics to engineers should be somewhat more
radical than has been the case within UK HE in recent years.

He cogently argued that promoting the use of statistics in engineering, rather
than statistics *per se*, should be the approach taken to making engineers stand up
and take note of the very powerful tools that they can utilize to improve any engineering process. Briefly he suggested that:

- The responsibility for adopting this approach rests squarely with management.
- There is a need for coaching in statistical engineering methods.
- These methods should be embedded in undergraduate curricula and professional experience requirements of our institutions.
- [Statistical Engineering] should be taught by engineers in the context of design and engineering, supported by first-class applied statisticians as necessary.
- These methods should not be taught on a separate course in statistics.

Leading up to and following the Parry-Jones's lecture, a good deal of discussion took place within the Ford Motor Company about how they could attempt to take forward his suggestions in a formal way. The momentum generated from the jointly organized Royal Statistical Society (RSS) Quality Improvement Committee (QIC) and Institute of Electrical and Electronic Engineering (IEEE) meetings gave rise to a further three exploratory ones, which took place between interested parties at Ford, the RSS and Dan Grove, an independent statistical consultant who has had a long history of involvement with training Ford engineers in statistical methods. These meetings were rather more focused on how at least some of the suggestions of Parry-Jones could be implemented at Ford.

Over summer 2000, Dan Grove, along with Ed Henshall of the Ford Design Institute and Tim Nicholls of Ford of Europe Education, Training and Development, using an engineering process/statistics model for delivery, wrote specific training materials using the Parry-Jones philosophy in the context of a generic engineering process. The material was created around realistic engineering scenarios, with each of 12 sections introduced by an engineering task based around the design and manufacture of a fuel filler flap. The sections and tasks build on each other in the context of the scenario storyline. Statistical concepts and tools that support the engineering task are taught in an engineering context and there is participant activity based on the engineering task for each section.

The following 12 engineering tasks given in Table 13.1 were designed, initially at least, as one and a half-hour sessions over an intensive three-day period.

As can be seen by scrutinizing the statistics 'syllabus' in the above table, what is learnt by adopting the case study/engineering process approach is very different, both in order of topics taught and content, from conventional introductory statistics courses. The approach enables 'harder' topics to be taught successfully assuming a much lower level of background knowledge. The approach relies much less heavily on traditional syllabuses that are often driven by demands of hand-computation, combined with an overemphasis on significance testing. The case study approach in each section uses hands-on participant activities that employ Microsoft Excel/Minitab for data analysis and display. The course is delivered with a minimum of theoretical input and uses graphically based techniques of analysis in preference to more mathematically based ones.

Table 13.1 Engineering tasks

Statistical engineering education

Section	Engineering task	Statistical tools
1	capture the voice of the customer	dot plots; introduction to frequency distributions
2	evaluate functionality of design concept	simple linear regression; least squares method
3	assess robustness of design concept	2-level designed experiments
4	quantify piec-to-piece variation	run charts; probability distributions; mean and standard deviation
5	optimize design	quadratic response surfaces; multiple regression
6	verify design	Weibull distributions; Weibull plot; estimation of percentiles
7	establish the engineering process	2-level designed experiments revisited; Daniel plots
8	estimate functionality of manufacturing process (1)	linear models/planar response surfaces; designing a response surface experiment; standard 3-level designs; optimal designs
9	evaluate functionality of manufacturing process (2)	residual analysis; statistical significance: t ratios, p-values
10	optimize process	Excel solver
11	validate the process	Shewart charts; control limits; capability
12	using knowledge gained	review of tools covered in the course

Supporting materials comprise:

- PowerPoint slide-based presentation materials for each statistical technique covered, with each presentation using (different) automotive engineering examples.
- Class notes based on the PowerPoint slide presentation materials.
- Participant exercises, each with a model answer.
- Teaching notes.

By February 2001 the training course had been delivered as two three-day pilots to engineers at Ford. The background academic knowledge required of these engineers was only GCSE Physics and Mathematics, and familiarity with Excel. However, the materials have been designed to be used in a flexible manner and so can form the basis of a more typical undergraduate course taught as a series of learning interactions over a longer period.

During early April the RSS hosted a day meeting in London designed to introduce the engineering statistics training materials to interested parties, and to consider how these might be used within the education of undergraduate and graduate engineers. The two LTSN Centres, Engineering (www.mathstore.ac.uk www.ltsneng.ac.uk) and Maths, Statistics and OR (www.mathstore.ac.uk), together with Ford, co-organized the day, with representatives from 13 universities attending. In addition there were four representatives from the RSS QIC, including Dan Grove and five from Ford.

Following an overview of the material and detailed scrutiny of one of the sections, the general view from everyone present was that the proposed approach to teaching engineering statistics was innovative and that it deserved careful consideration by engineering departments in the UK.

LTSN Engineering at Loughborough University volunteered to host the material, via a secure password-protected Web site, and interested engineering departments are being invited to look at the material with a view to running the course during the next two years. The following actions were agreed:

- Volunteer universities would be invited to take the developed material back to their departments.
- The material would be examined closely and consideration would be given to how it could be used as part of undergraduate and/or postgraduate teaching programmes.
- Suggested changes would be recorded.
- Consideration would be given to the delivery mechanism that best suits them, for example, as an intensive course, spread over one term, electronic, Web based, or a combination of these.
- Assessment issues should be thought through, including formative and summative ones.
- Different self-study/learning options should be entertained, such as how long the end of session exercises should take, and whether mini or full project work was appropriate.
- Extensions of the filler-cap scenario into other engineering applications should be thought about to take into account local needs within a department's portfolio.

Following the consultation period, feedback from those colleagues in HE institutions who expressed an interest in delivering the course to undergraduate and/or postgraduate students reveal that such an innovative approach to communicating and teaching statistics could be very popular. By the end of the 2001/2002 academic year, at least six universities will have tested this new way to teach statistics to engineers and the results will be reported in due course.

Conclusions

I have suggested several ideas that colleagues may wish to pursue, to try to enhance learning and teaching standards in statistics. A key theme throughout has been a strong suggestion that learning and teaching statistics can become livelier and more meaningful to students through the use of data. This is not new (see, for example, the excellent introductory book by Moore, 1997). The first edition of this book appeared in 1979, and in all editions the author has extolled the virtues of a data analytic approach to teaching statistics, especially to non-specialists. More people are recognizing the role real data can play to motivate learning. A recent study by Rice *et al* (2001), into the use of numeric data in learning and teaching in UK HE, reports the results of a national survey of teaching departments in universities. The report reveals that relatively few university teachers use real data such as those that can be supplied from national data services. Reasons for this are given and the five summary recommendations contained in the report are:

1. A broad initiative is recommended to promote subject-based statistical literacy for students, coupled with tangible support for academic teaching staff who wish to incorporate empirical data into substantive courses.
2. The development of high-quality teaching materials for major UK data sets must be funded adequately, in order to provide salience to subject matter and demonstrate relevant methods for coursework.
3. The national data services need to improve the usability of their data sets for learning and teaching.
4. A more concerted and coordinated promotion of the national data services could then follow, which is responsive to user demand.
5. Universities should develop IT strategies that include data services and support for staff and students, and integration of empirical data sets into learning technologies.

The LTSN Mathematics, Statistics and OR Network, through a number of projects being managed for it at the Royal Statistical Society for Statistical Education at Nottingham Trent University, has resonance with many of these recommendations. As I have described in this chapter, it is being proactive in promoting new ideas for enhancing learning and teaching through the use of real data. More significant progress could be made if the second recommendation about funding were acted upon. In particular the national data services could well benefit from joining with the LTSN Mathematics, Statistics and OR Network help us to go forward and develop the ideas reported here so that we can together further improve learning and teaching statistics in UK HE.

References

Bowman, A *et al* (1998) Computer-based learning in statistics: a problem solving approach, *Statistician*, **47**, pp 349–364

Chance, B, Garfield, J and delMas, R C, (1999) *Developing Statistical Reasoning about Sampling Distributions,* International Research Forum on Statistical Reasoning, Thinking and Literacy, Israel, July 1999

Cox, D R and Snell, E J (1982) *Applied Statistics: Principles and examples*, Chapman and Hall, London

Cropley, A (2001) *Creativity in Education and Learning: A guide for teachers and educators*, Kogan Page, London

Davies, N (2001) Feedback from the Stats/OR Community, *MSOR Connections*, **1**, pp 3–4

delMas, R C, Garfield J and Chance, B (1999) A model of classroom research in action: developing simulation activities to improve students' statistical reasoning, *Journal of Statistics Education,* **7**(3)

Fallows, S and Steven, C (2000) *Integrating Key Skills in Higher Education: Employability, transferable skills and learning for life*, Kogan Page, London

Forsyth, I (2001) *Teaching and Learning Materials and the Internet*, Kogan Page, London

Garfield, J (1995) How students learn statistics, *International Statistical Review*, **63**, pp 25–34

Greenfield, T (1993) Communicating Statistics, *Journal of the Royal Statistical Society A*, **156**, pp 287–97

Hand, D J *et al* (1994) *A Handbook of Small Data Sets* (with disk), Chapman and Hall, London

Hawkins, A, Jolliffe, F and Glickman, L (1992) *Teaching Statistical Concepts*, Longman, London

Jolliffe, A, Ritter, J and Stevens, D (2001) *The Online Learning Handbook*, Kogan Page, London

Laurillard, D (1993) *Rethinking University Teaching*, Routledge, London

Lindley, D V (2001) Letter to the Editor, *Teaching Statistics*, **23**, (3)

Moore, D (1997) *Statistics: Concepts and controversies*, 4th edn, W H Freeman, New York

Moore, D and McCabe, G P (1998) *Introduction to the Practice of Statistics*, W H Freeman, New York

Parry-Jones, R (1999) *Royal Academy of Manufacturing Engineering Annual Lecture* [online] http://www.raeng.co.uk/

Rice, R *et al* (2001) *An Enquiry into the Use of Numeric Data in Learning and Teaching* [online] http://datalib.ed.ac.uk/projects/datateach.html

Ripley, B (2001) The R project in statistical computing, *MSOR Connections*, **1**(1), pp 23–25

14

Proof and reasoning

Joseph Kyle

Introduction

What are the special and particular problems that lie in the way of effective teaching and learning in pure mathematics? If we restrict our attention to a context of higher education in the UK, there are a number of signals and signs that can be read. Among these are current issues in mathematical education, reported problems in contemporary literature (a good recent example is Brake, 2001) and – to a lesser extent – the results of the Assessment of the Quality of Education, which has recently been initiated by Quality Assurance Agency acting on the behalf of the funding bodies.

At the heart of the matter is the nature of the discipline itself. Everyone should have a working definition of their subject and there are a number of famous descriptions to hand. For example, if we consult the first edition of *Encyclopædia Britannica*, we find a relatively short but interesting entry under 'Mathematics':

> Mathematics are commonly distinguished into pure and speculative, which consider quantity abstractly; and mixed which treat of magnitude as subsisting in material bodies.

> Pure mathematics have one peculiar advantage … it is easy to put an end to controversies, by shewing either that our adversary has not stuck to his definitions, or has not laid down true premises, or else that he has drawn false conclusions from true principles.

> These disciplines … instruct by profitable rules … ensure and corroborate the mind to a constant diligence of study … perfectly subject us to the

government of right reason. The mind is abstracted and elevated … and the understanding raised and excited to more divine contemplation.

(*Encyclopædia Britannica*, 1771)

However, it is possibly the definitions of Bertrand Russell that catch the eye of the modern pure mathematician: 'Mathematics may be defined as the subject where we never know what we are talking about, nor whether what we are saying is true. … Mathematics is the study of "P implies Q"' (Russell, 1994). This leads us to a definition of mathematics as the science of reasoning and takes us to the heart of the challenges that lie in the way of teaching and learning in the subject. Readers might themselves wish to consider how they would define pure mathematics and the problems involved in teaching it: 'How would you define (pure) mathematics?', 'What are the problems in teaching it?', 'Think back to an examination board or departmental meeting'.

In this chapter, we examine two current issues in this challenging area of pure mathematics. One lies at the very threshold of pure mathematics for those in higher education in the UK. This is the issue of encouraging a mature approach to proof and reasoning. The other develops ideas introduced in Chapters 2 and 3 and is more international in flavour and explores a more theoretical investigation of how our students learn and engage with more advanced topics in pure mathematics. This involves a discussion of one contemporary theoretical educational analysis of pure mathematics, not necessarily because it possesses all the answers – it does not – but because it invites us in a very persuasive fashion to reflect on how students learn pure mathematics. In order to encourage this reflection on how students learn pure mathematics, also included within this chapter are a number of questions for the reader to consider.

Reasoning and proof at an elementary level

One of the clearest signs that there is a problem is the emergence of a considerable number of courses/modules and textbooks that have a specific and dedicated agenda of strengthening logic and reasoning skills among undergraduates reading single-honours degrees in mathematics (see, for example, Velleman, 1994; Eccles, 1998; Kahn, 2001). Some of these embraced a wider remit of raising the profile of those other essential skills: how to read and write mathematics with care and attention to detail.

So what can be said about these skills of reasoning and logic? What is the evidence that they are missing and what effective mechanisms are available to us in addressing this issue? Many of the, alas, unpublished, self-assessments that were produced by schools and departments in the discipline for the assessment of teaching quality within the UK refer explicitly to analytical and logical skills as being. perhaps, the transferable skill *sine qua non*. Indirect support for this might be found in the strong interest from a wide range of employers in attracting graduates with well-developed skills of this nature.

The first task, therefore, is that of inculcating good habits of reasoning and argument in our students upon arrival. The second fundamental attribute of pure mathematics is the creative reasoning faculty. This is less easy to define and has had much less attention than the other problem. At a very basic level, it might be defined as the ability to take two *prima facie* unrelated pieces of knowledge into a new context in which fresh deductions are then accurately driven to the solution of a problem. Here we may well have to deal with rather serious habits learnt earlier, or 'belief overhangs', to use the terminology of Daskalogianni and Simpson (2001).

The most serious manifestation of the problem is when work is presented as a series of disconnected mathematical statements. At best, this is a consequence of a sloppy and lazy approach in recording essentially correct reasoning. At its worst, unspoken and unspeakable errors in logic have compounded equally poor technical understanding and there is very little to define a strategy to help the student.

The next level involves some recognition that lines of mathematics should relate to one another. Unfortunately this often translates into a rather mindless use of the symbol $\Rightarrow$ at every available opportunity, which can mean little more for some students than a vague signpost on the page: an indication of where the next bit of mathematics is to be found. Indeed a good number of students will always use a $\rightarrow$, instead of the conventional implications sign. A typical few lines from such work looks reasonable at first glance:

$$..$$
$$..$$
$$\Rightarrow$$
$$\Rightarrow (x-2)(x-3) > 0$$
$$\Rightarrow x > 3 \text{ or } x < 2$$
$$\Rightarrow$$
$$..$$

Therefore the solution set is $(-\infty, 2) \cup (3, \infty)$.

It is interesting to note that in recent workshops the author has undertaken with teachers of A-level mathematics, 100 per cent in one session voted in secret that the proof above was correct. (A typical reaction in later discussion would be, 'Of course all the steps can be reversed, so what's all the fuss about'.) Only when it is pointed out that the following steps are equally valid and lead to a false conclusion is the point accepted:

..
$$\Rightarrow$$
$$\Rightarrow (x-2)(x-3) > 0$$
$$\Rightarrow x > 2.9 \text{ or } x < 2.1$$
$$\Rightarrow$$
..

Therefore the solution set is $(-\infty, 2.1) \cup (2.9, \infty)$.

Further 'progress' appears when, as a reaction to the mini-debate above, students look to meet the problem halfway. To cover all eventualities, all lines of mathematics are linked with $\Leftrightarrow$ on a rather misplaced 'belt and braces' principle. Of course, this might work well for the simple examples above but is doomed to fail sooner or later: 'How might you inculcate good practice in writing mathematics, particularly when presenting proofs?'

So what can be done? There is little evidence that a dry course in logic and reasoning itself will solve the problem. Some success may be possible if the skills of correctly reading and writing mathematics, together with the tools of correct reasoning, can be encouraged through the study of an appropriate ancillary vehicle. The first (and some would still claim the foremost) area was geometry. The standard attack of the popular Euclidean theorems was for many the *raison d'etre* of logic and reasoning. However, the teaching of geometry itself is in some state of crisis and there is little to be gained from an attempt to turn the clock back. It is worth noting however that the problems with $\Leftrightarrow$ and its relatives were not a feature of the traditional proof in these topics: most commonly lines were linked with 'therefore' (with a resulting improvement in the underlying 'grammar' of the proof as well). We have now seen the sad demise of 'therefore' and 'because', which were the standard features of geometrical proofs. At one time, introductory mathematical analysis was thought to be the ideal topic. Indeed for many the only reason to have early exposure to rigorous analysis was as a good grounding in proper reasoning. Few advance this case now. Indeed some workers in mathematical education have recently cast doubt on the need for proof itself in such introductions to analysis (see the work by Tall *et al*, especially Tall *et al*, 1999, where it is suggested that the benefits of appropriate use of information technology should be considered). Axiomatic group theory (and related algebraic topics) has rather taken over as possibly being more amenable. Unfortunately there is not the same scope for repeated use over large sets of the logical quantifiers and little need for contra-positive arguments. Number theory has also been tried with perhaps more success than some other topics. However, most success seems to come when the mathematics under discussion is well inside a certain 'comfort zone' so that technical failings do not become an obstacle to engagement with debate on reasoning and proof. This is the approach, for instance, adopted in Kahn (2001). Examples might include simple problems involving whole numbers, as opposed to formal number theory, quadratic equations and inequalities, and trigonometry.

At a simple level we can explore how we record the solutions of a straightforward quadratic equation. One might normally note that the solutions to $(x - 1) (x - 2)$ are $x = 1$ or 2. Or would you prefer $x = 1$ or $x = 2$? And what about $x = 1$ and $x = 2$? Is it pedantic to make the difference, or is there a danger of confusing the distinction between 'or' and 'and'? By the time the solution to the inequality $(x .-. 1) (x - 2) > 0$ is recorded as the intersection of two intervals rather than the union, things have probably gone beyond redemption. Recent experience of the author has indicated that creative use of computer aids bring these points much more forcefully to students whose answers may have been too generously 'interpreted' by human markers. First year students at the University of Birmingham find that the computer, algebra-based AIM system (http://www.mat.bham.ac.uk/aim) puts a rather unforgiving spotlight on sloppiness in language (see also a recent discussion by Brake, 2001).

One possible way forward, which has had some limited success, is to use a workshop style approach at least to early sessions when exploring these issues. But a real danger for such workshops at the start of university life lies in choosing examples or counter-examples that are too elaborate or precious. Equally it is very easy to puncture student confidence if some early progress is not made. Getting students to debate and justify proofs within a peer group can help here. One way of stimulating this is outlined in the workshop plan below.

Model for workshop/group discussion:

- Five or six 'theorems with proofs': some valid, others not.
- Vote in secret whether:
  - 'theorem' is correct;
  - 'proof' is valid.
- Voting in secret can be done with fancy information technology, but little slips of paper are just as good.
- Announce results and discuss.

One can also find much resource in the world of the legal profession. Much legislation, especially in the world of finance, goes to some length to express simple quantitative situations purely and simply in words. Untangling into symbolic mathematics is a good lesson in structure and connection. Further, one can always stimulate an interesting debate by comparing and contrasting proof in mathematics with proof as it is understood in a court of law.

Approaches to a theory

But suppose we wish to go beyond elementary workshops in the first year. What approaches have been suggested for more sophisticated levels of pure mathematics? Here we outline one recommended by Professor Ed Dubinsky when he addressed the International Congress of Mathematical Education (ICME) in 2000 (Dubinsky, 2000; see also Dubinsky and Macdonald, 2001).

At this meeting Dubinsky outlined the so-called APOS theory in mathematical education. As an example he chose the area of group theory. He asks one to consider the problem of teaching the concept of a coset in group theory. More specifically, you might want your students to understand what a coset is, to be able to find examples and non-examples, and to establish some properties, such as the lemmas leading up to Lagrange's theorem, as well as the theorem itself together with its applications. You might even want your students to be able to construct examples of quotient groups and prove theorems relating properties of a quotient group to properties of the original group.

There is no great difficulty in delivering all of these ideas to your students. There will be a standard lecture giving them definitions and examples. You can state theorems and give the proofs, or ask them to discover some of the arguments. You can go over various applications of the concept of cosets. All of this is done, traditionally, through lectures, tutorials and set exercises. Unfortunately, there is a certain amount of evidence, both experimental and anecdotal, that this does not work very well. Not only do relatively few students learn the concept of a coset very well, but this topic may tend to drive them away from studying further algebra or even any more pure mathematics.

Dubinsky offers a different approach. This hinges on a belief that it is possible, through a programme of research, to find out something about what might be going on in a student's mind when he or she is trying to learn a piece of mathematics. Teaching then focuses not directly on the mathematics, but on some model of how the topic in question can be learnt. A rich theory of learning can give direction where otherwise there is much confusing endeavour. Thus Dubinsky is led to the following question, 'What is a good theory of learning and what characteristics should it have?'

Replace the words 'of learning' with 'in mathematics' and most mathematicians could make a fair stab at answering these questions. A good 'theory' consists of definitions, examples, counter-examples, theorems and proofs. It should help solve problems, prove new theorems and make applications, both in and out of mathematics. In mathematical education, however, the matter is not so clear and there is usually controversy. Nonetheless, Dubinsky offers a set of characteristics. He then offers APOS theory (see below) as an example of one that fits the bill. Readers must judge for themselves whether the characteristics stand on their own or have been chosen because they fit well with APSO theory. Here then are Dubinsky's characteristics.

A good theory in mathematical education should:

- *Support prediction.* A theory should help us say that if certain phenomena, call them antecedents, are observed, then other phenomena are likely to occur as consequences. Ideally, these phenomena should be observable. Moreover, antecedents should be of such a nature that it is possible, through appropriate instructional treatments, to foster their occurrence in students. Finally, of course, the consequent phenomena should consist, essentially, of mathematical knowledge and understanding.

- *Possess explanatory power.* It should be possible to use the theory to explain, in both coarse and fine grain, specific successes and failures of individuals and groups of students in trying to learn mathematical topics.
- *Be applicable to a broad range of phenomena.* It is not enough to observe a phenomenon, or even a small set of phenomena, and then develop a theory to connect and observe them. It should be possible to apply a theory to phenomena very different from the ones used to develop it.
- *Help organize thinking about learning phenomena.* Thinking about learning tends to be ad hoc, anecdotal and restricted to descriptions of an individual's experiences as learner and/or teacher. Scientific investigation of a domain, such as learning mathematics, requires an organized structure, including definitions of theoretical concepts and relationships among them, that practitioners discipline themselves to follow.
- *Serve as a tool for analysing data.* One way to analyse a set of data is to immerse oneself in it, discuss it within a research team and use one's best thinking to make sense of it. A theory, however, should provide a more systematic method of analysis. It should tell the researchers what questions to ask of the data and how to interpret the answers.
- *Provide a language for communication about learning.* Research and curriculum development must go beyond a single person or team making investigations and obtaining results. The work must be communicated and this is best done if there is a generally accepted common language. A theory can provide such a communication tool.

One theory – APOS theory – is then tested against these criteria. APOS theory is a constructivist theory of how learning a mathematical concept might take place. It is based on certain hypotheses about the nature of mathematical knowledge and how it is developed. Essentially these assert that mathematical knowledge resides in a tendency to respond to perceived mathematical problems, constructs or reconstructs mathematical actions, processes and objects, and organizes these in schemas to use in dealing with the situations. APOS theory is thus an elaboration of the mental constructions of: Actions, Processes, Objects and Schemas.

Here is an informal description of the concept of cosets in terms of actions, processes, objects and schemas. Learning cosets would begin with an action conception consisting of forming cosets that can be described by listing their elements, such as the cosets of the subgroup of multiples of 4 in the group of integers mod 24 with addition mod 24 as the group operation. Calculations could be made of specific cosets and properties such as the number of elements in a coset. The idea of a quotient group would be essentially inaccessible. A higher level of understanding would involve the individual internalizing the actions. The student no longer requires explicit listings and calculations to perform operations but can imagine them or run through them mentally. Thus, given a group G, a subgroup H, and an element x in G, the individual can think of forming the group product of each with x (on the left, say). In moving towards thinking about properties of cosets and performing actions on them, the individual develops an object conception of cosets. At this point, ideas such as Lagrange's theorem become accessible to the student and he or she can think of constructing a binary operation on the set of cosets of a subgroup. In working with these concepts, it is important for the individual to pass easily from the object back to the process from which it came and then return to the object as needed to work with particular situations. Thus, having constructed (mentally) the set of cosets of a subgroup, the individual can think about a binary operation that takes two cosets and produces another coset. Such thoughts require an object conception of cosets. But to actually construct the binary operation (as the set of all products of two elements, one from each coset), the individual must return to the process conception. In many mathematical activities, it is necessary to go back and forth between process and object conceptions of a mathematical entity.

All of these conceptions of cosets together with properties that the individual understands are organized in what we call the individual's schema for cosets. A schema is a collection of actions, processes, objects and other schemas, together with their relationships, which the individual understands in connection with cosets. This collection will be coherent in the sense that the individual will have some means (explicit or implicit), perhaps the formal definition, of determining for any phenomenon encountered what relationship it has to her or his conception of cosets.

Dubinsky argues that computer activities can foster the mental constructions called for by the theoretical analysis. He also stresses cooperative learning as providing a social context in which the students can engage in the reflection referred to in the hypothesis given in the previous section. This results in less lecturing than in a traditional class. The instructional treatment is organized in what is called the so-called ACE Teaching Cycle:

- Activities to be done (for Dubinsky, usually on the computer).
- Classroom discussions.
- Exercises to be done with pencil and paper.

For example, to help the students construct an action understanding of cosets, they might be asked to write code to construct the additive group of integers mod 20, calculate one example of the operation in this group, to form a certain subgroup H, and determine the coset K = 3 + H. Finally, to help the students construct an object conception of cosets, they might be asked to write a program that will accept any two cosets and return their product. This program can then be applied by the student to specific examples and used to investigate properties that the coset product may or may not possess, such as commutativity (for more information on this way of using computers, see Dubinsky, 1995). In the classroom sessions, the students are given specific mathematical tasks to perform, based on the mental constructions they have made on the computer. Finally, exercises are assigned to do as homework. These are fairly traditional drill and practice, as well as problems that require deeper thought. The reinforcement that comes from practice does not take place until the possibility of reinforcing misconceptions is reduced as much as possible.

Weller *et al* (2001) quote several instances supporting the claim that APOS meets many of the characteristics outlined earlier. He also indicates that the approach has a wide spectrum of applicability: from abstract algebra to pre-calculus. In summarizing some dozen or so studies it is claimed that in essentially every single category under consideration, students from the experimental (APOS) groups achieved a higher level of performance than did students from the traditional groups.

There is no doubting that Dubinsky is a powerful advocate and has had some success himself with this approach. Nonetheless, there is some scepticism, even among those who are persuaded of the case in theory:

> There are still problems if one begins to apply these new methods from an empty table. Should one use the new methods for all students or for a special group of students? What about the lack of experts on the matter? It may not be enough to study these methods a day or two from books and articles and then to try them in practice.
>
> (Anon, 2001)

What cannot be in doubt is the fact that Dubinsky has sketched out an agenda for reflecting upon teaching and learning in pure mathematics that will allow a more informed debate to take place.

Conclusion

There are no easy answers. There are no '100 effective and efficient tips' to teach a mature attitude to proof and reasoning. There is hope if we first recognize the problem and address it with the students outside a culture of blame. It is worth engaging students in some of the topics below:

- Encourage translation from symbols to words and vice versa.
- Do some mathematics entirely in words.
- Remember 'therefore'.
- Distinguish between finding the proof, which will often be rough and informal, and writing out the proof, which should be watertight and formal, and note how often the flow reverses in these two processes.
- Similarly explore uses and abuses of pictures.

As a practitioner, I have found it useful at least to explore some of the contemporary writing in mathematical education, such as Dubinsky's work outlined above. There are, without doubt, two cultures: that of mathematics and that of mathematical education, but each has a responsibility to respect the other. In the words of Morgens Niss at ICME-9:

> One observation that a mathematics educator can hardly avoid to make is the widening gap between researchers and practitioners in mathematical education. The existence of a gap is neither surprising nor worrying.
>
> The cause for concern is that it is widening. If we are unsuccessful, research on mathematical education runs the risk of becoming barren dry swimming ... while the practice of teaching runs the risk of becoming more naïve, narrow-minded and inefficient than necessary and desirable.

(Niss, 2000)

References

Anon (2001) Evaluation (accessed 13 November 2001) [online] http://www.joensuu.fi/sciences/mathematics/DidMat/DubEval/Report01.html

Brake, W (2001) Logic, language and life, *Mathematical Gazette*, **85**(503)

Daskalogianni, K and Simpson, A (2001) Beliefs overhang: the transition from school to university, in *Proceedings of 5th British Conference on Mathematics Education*, (forthcoming)

Dubinsky, E (1995) ISETL (Interactive SET Language): a programming language for learning mathematics, *Communications in Pure and Applied Mathematics*, **48**, pp 1–25

Dubinsky, E (2000) Towards a theory of learning advanced mathematical concepts, in *Proceedings of the 9th International Conference on Mathematics Education*, (forthcoming)

Eccles, P J (1998) *An Introduction to Mathematical Reasoning: Numbers, sets and functions*, Cambridge, Cambridge University Press

Encyclop'dia Britannica (1771) 1st edn, Edinburgh

Kahn, P E (2001) *Studying mathematics and its applications*, Palgrave, Basingstoke

Niss, M (2000) Key issues and trends in research on mathematical education, in *Proceedings of the 9th International Conference on Mathematics Education*, (forthcoming)

Russell, B (1994) *The Collected Papers of Bertrand Russell, vol 3*, Routledge, London

Tall, D (1999) The cognitive development of proof: is mathematical proof for all or for some?, in *Developments in School Mathematics Education Around the World, vol 4*, ed Z Usiskin, pp 117–136, National Council of Teachers of Mathematics, Virginia

Tall, D et al (1999) *Knowledge Construction and Diverging Thinking in Elementary and Advanced Mathematics*, Educational Studies in Mathematics, **38**, (1–3), pp 111–13

Velleman, D J (1994) *How to Prove it: A structured approach*, Cambridge University Press, Cambridge

Weller, K et al (2001) *In Review, an Examination of Student Performance Data in Recent Research in Undergraduate Mathematics Community (RUMEC) studies*

15

Making learning and teaching more effective

Peter Kahn and Joseph Kyle

Introduction

What makes for effective learning and teaching in mathematics and its applications? We only need to consider some of the concerns about learning and teaching that have been raised in recent years to realize that this is an important question. Within higher education, there have been difficulties with recruiting and retaining sufficient numbers of students (see, for example, Thomas, 2000; Quality Assurance Agency for Higher Education, 2000). Various reports have pointed to the inadequate mathematical preparation of students for existing degree programmes (London Mathematical Society, 1996; Engineering Council, 2000). At the same time there is in many places a shortage of mathematically qualified teachers in schools (Tikly and Wolf, 2000). Concerns over such issues are closely linked to the recognition that modern economies need a large number of individuals with understanding of mathematics and its applications if they are to thrive. And while making learning and teaching in higher education more effective is only likely to provide one element in any moves to improve mathematical education more widely, it remains an important element.

We therefore need to address the question of how to make learning and teaching in mathematics and its applications more effective. What is evident from the earlier chapters is that, while it is essential to consider the particular context, effective learning and teaching in mathematics and its applications are likely to be marked by a number of characteristics. Foremost among these characteristics is the recognition that the practice needs to be shaped by the nature of mathematics and its applications. And yet other features have also been seen as important. Learning and teaching clearly need to take into account the background of the students concerned. It is also apparent that learning mathematics involves students engaging with a process rather than simply absorbing mathematical products. Teaching thus needs to directly support students in carrying out the relevant processes for themselves. The importance of technology is also evident, with a clear recognition that its use needs to be effectively integrated into the rest of the provision. While these further characteristics of effective learning and teaching are closely linked to mathematical considerations, they also require a focus that extend far beyond mathematical ideas themselves. And more widely, it is also evident from the earlier chapters that the outcomes of learning and teaching need to meet a wider agenda than simply understanding mathematical ideas.

This chapter now takes each of these characteristics in turn, drawing out their role in effective learning and teaching and looking to see how future practice might take greater account of them. As professionals engaged in teaching and supporting learning, however, it is not enough to be aware of these characteristics. It is also essential that this awareness is translated into practice. This chapter therefore also looks at the nature of professionalism, before concluding by considering how the mathematical community as a whole might seek to make its practice of learning and teaching more effective.

The nature of mathematics

Learning and teaching in mathematics and its applications clearly need to be rooted within the subject matter itself. This is particularly evident in Part B of the book, where learning and teaching are more directly addressed with respect to specific areas of mathematics and its applications. For instance, in Chapter 12 the modelling process itself helps to shape the way in which mathematical modelling is both learnt and taught, while in Chapter 13 we see the relevance of using real data when teaching statistics.

However, it is also true across the book as a whole that the nature of mathematics needs to be taken into account if learning and teaching are to be effective. We can point to the importance of connections between ideas, the hierarchical nature of mathematics, the logical underpinnings of the subject and the way in which mathematics is applied to the real world. For example, the importance of making connections when studying mathematics cannot be underestimated, as has been widely noted. The role of connections is, for example, seen through generalization in Chapter 2, in linking mathematics with the real world in Chapter 12 and in using computer algebra systems to promote understanding in Chapter 5. In general, teaching needs to highlight these connections and to enable students to develop their own rich networks of ideas. We need to find further ways to ensure that students know how to make the relevant connections for themselves. We similarly will need to find additional ways to ensure that students appreciate other features of mathematics. For instance, we might want to draw on a tool such as concept analysis (for use of this tool in a related context see Novak, 1990), so that students are able to appreciate more fully the hierarchical nature of mathematics.

More widely, we can note the way in which practices developed in the context of other disciplines will need either to be illustrated with examples from or adapted to the mathematical context if they are to be applied to learning and teaching mathematics. For instance in Chapter 3 we see a theory of curriculum orientations illustrated with reference to the mathematical context, helping to provide a basis for active learning. Alternatively, one of the case studies in Chapter 7 seeks to adapt problem-based learning to a mathematical context. Rather than ignoring innovative practices that do not translate easily into a mathematical context, the challenge is to explore their relevance. It will be important for teaching and learning in mathematics and its applications to draw regularly on approaches within the context of other disciplines, given the wide range of innovations in other disciplines.

The student background

The hierarchical nature of mathematics typically leaves little room for students to learn more advanced mathematical content when more basic ideas have not been mastered. It will after all be a challenge trying to teach elementary algebra to students who have not grasped the rules of arithmetic. The implications of this reality are particularly evident in the transition to higher education in Chapter 1 and for non-specialist students of mathematics in Chapter 11. Diagnostic testing at the point of this transition is therefore likely to form an important element in responses to gaps in students' understanding of any given area of mathematics and its applications.

However, we need to take into account more than simply which areas of mathematics or its applications students have already covered, as we have seen in various chapters. In order to learn mathematics or one of its applications effectively, students need to possess a range of understanding and skills. This will include sufficient understanding of logic and mathematical reasoning, as well as the ability to solve problems and to use information and communication technology effectively. Students also need effective study skills. Take for instance the ability to interpret visual information appropriately, which one might regard as a study skill (see, for example, Northedge *et al*, 1997). It is certainly important that students are able to do this, but are we sure that students do in fact possess this skill to a sufficient level? We cannot assume that students will develop the necessary expertise simply as a result of trying to master given areas of mathematics, particularly when dealing with mass higher education.

Finally, attitudes to mathematics and its applications also form part of the students' background. Where frustration and anxiety have previously been hallmarks of a student's experience of studying mathematics, then effective learning and teaching will need to take this into account. Where numeracy is concerned, focusing provision on employment seems to be one way of addressing the perceived lack of relevance of mathematics to the students' concerns as evident in

Chapter 10. Similarly, in Chapter 11, relating the provision to the host subject may also help foster positive attitudes towards study. Then in Chapter 8 we also saw the importance of the wider environment in which learning occurs. We will also need to find ways to build students' confidence for their study. Revisiting specific material that has been covered earlier in the course, rather than simply making use of the material in the context of more advanced ideas, would be one way in which this could occur, drawing on ideas of the spiral curriculum developed by Bruner (1966). If a concept is sufficiently important then revisiting its definition and looking at further examples is surely warranted.

The importance of process

It is well established in the research literature that in order to learn mathematics effectively students need to engage in a process that leads to the construction of their own mathematical understanding. This should involve far more than simply presenting students with the products of mathematical thought (see, for example, Tall, 1991: xiv; Skemp, 1971). Simply giving lectures in which ideas are presented in a deductive order and then requiring students to solve problems is unlikely to suffice, unless perhaps the students themselves are highly motivated. Definitions and theorems, for instance, can be memorized rather than fully understood. Model solutions to problems can be adapted and friends can assist in the process. There are a whole range of ways in which students can avoid genuine engagement with mathematical content.

The challenge is to find ways of engaging students with the process of learning mathematics. It is worth, then, emphasizing that earlier chapters have proposed a variety of possible ways forward. In Chapter 2 in particular we considered a variety of different processes that all contributed to the genesis of mathematical under-standing, including pattern recognition, conjecture, special cases and the role of historical insights. Similarly, the more practical focus of Chapter 3 took in various activities for students. Other chapters also sought to help students engage in the process of learning mathematics, whether through making use of assessment involving computer algebra systems, adopting elements of problem-based learning, taking into account the wider support needed to learn mathematics, focusing on the modelling cycle, making use of statistical data or so on.

However, it is not only necessary for students to be led through the process by their tutors. It is worth emphasizing again that students also need to have explicit attention devoted to their ability to engage in these processes for themselves. For instance, we may well need to explicitly teach students how to choose their own examples of concepts, rather than simply provide them with a set of examples (see, for example, Kahn, 2001). Adopting relevant skills as learning outcomes for early courses in undergraduate programmes provides one means of teaching this kind of skill, although dedicated provision is another option (Toohey, 1999). Skills need to be sufficiently valued if they are to be developed and this implies some form of explicit attention and even assessment.

The emphasis needs to be not only on the mathematical product but also on the process of coming to understand that product, as Tall again notes (Tall, 1991: 3). This is an area where evident scope still remains for development, particularly for departments where teaching is dominated by lecturing and formal examinations. The evidence from this book is that there is a great deal of good practice on which to draw. The challenge now is to integrate this into practice more widely.

The role of technology

Technology is playing an increasingly important role in the study of mathematics and its applications, as evident for instance in the use of computer-based assessment, computer algebra systems and so on. Applications of mathematics offer particular scope for using further tools with students. Furthermore, the ability to use information and communication technology is in itself a valuable transferable skill, as noted in Chapter 6. And there are clearly many more developments that this book has not had space to address.

In many ways the challenge is to integrate the use of technology into the wider process of learning and teaching, as has been widely recognized (see, for example, Burton and Jaworski, 1995). This focus is especially evident in Chapters 5 where the use of computer algebra systems is addressed. But other chapters also display a concern for such integration. For instance, as outlined in Chapter 14, when applying APOS theory, technology is used to assist in helping students to carry out actions on mathematical objects. Similarly in Chapters 12 and 13, technology is seen to play an important part in helping students to develop and make use of their own mathematical models. Given the pace at which technology is developing, the appropriate integration of technology into learning and teaching will remain an ongoing concern.

Meeting a wider agenda

A further characteristic of effective learning and teaching that is evident in this book is that we cannot ignore the wider agenda. To concentrate only on mathematics and its applications is to ignore a number of needs. In particular, the product that courses in mathematics and its applications offer needs to go beyond subject content. If one views this product in terms of the outcomes of learning, then we can see a range of outcomes addressed in many of the chapters. Transferable skills, including the ability to use technology, the development of attitudes and values more widely, and an appreciation for meta-mathematical principles are all relevant, as seen in various chapters.

This wider agenda is closely related to students' personal and professional development. It is worth noting that a similar concern for such development has been evident across the whole of higher education in recent years (National Committee of Enquiry into Higher Education, 1997). One way in which this has manifested itself is through the use of development planning, in which students are guided by a tutor in planning for their own development. While this can operate in isolation from academic work, many systems address planning for personal and academic development as a whole (Bull and Otter, 1994). As far as the study of mathematics and its applications is concerned, however, relatively little attention has been given to such integration. But clearly there is scope in this context for the use of diagnostic testing throughout a degree programme, for a focus on study skills and to address issues more directly related to a student's aspirations for future employment, as well as for students to take responsibility, for instance, for developing transferable skills.

Professionalism

While it is relatively straightforward to draw out various characteristics of effective learning and teaching, it is more challenging to ensure that one's own practice is in fact effective. One might argue that it is sufficient for most lecturers to be able to teach competently, and that there is no need to take matters further. Given, however, the current state of education in mathematics this is surely an inadequate response. In the UK, for instance, we need only consider the inadequate supply of mathematics teachers for schools (Tikly and Wolf, 2000) to realize that more is needed than competence. Furthermore, the rate at which the higher education sector is changing also calls for ongoing development, with widening access to higher education, the changes in technology already noted and a growing body of knowledge on what makes for effective learning and teaching.

We thus need to consider the professional development of lecturers and tutors with regard to their teaching. There are two groups of people to whom one might initially turn: those providing professional development across the university as a whole and educational researchers. More general professional development, however, usually requires individual lecturers themselves to apply or adapt pedagogical practices to their own context. Educational researchers, meanwhile, are often more concerned with developing theoretical understanding rather than exploring the implications for practice of existing theory. While both of these groups will have a role to play, it is difficult to avoid the conclusion that ultimate responsibility lies with the mathematics community in general and the individual lecturer in particular to ensure that practice is effective. In the remainder of this section we will briefly consider how the individual lecturer might take such professional responsibility for his or her own practice, while in the final section we will consider ways in which the mathematics community as a whole might seek to make its practice more effective.

There are two related concepts that are of particular use in helping the individual lecturer to take these ideas forward on a more practical level. The first of these is the idea of reflective practice, which was considered at length in Chapter 9. We saw that sustained attention needs to be paid to systematically reflecting upon practice, so that practice can be evaluated and subsequently adapted (see, for example, Brown, 1999). This is true not only of existing practice, but also of more innovative approaches. It is not enough to simply introduce an innovation: innovations also needs to be reflected upon. The second and related concept is that of the scholarship of teaching. Scholarly teachers are those who gain knowledge of pedagogical practice, implement new developments and evaluate their effectiveness (Trigwell *et al*, 2000). Furthermore, they disseminate the knowledge that is thus developed so that their understanding is both subjected to the scrutiny of their peers and so that others can benefit. In this way, individuals play their role in ensuring that the practice of the community as a whole is effective.

Conclusion

It is the contention of this chapter that it falls to those engaged in teaching and learning mathematics to ensure that their own practice is effective. It is our responsibility to develop new approaches to the study of mathematics that are effective for the changing circumstances in which we find ourselves. This is true on the individual level, as considered in the previous section, but it is also the case that as a community we need to encourage mathematicians to develop their practice of teaching and learning. It is therefore worth concluding this chapter by considering a number of ways in which this might be achieved more comprehensively.

We first of all need to support and reward individuals and departments that develop more effective practices of teaching and learning. This book as a whole has advanced a number of potentially effective practices, some of which have yet to be fully tried out or incorporated more widely. Clearly, such ideas will be adapted in any process of implementation, but we need staff who are prepared to invest their energy in this process. Additional time, resources and money all need to be made available on an ongoing basis. We will need to see national and local awards for teaching mathematics, senior posts within departments for developing teaching, increased sponsorship from companies, recognition for the development of practices that are widely adopted elsewhere and so on. Within the UK, the LTSN Mathematics, Statistics and Operational Research Network may provide a focus for this to occur in part, but this is something that every department and relevant national organization needs to take seriously.

However, in addition to a focus on making the practice of teaching and supporting learning more effective, we also need as a community to address a range of wider issues, as proposed by Tikly and Wolf (2000). Teaching and learning are not carried out in isolation from the rest of the education system and from society more widely. We need to convince potential students of the vocational relevance of studying mathematics. Education in schools needs a wider focus than numeracy, so that larger numbers of students receive an advanced mathematical education. Government and funding bodies need to be convinced of the importance of mathematics to a modern economy, putting in place further incentives for people to study and teach mathematics and for those developing education in the numerate disciplines.

This book seeks to help both individual lecturers and the mathematics community as a whole to take forward the practice of teaching and learning. This is not something that can be achieved quickly and easily. The question is whether we value the mathematical education of our students and the needs of our society sufficiently to invest the resources needed to make learning and teaching more effective.

References

Brown, M, Fry, H and Marshall, S (1999) Reflective Practice, in *A Handbook for Teaching and Learning in Higher Education*, eds H Fry, S Ketteridge and S Marshall, Kogan Page, London

Bruner, J S (1966) *Towards a Theory of Instruction*, Harvard University Press, Cambridge, Mass

Bull, J and Otter, S (1994) *Recording Achievement: Potential for higher education*, Committee of Vice-chancellors and Principals of the Universities, Sheffield

Burton, L and Jaworski, B (eds) (1995) *Technology in Mathematics Teaching*, Chartwell–Bratt, Bromley

Engineering Council (2000) *Measuring the Mathematics Problem*, Engineering Council, London

Kahn, P E (2001) *Studying Mathematics and its Applications*, Palgrave, Basingstoke

London Mathematical Society (1996) *Tackling the Mathematics Problem*, London Mathematical Society, London

National Committee of Enquiry into Higher Education (1997) *Higher Education in the Learning Society (The Dearing Report)*, HMSO, London

Northedge, A *et al* (1997) *The Sciences Good Study Guide*, The Open University, Milton Keynes

Novak, J (1990) Concept mapping: a useful tool for science education, *Journal of Research in Science Teaching*, **27**(10), pp 937–49

Quality Assurance Agency for Higher Education (2000) *Subject Overview Report: Mathematics, Statistics and Operational Research*, Quality Assurance Agency for Higher Education, Bristol

Skemp, R (1971) *The Psychology of Learning Mathematics*, Penguin, London

Tall, D (ed) (1991) *Advanced Mathematical Thinking*, Kluwer Academic, London

Thomas, J (2000) *Mathematical Sciences in Australia: Looking for a future*, Federation of Australian Scientific and Technological Societies, Deakin West

Tikly, C and Wolf, A (2000a) The state of mathematics education, in *The Maths We Need Now: Demands, deficits and remedies*, eds C Tikly and A Wolf, pp 1–25, Institute of Education, London

Tikly, C and Wolf, A (eds) (2000b) *The Maths We Need Now: Demands, deficits and remedies*, Institute of Education, London

Toohey, S (1999) *Designing Courses for Higher Education*, Society for Research into Higher Education/Open University Press, Buckingham

Trigwell K *et al* (2000) Scholarship of teaching: a model, *Higher Education Research and Development*, **19**(2), pp 155–68

Appendix: a guide to mathematics resources on the Internet

This is a guide to some of the ways in which the World Wide Web can be used as a resource for teachers and learners of mathematics. Browsing the Internet can be very time-consuming, so this is just one person's selection of tutorials, interactive materials and mathematical tools. The selection given here, along with the accompanying notes, was collated by Pam Bishop, Assistant Director of the LTSN Mathematics, Statistics and Operational Research (OR) Network (see http://ltsn.mathstore.ac.uk/workshops/induction2001/resources.htm#uk for the original version).

Recently the Mathematics, Statistics and OR Network has added a section to its Web site, 'Accessing Maths and Stats By Other Means' (http://ltsn. mathstore.ac.uk/access/accessmsor.htm), which includes tools for students with disability. Help with finding mathematical sites on the Internet is available via the online tutorial 'The Internet Mathematician' (http://www.eevl.ac.uk/vts/maths/index.htm).

Some of these sites use special browsers or plug-ins which have to be installed as part of Netscape or Internet Explorer. If you want to take advantage of such facilities on machines in your own institution, you (or a network manager) may have to download and install the correct version for your machine or network.

Many other sites can be searched for within the Network's resource database at http://www.ltsn.gla.ac.uk/resources or the 'Internet Guide to Mathematics' at http://www.eevl.ac.uk/mathematics.

Given the dynamic nature of the Web, URLs and site content are liable to change but the information here was correct at the time of publication.

Selection of UK sites containing tutorial materials

UCL Geomaths MathHelp project.
http://www.ucl.ac.uk/Mathematics/geomath/
Based at University College London, this is a joint Geological Sciences/Mathematics project funded by the HEFCE as part of the Fund for the Development of Teaching and Learning (FDTL) programme.

Coventry Mathematics Support Centre.
http://www.mis.cov.ac.uk/maths_centre/index.html
Support for students at Coventry University. Includes interactive online resources and online tests.

Plymouth Mathematics Support Materials.
http://www.tech.plym.ac.uk/maths/resources/PDFLaTeX/mathaid.html
A library of portable, interactive, Web-based support packages in pdf format to help students learn various mathematical ideas and techniques and to support classroom teaching.

Loughborough's Engineering Pre-session Mathematics Refresher Programme.
http://www.lboro.ac.uk/faculty/eng/maths/
Revision mathematics course at Loughborough University.

LMS Undergraduate Project Archive.
http://www.maths.abdn.ac.uk/maths/department/services/lms/projread.html
A stock of topics for undergraduate project work that has been successfully used. There are two lists. One consists of a clear description of the work involved in the project, a good set of appropriate references and some indication of the length, level and prerequisites of the project. The other is a simple list of topics in the hope that it sparks off ideas in the mind of the reader.

Maple4students.co.uk
http://www.adeptscience.co.uk/products/mathsim/maple/students/
For engineering, mathematics and science students who use Maple. Full of free resources including tutorials, course-specific examples and general reference information, as well as diversionary content intended to make mathematics more appealing and interesting for students. Teachers and lecturers can also take advantage of the site with links to educational PowerTools and Waterloo Maple's suite of free, full-powered add-on packages. These include complete sets of curriculum material for various college and university-level courses, including calculus, linear algebra and engineering mathematics.

Fibonacci numbers and the Golden Section.
http://www.mcs.surrey.ac.uk/Personal/R.Knott/Fibonacci/fib.html
Here you can find out who Fibonacci was, look at the Fibonacci series of numbers and some of their numerical properties, and all the places that it turns up in nature. There is another page on some puzzles where the answers all seem to involve the Fibonacci numbers and a page to show where the Fibonacci numbers have been used in art, in architecture and in music. Compiled at the University of Surrey.

History of Mathematics.
http://www-groups.dcs.st-and.ac.uk/ history/
Award-winning archive based at the University of St Andrews.

Sites presenting tutorial material using Java

MathinSite.
http://mathinsite.bmth.ac.uk/
Mathematics Java applets linked to worksheets, prepared by Peter Edwards, one of the first UK National Teaching Fellows. The philosophy behind the applet/worksheet combination is to guide users into 'discovering' aspects of mathematics, not necessarily obvious using chalk-and-talk or from reading a book. Interaction with the software should promote a deeper insight into each topic and so enhance the users' mathematics learning experience.
An introduction to Power Series.
http://www.mat.bham.ac.uk/P.J.Flavell/MSM130/lectures/PowerSeriesOld/Preface.htm
Interactive presentations on Power Series, developed for an electronic engineering course at the University of Birmingham.
Gallery of Mathematics.
http://info.lut.ac.uk/departments/ma/gallery/index.html
Within the Department of Mathematical Sciences at Loughborough University.
Non-Euclidean Geometry.
http://cvu.strath.ac.uk/courseware/info/noneucgeom.html
Part of the Clyde Virtual University.

Selection of sites containing assessment resources

Report of workshop on computer-aided assessment in mathematics.
http://ltsn.mathstore.ac.uk/workshops/maths-caa/report.htm
The Mathematics, Statistics and OR Network presented this workshop in May 2000. The report includes contributions from presenters who are actively using computer-aided assessment in undergraduate mathematics courses.
Discussions of computer-aided assessment in mathematics.
http://ltsn.mathstore.ac.uk/articles/maths-caa-series/index.htm
A series of monthly articles on this topic began in July 2001, and there is an opportunity to respond via an e-mail discussion list.
AIM server at Birmingham.
http://mat-nt2.bham.ac.uk:8080/index.html
Some sample tests using the Alice Interactive Mathematics (AIM) system.
Perception server at Birmingham.
http://mat-nt2.bham.ac.uk/qm/open.dll
Tests and questionnaires using Question Mark Perception. This includes the MidMath suite of diagnostic tests.
Mathematical Assessment on the Web.
http://www.icbl.hw.ac.uk/marble/maths/public/assessment.html
This page delivers a multiple-choice mathematical test.
CalMaeth.
http://calmaeth.maths.uwa.edu.au/
Computer Aided Assessment and Learning of Mathematical Methods at the University of Western Australia.

Educational sites for some of the standard packages

MathSoft's educational site.
http://www.mathsoft.com/eduindex.html
Mathcad educational files, including the Mathcad Explorer for reading Mathcad files on the Web.
Maple Application Centre.
http://www.mapleapps.com/index.html
Contributions submitted by Maple users including educational applications.
MathSource.
http://www.mathsource.com/Content/Applications/Mathematics
Wolfram Research archive of materials using Mathematica, including the MathReader.
Eric's Treasure Trove of Mathematics.
http://mathworld.wolfram.com/
A very useful and popular online mathematics dictionary originally produced at the University of Virginia and now sponsored by Wolfram Research.
LiveMath.
http://www.livemath.com/
Educational material written in MathView, previously known as Theorist or MathPlus. The interactive material on this site requires the use of the LiveMath plug-in, which can be freely downloaded.
Design Science.
http://www.dessci.com/
Details of resources that will help in publishing your own documents, Web pages, presentations, TeX and LaTeX, and MathML documents including MathType, WebEQ and TeXaide.

Other sites with a substantial collection of maths resources

Mathematics Archives.
http://archives.math.utk.edu/index.html
A collection of resources, including a searchable database of teaching materials, software and WWW links organized by Mathematical Topics. The software section on public domain and shareware software is now available from the UK Mirror Service
http://www.mirror.ac.uk/sites/archives.math.utk.edu/software/
MATH Database 1931–1996.
http://www.emis.de/ZMATH/
A service of the European Mathematical Society providing a bibliographic search facility.
The Mathematical Modellers Database.
http://www.hull.ac.uk/mathskills/themes/theme2/mmdb/index.html
An international catalogue of people who are involved in mathematical modelling, developed at the University of Ulster as part of the MathSkills project.

Electronic catalogue of teaching innovations.
http://www.hull.ac.uk/mathskills/themes/theme3/
Again developed at the University of Ulster, the aim is to provide a searchable database on the MathSkills' Web pages, which mathematics lecturers can use to obtain ideas and advice on new methods of teaching or assessment, not necessarily relating to the use of technology.

Internet Center for Mathematics Problems.
http://www.mathpropress.com/mathCenter.html
MathPro Press searches journals and other media to set up this page, which identifies and lists all sources of mathematics problems on the Internet and related information.

Spreadsheets in Mathematics, Science and Statistics Education (Austria).
http://sunsite.univie.ac.at/Spreadsite/
This Web page tries to collect some information about spreadsheets with an emphasis on mathematics and statistics education.

The following five Web sites consist of searchable collections of documents relating to mathematics.

Math-Net.
http://www.math-net.org/
MathGuide.
http://www.mathguide.de/
WWW Virtual Library: Mathematics.
http://euclid.math.fsu.edu/Science/math.html
Yahoo – Science: Mathematics.
http://dir.yahoo.com/Science/mathematics/
MathSearch (Sydney).
http://www.maths.usyd.edu.au:8000/MathSearch.html

The future of mathematics on the Web

Some of the latest information on MathML.
http://ltsn.mathstore.ac.uk/mathml/index.htm
Collated by the Mathematics, Statistics and OR Network.
Putting mathematical notation on the Web.
http://www.bham.ac.uk/ctimath/workshops/mathml.htm
This is the report of a workshop that took place in 1999, much of which is still valid. It includes a very valuable hands-on session on techExplorer from Francis Wright of Queen Mary and Westfield College.

Acknowledgement

The editors are grateful to the LTSN Mathematics, Statistics and Operational Research Network for permission to reprint the material contained in this appendix.

Further reading

Baumslag, B (2000) *Fundamentals of Teaching Mathematics at University Level*, Imperial College Press, London

Burn, R, Appleby, J and Maher, P (1998) *Teaching Undergraduate Mathematics*, Imperial College Press, London

Exner, G R (1996) *An Accompaniment to Higher Mathematics*, Springer, New York

Holton, D (ed) (2001) *The Teaching and Learning of Mathematics at University Level: An International Commission on Mathematical Instruction (ICMI) study*, Kluwer Academic, Dordrecht

Kahn, P E (2001) *Studying Mathematics and its Applications*, Palgrave, Basingstoke

Kent, P, Ramsden, P and Wood, J (1996) *Experiments in Undergraduate Mathematics: A Mathematica-based approach*, Imperial College Press, London

Krantz, S (1999) *How to Teach Mathematics*, American Mathematical Society, Providence, RI

Mason, J (1999) *Learning and Doing Mathematics*, 2nd edn, QED, York

Mason, J (2001) *Mathematics Teaching Practice: A guide for university and college lecturers*, Horwood Publishing, Chichester

Pólya, G (1957) *How to Solve It*, 2nd edn, Penguin, London

Skemp, R (1971) *The Psychology of Learning Mathematics*, Penguin, London

Tall, D (ed) (1991) *Advanced Mathematical Thinking*, Kluwer Academic Press, Dordrecht

Index